AF870033

SWEEPING THROUGH THE LAND

Roger & Freddie,

Our association with you folks over the past four & one half years is something we will forever cherish. Keep your enthusiasm alive and you will always land on your feet.

I wish you the best for 90/91 and only wish we could be here to serve along side you.

We love you both Very Much.

Sincerely

Tom & Sue

5-23-90

Sweeping through the Land

A HISTORY OF THE SALVATION ARMY IN THE SOUTHERN UNITED STATES

By
Allen Satterlee

THE SALVATION ARMY SUPPLIES
Atlanta, Georgia

Published by
The Salvation Army Supplies
1424 Northeast Expressway
Atlanta, Georgia 30329

Available through
Salvation Army Supplies
or local bookstores

ISBN; 0-86544-054-9
Printed in the United States of America
First Printing, September 1989

Dedicated to
The Pioneers
Of Each Generation
Who Have Toiled in Lonely Places,
Endured Misunderstanding,
But Have Been Victorious
Through the Lord They Serve.

We are sweeping through the land,
    With the sword of God in hand,
We are watching and we're praying while we fight;
    On wings of love we'll fly
    To the souls about to die,
And we'll lead them to behold the precious light.

CHORUS:
With the conquering Son of God
Who has washed us in His blood,
Dangers braving, sinners saving,
We are sweeping through the land.

O the blessed Lord of light,
    We will serve Him with our might,
And His arm shall bring salvation to the poor!
    They shall lean upon his breast,
    Know the sweetness of His rest;
Of His pardon, He the vilest will assure.

We are sweeping on to win
    Perfect victory over sin,
And we'll shout the Savior's praises evermore;
    When the strife on earth is done,
    And the final victory's won,
We'll rejoin our conquering comrades gone before.

—George Scott Railton

TABLE OF CONTENTS

FOREWORD

Sweeping Through The Land: A History Of The Salvation Army in the Southern United States is a sweeping survey and substantive study of the scintillating progress of the Army since 1927 in the Southland.

Begun years ago as a project of love by Mrs. Colonel (Dr.) William Noble (nee Lillian Hansen), this immense and impressive compendium of facts and figures was carried through to literary completion by Captain Allen Satterlee. His prodigious penchant for details and anecdotes is obvious in this historic review. A gifted writer, Captain Satterlee has succeeded in presenting much more than a resource and reference tome. He has captured and conveyed the glorious spirit of the Southland and its forward-marching Army of Salvation.

In enthusiastically endorsing the book, I also commend both the Literary Council and the Supplies Department for their strong support of the author in the production process.

Indeed *Sweeping Through The Land* is a monumental and masterful literary tour de force.

God bless this book!

God bless The Salvation Army in the Southland!

James Osborne

Commissioner James Osborne
TERRITORIAL COMMANDER

Atlanta, Georgia
September 1989

PREFACE

THE SALVATION ARMY was not readily welcomed to the South. When it came the South was generally suspicious of anything which originated outside of its borders. But the South's lack of enthusiasm for the Salvationists was for deeper reasons. If the Army had chosen, it could have hardly taken positions which were more offensive to many white Southerners. Just consider the Army's features and beliefs.

When tobacco was the number two cash crop, the Army spoke against its use, calling it a narcotic. Imbibing in alcoholic spirits was an accepted part of much Southern life but the Salvationists denounced it in terrific tirades, rejecting any use of the "liquid damnation." When the Army came marching South it wore blue serge uniforms—almost identical to the heathen hordes of Yankees who had destroyed the South fifteen years before. It also preached an unpopular Christian message which included the belief that salvation was not necessarily eternal—that the believer had a responsibility to remain obedient to Christ or risk losing his salvation. With this was the message of Wesleyan holiness which included ethical obligations. That is, to be a Christian meant to interpret that experience in everyday life. You could not claim a life of victory while exploiting the sharecropper on your land.

In the heavily Calvinistic South these messages were often far from welcome.

More offensive than even these stands was the Army's belief that women were the equals of men and, as such, had every right to preach the Gospel. Southern sensitivities were shocked when dainty ladies stood on dusty streets to preach. The ideal of Southern womanhood could not be reconciled with this blasphemous use of the weaker sex. The Army was not deterred by the reactions. In fact, the Army's use of women leaders in the South was so widespread that, of the corps existing today, more than half were opened by women officers and over three-fourth have had women in command at one time or another.

A final irritation came with the Army's view of race. Though no one in the South seriously advocated a return to slavery, the black was always a step below the white. He never had rights but only privileges which could be arbitrarily revoked.

The Salvation Army confidently asserted its belief in the equality of the races and set itself to reach the black. When change began to sweep across the South, the Army had already settled in its heart that the black would be welcome in its ranks.

The Army was as hamstrung as the region because of the woeful economic conditions which existed for generations following the Civil War. It was misunderstood and misrepresented, looked down on and looked to. It stubbornly continued its spiritual assault on the South first as an intruder, then as something to be tolerated, and finally as a part of Southern life itself. I have met people who have not traveled outside the South who assume that the Army was indigenous to this part of the country, so completely has the Army been accepted where it was before unwelcome. I hope you will find it as fascinating in your reading as I have in the research.

I owe a debt of gratitude to a number of individuals. Captain Frank Duracher reviewed the manuscript and made helpful notes and suggestions. Major Omer McKinney's historical knowledge served me well in keeping the facts in proper order. While working on this manuscript I had the privilege of serving as the corps officer in two communities—Roanoke, Va. and Selma, Ala. I am grateful to the staffs in both corps and the kind support of my soldiers. In these commands I have served with three divisional commanders; Lt. Colonel B. Gordon Swyers, Lt. Colonel W. Edward Laity, and Lt. Colonel Jack T. Waters. Each will know the measure of support and encouragement they have given.

For this project of the Southern Territorial Headquarters, I appreciate the confidence given me as an essentially unproven writer to handle this work, especially as demonstrated by Commissioner Andrew S. Miller and Commissioner James Osborne. I worked closely with the Program Secretary, Lt. Colonel Orville Salmon. It was an honor to work with a man so supportive and helpful.

A few years back, Mrs. Colonel William (Lillian Hansen) Noble was to have written this history. She conducted months of research, compiling hundreds of pages of notes and drawers of material. Because of the declining health of her husband, she was unable to finish the project. When she learned of my involvement, Mrs. Noble magnanimously encouraged me and turned over her research materials. That alone probably saved a year's work. I cannot properly express my appreciation for this. Also, Mrs. Frances Garrison shared valuable materials. The Salvation Army National Archives and Research Center's staff provided invaluable assistance, especially Ms. Judith Johnston and Mr. Tom Wilsted.

I appreciate all who shared information in correspondence and interviews. At the same time, I acknowledge that constraints of time and space limited including material some readers may have considered essential. Perhaps this can be done in a future edition or by another author.

Finally, I thank God for reaffirming in wonderful and touching ways that God not only has His hand upon the Salvation Army in the Southern United States, but is far from being finished with it.

God bless you. God bless The Salvation Army.

Allen Satterlee
Captain

September, 1989

CHAPTER 1

THE STRUGGLE BEGINS
(1865–1879)

ON MAY 26, 1865, General Edward Kirby-Smith surrendered the last army of the vanquished Confederate States of America. Passing through his ranks he saw the empty eyes of beaten soldiers, the silent cannons, the motionless caissons. His army would dissolve around him as the soldiers made their way back home. He was a general without an army. If he had chosen to cross the South he could have seen the charred ruins of Atlanta or the dusty rubble of Richmond. He could have seen steel twisted around tree trunks where railroads once lay. Blasted fields prophesied the coming starvation of the war-weary population. His pockets were full of worthless currency and his heart festered with the bitter gall of defeat. General Kirby-Smith could have walked across land that represented the corpse of the Confederacy. Reconciliation of brother to brother had come at a terrible price of blood. Now the war was over. He was forced to lay down his sword.

Scarcely a month later another general walked across another battlefield. The shattered victims of war lay in their prostrated positions too weakened in their condition to separate themselves from the filth around them. He could hear the stray curse, see the empty eyes of the crushed. Everywhere he looked he could see the ruin of war. He was a general without an army. The pressure mounted inside his head to say something, something to spark the flame of forgotten hope in this mass of scarred humanity.

And so, William Booth stood in London's Mile End Waste and lifted his voice above the din to tell these casualties that the price of slavery and the reconciliation of rebels had come at the price of the Blood of the Lamb. For Booth the war was just beginning. Here, on July 2, 1865, he picked up his sword.

Booth's Army would come to America in 1879 and invade the South two years later. But it would be the turn of the century before his soldiers made substantial progress in the region.

Booth had been born thirty-six years earlier on April 10, 1829 in Nottingham, England. His father was a man who had apparently made and lost great wealth. While William was still a boy his father died leaving his family in near poverty. His mother, thought to be part Jewish, earned money as she could but never successfuly enough to rid the home of the threat of poverty. As was customary in that day, William was expected to learn a trade. He was apprenticed to a pawnbroker, a profession he immediately learned to loathe.

It was in this position he could see human misery more graphically than the streets themselves bore witness to in Victorian England. Here he could see men selling the last of all that was precious. Sometimes it was for rent, sometimes for food, but, most detestable of all, too often for liquor.

In a sort of perverted logic the lawmakers of England sought to address the misery of the masses by making liquor cheap and abundantly available. Day after day the anesthetized alcoholics came into the pawnshop turning possessions into money and then money into rum.

Driven both by these sights and the depth of his Christian values growing since his conversion at age fifteen, William went to the streets with the message of a fuller life to the victims of the Industrial Revolution. He left his pawnshop to speak in cottages, in chapels or in the open-air. He impatiently marked the time for his apprenticeship to end and so, when it was finally over at the age of nineteen, he was ready to launch his crusade.

Having left his employment forever Booth ventured into London. Here he had the good fortune to meet Edward Harris Rabbits who agreed to sponsor Booth for three months as a preacher. It was also through Mr. Rabbits that young William met and fell in love with a young woman named Catherine Mumford. At a party hosted by Mr. Rabbits he had recited a poem entitled, "A Grog Seller's Dream."

She impressed by his intensity, and he impressed with her sensitivity, they testified later that they fell in love with each other that afternoon while walking with a group of other young people. But it was to be far more than a quaint love story. Catherine Mumford was to leave an indelible mark on the movement that she and William would birth together.

Catherine Mumford was born January 17, 1829. She was soon besieged with long spells of poor health which made her, even in childhood, a near invalid. Lengthy confinements to bed drove her to the world of books where her brilliant mind fed on the thoughts of the great writers of the past and present. She was particularly drawn to the Bible and other religious literature which inspired and challenged soul and mind.

Even in the thrill of literature she was faced with the illogical conviction of the day that women, while enjoying equality of religious experience, were denied equality of religious expression. Her own gifts and deepening convictions of woman's perfect equality with man chafed against her shy nature. But what had been conceived in the lonely hours of suffering had to find full expression. That would come with the help of a man who not only valued her love and devotion but would encourage her to her full potential.

The courtship was a strange one by modern standards. William was often away preaching somewhere, writing when he could to his dear Catherine. She, now on the sidelines, would write back encouraging him to carry on, counseling him on matters of physical and spiritual health. Each letter and its reply witnessed deepening of love and commitment.

William Booth had now received an appointment with the Methodist New Connexion. Because of the excellence of his ministry the mandatory waiting period for marriage was shortened. William and Catherine were married in June 1855. Appointed to Gateshead, England, the Booths found a church with an average attendance of 120 blossom to 2,000 in the three years they were there.

It was at Gateshead that events not only changed the lives of the Booths but would impact hundreds of thousands. Here the Booths claimed the experience of personal holiness, as first popularized by John Wesley.

Known variously as the experience of holiness, full salvation, sanctification, baptism with the Holy Spirit, and other names, the teaching includes the belief in a second experience of grace subsequent to receiving Christ as Savior. The deeper commitment to God is accompanied by a cleansing from sin and a filling with the Holy Spirit. Although not free from temptation and the possibility of sin, the claimants of this experience believe that this will allow for a life of spiritual victory.

The second event was precipitated when a pamphlet was published in 1860 by the Reverend Arthur Augustus outlining the reasons why women should not be allowed to preach. Incensed by what she felt was a violation of Scripture to prove his point, she wrote a response defending women's rights with regard to the proclamation of the Gospel. Convicted by her own writing, she was in turmoil about her personal unwillingness to speak publicly though her husband had urged her repeatedly to exercise her gifts.

At the end of a Sunday evening service on May 29, 1860, she got her husband's attention. He announced to the confused congregation, "My wife would like to say a word." With that Catherine's platform ministry began. She was warmly received by the congregation, frequently speaking there and finding herself in demand as a speaker across England.

The envy of other ministers in the church brought an inevitable showdown. Feeling that their ministry was best fulfilled through evangelism, the Booths had requested a change to a revival ministry. This had been agreed to in principle by the leaders of the New Connexion and was to be inaugurated at the church conference when appointments were announced.

In the meantime, pressure was exerted to see the Booths accept an obscure position with a circuit of churches. When this latter appointment was revealed, the Booths promptly resigned and walked away. What could have been considered foolhardy was to the Booths the proof of their faith.

For a time both William and Catherine accepted preaching engagements whenever possible. It was a week to week existence. This was particularly precarious because they had already begun a family to which eight children would be born.

In 1865 Catherine was ministering in London. Here she came in contact with the Midnight Movement, a ministry to "fallen women." At the same time William had made application to work with the East London Revival Society, a small evangelistic outreach based in the appalling slums of Mile End Waste. It was while engaged by this group that the Lord's ultimate purpose for him began to crystalize in his heart and mind.

He was heartsick as he moved through streets littered

with the bodies of drunken children, unconscious mothers and vomit-encrusted fathers. He heard the slurred songs from the pubs, the only place where these pitiful people were welcome. He avoided the looks of the prostitutes and stepped over the filth. These scenes haunted and then beckoned him.

Finally at home he announced to his wife, "Oh, Kate, I have found my destiny. These are the people whose salvation I have been longing for all these years. As I passed by the doors of the flaming gin-palaces tonight I seemed to hear a voice sounding in my ears, 'Where can you go and find such heathen as these, and where is there so great a need for your labors?' And there and then in my soul I offered up myself and you and the children to this great work. These people shall be our people, and they shall have our God for their God."

Mrs. Booth recalled later, "I remember the emotion that this produced in my soul. I sat gazing at the fire, and the Devil whispered to me, 'This is another departure, another start in life!' The question of our support constituted a serious difficulty. Hitherto we had been able to meet our expenses out of the collections which we had made from our more respectable audiences. But it was impossible to suppose that we could do so among the poverty-stricken East-Enders—we were afraid to even ask for a collection in such a locality.

"Nevertheless I did not answer discouragingly. After a momentary pause for thought and prayer, I replied, 'Well, if you feel you ought to stay, stay. We have trusted the Lord once for our support, and we can trust Him again!' "

Taking a fulltime position with the revival society, he began his efforts in a tent erected at an unused Quaker cemetery. The meetings were an immediate success with the crude people of East London and the tent was the scene of many remarkable conversions. This ended when the tent was destroyed by bad weather. Booth then moved to an old dancing hall and so began an early tradition to use any building that was available and accessible to those who needed to hear the message.

The most perplexing difficulty came with the converts. This problem was to be the main force in the spontaneous birth of what would become The Salvation Army. Writing soon after this Booth said:

> My first idea was simply to get the people saved, and send them to the churches. This proved at the outset impracticable.
>
> 1st—they would not go when sent.
>
> 2nd—they were not wanted.
>
> 3rd—We wanted some of them to help in the business of saving others.

As the work grew it changed in name and character. Eventually the more democratic conference form of government was abandoned in favor of work under the sole direction of a general superintendent. To this position Booth was named since by this time he was the unquestioned leader of the blossoming ministry. The name was first changed to the East London Christian Mission, but Booth found himself heading a movement too dynamic to accept the boundaries of one area of one city. It went to the suburbs of London and then out into England as a whole, forcing a name change to "The Christian Mission."

It was marked by distinctive use of open-air meetings, "free and easy" style worship services (diagnosed as vulgar by the religious establishment), and the use of women as equals with men. The latter innovation not only helped toward solving the personnel shortage but Booth found the women quite capable. It was also discovered that women in some settings were more effective than their male counterparts. The very novelty of seeing an unlearned woman heading up a mission station created a stir that brought the curious into the meetings.

This combination of features, with the unbridled religious zeal of the mission's converts, struck a responsive chord with the poor and working classes. Here they were more than welcome—they were wanted. Here they were not to be passive worshippers who had to watch lest their ignorance be revealed in their speech. They were encouraged to sing their old tavern tunes with salvation lyrics; to stand and give their testimonies in the unfinished eloquence which made the Gospel message so very real.

The movement took on an increasingly militant feeling. So it was only natural that in 1878 the name was changed to reflect this. With the change of name to "The Salvation Army", the evangelism was now "warfare" against the "enemy", the Devil. The members became "soldiers", the evangelists became "officers" of varying rank. Booth himself ceased to be General Superintendent and was the "General." The mission stations were "barracks" or "citadels." Membership was confirmed by the signing of a statement of faith and commitment called the "Articles of War."

Even the meeting collections changed name—instead of offering envelopes they became "cartridges" to be "fired" as the plate went by. A flag and uniform were designed. The unique character was a source of derision and persecution for over a generation around the world. But to those in this new Salvation Army the war was no laughing matter. Time would confirm the resolve of this new Army.

****

When the last shot of the Civil War was fired the South lay prostrate. Any good thing which had existed before the war was now gone, either taken for the war effort or destroyed by the invading Federal armies. No part of the dead Confederacy had escaped the effects of the war.

When the Confederacy yielded up its life it died with one fourth of the soldiers who had marched to establish its independence. As W. J. Cash wrote, ". . . (The soldiers) had manured the land with their dead, often enough with their own limbs." Those who did come back from fighting for the Lost Cause found widespread devastation.

Richmond had not only been the victim of siege but saw its business district in ruins. Atlanta was burned to the ground. Galveston was known as "a city of dogs and desolation." If any roads existed they were often impassable. Bridges simply weren't there anymore. In all the South there weren't enough engines and cars to make a decent train. Had there been the railroad tracks that were left in usable condition amounted to less than seven hundred miles.

When the Union armies reached the South they were determined to make further fighting by the Confederates impossible. What could not be used by the armies was destroyed. With this the civilian population suffered, causing Southern hatred to seethe for those who had ignored the "honorable conduct" of war.

In many sections of the South law ceased to exist. Portions of Alabama were terrorized by deserters and guerillas for over a year after the official fighting stopped. Virtual war zones existed in Texas and Arkansas.

The poverty that follows in the wake of war was further heightened by the collapse of the economy. An observer from Maine, Mr. James S. Pike, wrote, "Everything went into Confederate securities; everything to eat and everything to wear was consumed, and when the war suddenly ended there was nothing but absolute poverty."

This state of affairs received little sympathy or tangible assistance from the reestablished authority of the United States government. For public works in 1865 the State of Kentucky received $25,000 while its northern neighbor Ohio received over a million dollars. Maine received over $3,000,000 while Mississippi received $136,000.

The Congress was dominated by "radical Republicans" who sought to punish the rebels in every conceivable way. Any voice of moderation was considered treasonous. When President Andrew Johnson attempted to restrain the radical elements he became the only president in American history to face impeachment proceedings. The period that followed the war was known as Reconstruction. While it may have succeeded in clearing the rubble and restoring some order, it was at the price of an abiding hatred that Southerners had for their Northern countrymen.

The South, still smarting from the humiliation of military defeat and destruction of its nation, now found most of its experienced leaders disenfranchised. The vacuum was filled by opportunists who swept into leadership. Those from outside the South were dubbed carpetbaggers, so named because of the carpetbags that they carried their belongings in when they came. Those from inside the South were scalawags. These were considered by Southerners to be traitors, collaborators with the conquerors.

Augmenting them were the freedmen who in slavery were denied even the most basic education but who now were called upon to make decisions in behalf of the impoverished blacks and whites who made up their constituency.

The role of the freed slave contributed to the chaos of the South. After yearning for freedom for so many years, when it came there were few who knew how to take advantage of it. Their former masters could not afford to employ them because of their own economic destitution. There was also a universal inferiority complex that had been preached and reinforced with chains for generations. When opportunities came many just did not have the confidence in themselves to take advantage of them.

Even though the white Southerner had lost the institution of slavery he still would not surrender his feeling of superiority over the black. No matter how bad things were he consoled himself into believing he was still better than any black man. And he was determined to make sure that the black never forgot his "place."

In this setting of the Reconstruction violence against blacks became a way of venting frustrations and striking back at the government which had given blacks their freedom. While many organizations were raised to accomplish this end, the Ku Klux Klan became the strongest and most famous. Supposedly a patriotic fraternity organized to protect the Christian values as defined by the white South, it became a terrorist organization instead. If the law would not deal swift judgment against the upstart blacks, then the Klan would.

Blacks found themselves victimized by petty men who found strength under the cloak of white sheets and tenets of white supremacy. For crimes, real or imaginary, the hapless black might find himself abducted in the night with his last sight being a mob demanding his death. It is significant that when the National Association for the Advancement of Colored People (NAACP) was formed its first priority was not the equality of blacks but to stop the lynching.

The South was a tragedy in the years of Reconstruction. It is difficult to find any positive fact during the period of 1865-1880. The weakened South fell prey to corruption. When Reconstruction ended, the indebtedness of the South was more than the value of all its land as assessed in 1865. Eventually the old ruling class came back into power and with it civil rights of blacks and poor whites were restricted so completely that it would take a hundred years of struggle to attempt to reverse the effects of disenfranchisement.

****

The currents of the parallel histories of the surging Army of Salvation and the sunken form of the South were about to be inextricably merged forever. It was already on its way to happening in 1879 when an unnoticed immigrant from England landed in America.

CHAPTER 2

INVASION

(1879–1884)

GENERAL WILLIAM BOOTH did not want America. Not in 1879. He was riding herd on a swelling Salvation Army which captured souls by first capturing the imagination of England. While every day provided more exciting news of advances on Satan's kingdom, the thought of this Army leaping the ocean's boundary was too much even for the visionary Booth.

He had not even begun to consolidate the gains in Great Britain. The leaders of the movement, while emerging, were still too few to allow him to delegate many of the major responsibilities. He had set his sights on East London, then England. He was not ready to consider the world. His hand was forced by a teenage girl.

Lt. Eliza Shirley was typical of the officers who led the fledgling Salvation Army. Though only sixteen, she had proven herself a capable leader with platform skills which demonstrated her ability to reach the hearts of the people the Army was pledged to save. Her father had emigrated to America in 1878 to take a position as a foreman in a silk factory in the Philadelphia suburb of Kensington.

After arriving there he wrote to England urging his wife and daughter to join him. After some deliberation, the family decided to be reunited in the New World. When this decision was communicated to headquarters, General Booth immediately dispatched his son Herbert to try to dissuade Eliza from making this move.

General Booth wrote his young officer and tried again to convince her that he needed her in England. Perhaps realizing how resolute his young lieutenant was, he concluded, ". . . if you are determined to go to America and you are determined to begin a religious work, you will do well to organize it along the lines of the Army at home. If you do this, you have my permission to call it The Salvation Army. If it succeeds, and I believe it will, we may later see fit to take over the work you have started and continue it."

Buoyed by this promise and endorsement, Eliza set sail with her mother. The America she was to find was a strange mixture of beauty and ugliness, of rising hopes and crushed dreams, of open-armed reception and closed-minded bigotry.

In 1879 America was the emerging giant. The population of over fifty million would swell in the next decade by natural growth and by the influx of five million fellow immigrants like Eliza Shirley. Beginning to enter the field of technology with what was then even known as "Yankee ingenuity," America boasted not only the birthplace of the telephone but also the first intercity phone service in 1879. The first city-wide power plant was being built in New York City which would power that novel Edison invention of the practical incandescent light bulb. The recently introduced typewriter was changing the work place forever.

The railroads opened the country to trade and corruption. Monopolies like Standard Oil built their empires by crushing competitors. Labor became restive as workers saw themselves paid pitiful wages, used up and finally destroyed by those who held the reins of power.

The level of corruption in government which marked the

two administrations of President Grant were eclipsed by the stolen election of 1876. Tilden had won but, in double dealing with Southern states, Rutherford B. Hayes was declared the winner. Everything had a price tag.

The Philadelphia which the Shirleys found was a slice of this America. Eliza soon realized that there was nothing here which she had not seen in her native land. And the Army worked there. It had to work here.

While her father worked, Eliza and her mother searched the streets of Philadelphia for a building in which to reach the lost and raise up an Army. They finally found an abandoned chair factory with broken windows, gaping holes in the roof, and a pathetic old horse tied up in the corner. When they told the landlord their purpose, he hesitated. Women preachers might have worked in England but they would never work here. He relented the next day, and the Shirley family set to work on a building which they affectionately dubbed "the manger."

When the day came for the work to begin, they found that the Americans greeted this Army, on the whole, with indifference. The first meeting had only twelve people present. The open-air meetings and marches back to the "barracks" continued to be ignored, unless you count the rotten vegetables thrown at the Shirleys.

Finally, they reached a man heavily under the influence of alcohol and marched him back to the building. This stirred the imagination of bystanders. That night the building was full and, while their captive slept off some of the effects of the liquor, the meeting went on. At the conclusion, they woke their friend and he knelt at the altar and was saved. This was the break they needed.

The building was filled night after night. A second corps was opened across the city. Lt. Eliza Shirley had proven the viability of the Army to herself and now had reason to write to the General that America was ready for a full scale invasion. The success with the Shirleys had been watched with intense interest in England. It especially touched thirty year old George Scott Railton.

Railton, colorful and gifted, had found in The Salvation Army the ideals of his own heart. He had himself launched out on an effort for world evangelism some years earlier when he staged a one man invasion of Morocco to win the Moslems. This aborted attempt did not discourage him. When he had read a booklet by Booth entitled, *How to Reach the Masses with the Gospel,* he immediately offered his services to the General.

His keen mind collaborated with Catherine Booth. Together they helped refine many of the doctrinal and governmental issues which faced the new movement. The very personification of self-denial, he was one who "rode the third class section of the trains because there was no fourth class available." He was particularly adept at understanding new cultures and was a gifted linguist. This movement in America was made to order for him.

Writing to the Founder, he said, "I feel sure that our own affair in Philadelphia will go with such a sweep that unless we get hold of it, and lead, and go in at full speed at once, I doubt if we should ever be able to get the reins at all. Then it will be a wild affair with no competent direction, and there will be after a while as complete a lull as follows almost all such things . . . I do not see why they should not let me go."

Convinced by the irrefutable facts and the pleading of Railton, General Booth decided it was time to invade America officially. Railton was his man.

In choosing his invasion force, Railton asked for women. He knew women officers were more readily available and he would need to build the Army in America with Americans. Preparations were completed. The Salvation Army was about to become international forever. This event deserved only the best send-off that could be offered. The forces were mustered to witness history.

For the occasion, Railton wore the first official men's uniform of The Salvation Army. The Army Mother, Catherine Booth, presented him with two Salvation Army flags with a small American flag sewn in the upper corner—one for the first New York corps Railton and his Hallelujah lassies would pioneer and the other for the corps in Philadelphia.

The eccentric Elijah Cadman, in his prayer of dedication said, "Lord, these ladies are going to America to preach the Gospel. If they are fully given up to Thee, be with them and bless them, and grant them success. But if they are not faithful, drown 'em, Lord! Drown 'em!"

In his farewell remarks to the party, General Booth announced plans were being finalized for the invasion of Sweden and France. Reminding the pioneer party of their responsibility he said, ". . . last but not least are the blessed negroes."

The trip over was a difficult one which resulted in the ship limping into New York. But upon arrival, Railton, in his typical style, stepped onto the land and proclaimed before the waiting press and passersby that he had claimed America for God.

A reporter said, ". . . They created quite a sensation in the Garden and subsequently in the streets as they proceeded to the lodging house that had been provided for them. They were all attired in a uniform of dark blue cloth, edged with bright yellow binding, and around their hats were broad bands of scarlet ribbon inscribed with the words: 'The Salvation Army' in gilt letters. . . . The band gave a service of song in the Garden yesterday. It was noticeable that some of their hymns were set to American tunes such as 'Way Down Upon the Swanee River' and 'My Old Kentucky Home'. . . . They intend to spread themselves throughout the principal cities of the Union . . ."

The coming of The Salvation Army to America continued to create interest. Before long it also created controversy. A well established Army practice of going where the sinners could be found led Railton to accept an invitation to appear with the "Magnificent Seven", as he called them, at Harry Hill's Variety Theatre, a notorious showplace. A pastor had warned them, "That is the most disreputable den in the United States. Go there and you will lose your reputation."

"Then that's the place for us," replied Railton. The propietor thought he was getting a minstrel show. When the Gospel was preached it surprised not only the patrons but the religious community as well.

There were no converts inside the theatre but outside a man, much the worse for drink, listened. He did not have enough money to pay to get inside, but he heard enough to be converted. His name was Jimmy Kemp, but he was better known as "Ash Barrel Jimmy." The nickname befit his condition. But now he was saved and he stayed saved. Later he became a Salvation Army officer and was faithful to the Army until his death.

Railton soon ran afoul of the City of New York. When he was prevented from holding street services, he delivered an ultimatum to the mayor of New York, informing him that if he did not relent on the question of open-air meetings the national headquarters of the Army would move out of New York. This captured the imagination of the press and the next day's newspaper showed the mayor encircled by uniformed female Salvationists with the caption "Past praying for."

The mayor did not change his mind and Railton, true to his word, left New York and headed for St. Louis. He was no more successful in St. Louis. The corps he established there folded within a year.

It was during this time that the first shots were fired south of the Mason-Dixon line. A couple of young men Salvationists in something of a freelancing effort, opened fire in Baltimore as reported in the *Baltimore Sun* on October 17, 1880.

"The advance guard of The Salvation Army opened the campaign in Baltimore yesterday by holding meetings, afternoon and evening, in William Street Independent Methodist Church. The names of the two guards were Theodore Jones and Charles Bentley, aged respectively, 23 and 22." *The Sun* further reported the next day, ". . . other Salvationists are expected in a short time . . . then they would use the Gospel broom and sweep the devil back to his headquarters."

Railton came to inspect this work and, since it was allowed to continue, he must have approved of what he saw. But this work was not to last. Jones and Bentley left the Army in January 1881 to start an independent revival work.

Amos Shirley, father of Eliza, had been made a Captain when Railton landed in America, becoming the first officer commissioned in the country. He and his wife were dispatched to Baltimore in May 1881 to reopen the work.

The War Cry reported, "The Salvation Army has advanced on Baltimore. Large crowds are attending the meetings, which feature preaching, reading and singing." However, that did not tell the whole story. Here, in this first corps in the South, was also the first taste of persecution. An early day warrior recalled:

> The 'toughs' of the early days of The Salvation Army in Baltimore were certainly most ingenious in their methods of annoying the officers and soldiers in their work. Rotten eggs, stale vegetation, dead cats, stones and such like were not sufficient, in their estimation. It was in the days when Salvationists

> used to march backwards and the toughs took delight in stretching wires and ropes across the street, close to the ground, the result being that frequently the entire march was thrown to the ground in hopeless confusion . . .
>
> It was a frequent occurrence for stones to come flying through the windows of the hall while the meeting was in progress, or for people to be suddenly left in utter darkness as the boys turned off the gas at the meter, or for everyone to be seized with a violent fit of coughing and sneezing on account of black or red pepper plentifully sprinkled on the stove by some sly tough or blown into the room through the doors and windows. Such things, I say, were common, and yet despite them, souls were saved by the score, many of them becoming out-and-out Blood and Fire soldiers under the yellow, red and blue . . .

By this time Railton had been ordered back to England. Despite his strenuous objections, the Founder was firm. The Salvation Army was growing faster than ever and Booth needed his faithful and resourceful Railton by his side. To replace him Booth sent Major Thomas Moore.

Moore, a short man with a dark beard, was a gifted evangelist with a colorful cockney accent. He was known for his aggressiveness and showed that Salvation Army survival spirit which knew how to capitalize on adversity and use it to reach the hearts of people. He was weak in administrative ability but, with only five corps existing manned by eleven officers, the need was minimal for administrative skills. He was sent to make the Army grow and that he did. By May, 1884 the number had jumped to 120 corps and 230 officers.

The Salvation Army had been born in the shadow of the factory and in view of the coal mines of Great Britain. It was among the blue collar workers that it showed its greatest effectiveness. As in its birthplace, it was in similar settings that the Army enjoyed its early success in America. This made the South in the beginning largely unattractive.

The South was still recovering from the destruction of the Civil War and the humiliation of Reconstruction. The poverty of the South was too strong even for an Army which built itself with the poor. Ventures into the South were limited to states which had not been part of the Confederacy.

The Salvation Army crossed the Ohio River and entered Louisville in 1883. Occupying a building known as Bowles Hall, the Army enjoyed some early success. As winter approached the Army's strength began to fade. A reporter for *The Louisville Courier-Journal* filed the following report:

> The Salvation Army is on its last legs in this city. A more forsaken looking crowd could not have been seen in all the city than the division of the Army which camped in Bowles Hall yesterday afternoon. About twenty-five forlorn and shivering men and women gathered about a broken stove and sang and prayed. The snow drifted in through one of the broken windows, and the wind whistled and howled about the corner of the building, taking up one loose glass in its strong, fierce grasp and shaking it sturdily. A crowd of boys were ranged in front of the building and amused themselves by throwing snowballs at the door. The heavy thump, thump of the masses of snow as they hit the open doors gave a not very cheering emphasis to a prayer or song . . .
>
> The speaking was frequently interrupted by hymns. At least they were intended to be hymns, although the orthodox would have repudiated the name indignantly. They consisted of a jumble of almost meaningless doggerel songs to the tunes that are favorites on the variety stage . . .

One hundred years after these cynical lines were written, a grateful city would dedicate General William Booth Park on the site of Bowles Hall.

The Army made a similar advance into West Virginia, opening its work in Wheeling in 1883. The work must have appeared akin to missionary endeavor from *The War Cry* report in the May 31, 1883 issue: "In this land of tobacco and bad whiskey, it means something for men to give up these things; and nothing but the Holy Ghost can enable men to do it; but God did so reveal Himself to hearts there that out of love to Him, they flung their idols down and filthy habits away."

By 1884 no further efforts had been made to reach the South. What was accomplished was destroyed by the events which followed later that year.

CHAPTER 3

THE LOST TRIBE

(1884–1891)

THE SWEEP of The Salvation Army had met great opposition but its unity was one of the secrets of its outstanding success. The first test of that unity would come through a rebellion in America late in 1884.

There was not even a murmur of dissension at the beginning of the year. In a pamphlet published in early 1884 entitled *All About The Salvation Army,* Major Moore boasted, "We have over 1,700 officers, and thousands of rank and file, who are so far disciplined as to regularly discharge any duty, or who are willing to go to any part of the world, simply at the word of command." Even as these words were written, a rift was widening between Moore and headquarters in London.

The first question came about the ownership of Salvation Army property. Booth preferred that the Army not own buildings and land in order to preserve its financial resources and its mobility. But on occasion it was necessary for the Army to own real estate. When this was necessary, Booth had all land in Great Britain titled to himself as the head of the movement. He wanted the same thing done in America.

The problem with this was that much of American law prohibited aliens from owning property in the United States. An example of this is the wording from the *Revised Statutes of the State of New York* (1881) which said, "An alien is not able to own land in New York unless he makes a deposition that he is a resident or always intends to reside in the United States and that he has taken steps to secure naturalization."

Moore tried repeatedly to communicate this both to Booth and to his subordinates. Even his arrest in New Jersey on a charge related to this problem did not convince International Headquarters that American law had to be satisfied.

While this was going on, auditors arrived from International Headquarters for a routine review of the financial records. They found that, while Moore was a beloved leader and effective evangelist, he was no administrator. The books were in disarray. There was no inference that Moore had been dishonest but he was simply unable to properly administer the Army in America. General Booth decided he would transfer Moore from the United States to the newly invaded country of South Africa.

Moore rejected the orders. He called a meeting attended by about 120 officers at the headquarters in New York City, carefully excluding any known to be in opposition to him. In the meeting he proposed that the Army in America incorporate and effect a split from the rest of The Salvation Army. This proposal was received enthusiastically by all but a few loyal to Booth.

The next day, October 24, 1884, Moore incorporated the movement as The Salvation Army of America. With that, he copyrighted the Salvation Army Crest (logo), the name of the Army magazine, *The War Cry,* and took all properties and inventories. He proclaimed himself to be the general of this Army. Of the corps then operating in the United States, over sixty joined him, seventeen remained loyal to Booth and nearly fifty others simply perished in the confusion.

In the South this rift extinguished the fledgling corps that was in Louisville, while the corps in Wellsburg and Wheeling,

W.Va. left with Moore. There were two corps in Baltimore: the original corps pioneered by the Shirleys and the first "colored" corps in the United States, opened only weeks before the schism.

Both corps went over with Moore. Five soldiers in the older corps refused. Led by Sister Yaegge, an immigrant who could speak only a few words of English, the five secured a building in West Baltimore and reported to the fragments of the Army still loyal to General Booth.

The new Army started out with a flourish. By becoming "American", the fledgling organization Army appealed to the strong nationalism of the late nineteenth century. This, coupled with the widespread, rabid hatred for Great Britain then exhibited in the United States, made the act of declared independence all the sweeter.

The Moore Army, while keeping most of the features of the Worldwide Salvation Army (as it called itself to distinguish itself from the dissenters), differed from the parent movement by establishing a democratic form of government to elect the General and the trustees. In addition, it was quick to add the sacraments of baptism (by immersion) and the Lord's Supper, sacraments which the Worldwide Army, emphasizing a deep personal relationship and commitment to Christ, had abandoned some years before.

William Booth and the Worldwide Salvation Army had looked upon the sacraments positively. They affirmed, however, the spiritual realities to which they pointed, simply stating these realities permeated their lives. To them the sacraments were offered daily, hourly, moment by moment in their living. As a later poet-general, Albert Orsborn, was to say, "My life must be Christ's broken bread, my love his outpoured wine," . . . a constant dipping of Spirit baptism and a continuing fellowship with our Lord and his family at the table.

While much happened with the splinter movement, the most fascinating aspect of the Moore Army was what happened in the South.

At the end of 1886 the Moore Army made its first appearance in the South when General Moore came to Chattanooga, and proclaimed to the newspapers that "Chattanooga would be headquarters for this part of the country at least, and possibly for the United States." The problem with this was that Chattanooga was not particularly hospitable to Moore's Army. There was a succession of officers who abandoned his army, causing considerable embarrassment. Although the work continued there, it never prospered.

Greater success was to be found in Atlanta. But even there the reception was cool as reported in *The Atlanta Journal* (January 20, 1887), "Last night the work of The Salvation Army was thoroughly inaugurated in Atlanta for the first time by a corps of five in command of Captain Ella Bruckner . . . The singing was decidedly more weird and loud than musical and the remarks more pathetic and earnest than scholastic."

In a major departure from the parent movement, it was soon evident that this branch of Moore's Army was willing to conform to prevailing conditions in the South. *The Atlanta Journal* reported, "For their hall meetings they have adopted rules, which are rigidly adhered to . . . No colored people are admitted."

This new corps enjoyed immediate success. Within a month it had moved to a larger building where 1,000 people could be seated. *The Atlanta Constitution* reported that the building was packed with over 1,200 people and approvingly noted the number of the city's most notable sinners who had been converted under the Army's leadership.

Even with the success there was opposition. In Athens, Ga., a minister "showed by the Bible that their (the Army's) way of doing business was not orthodox, and made a strong appeal to the church to keep clear of all such freaks."

Sometime in 1887, General Moore appointed Colonel Milton K. Light to oversee the fast developing work in the South. Colonel Light was to prove to be one of the ablest leaders of Moore's Army. He had been at headquarters when the split occurred and left with Moore. Advancing in rank rapidly, he proved his ability to organize and to attract people to the Army. He was extremely innovative and a persuasive speaker. Dispatching him to the South was to guarantee the continued prosperity of the work there, even though the Moore Army was now retreating in the East before the continued advances of the Worldwide Salvation Army.

In a meeting with reporters, Light announced, "Owing to the remarkable progress of our work in the South, we are confronted with the necessity of the early establishment of Southern headquarters and a training school for officers in connection therewith." He went on to report that the Army had established two corps in Atlanta while also operating in Columbia, S.C.; Augusta, Macon, Savannah, Columbus, and Athens, in Georgia; Nashville, Knoxville, Chattanooga and Bristol, in Tennessee.

At the same time this announcement was made the Moore Army had its first mass baptism in the South. The following account appeared in *The Atlanta Constitution*, June 13, 1887:

> At half past three the members of the Army . . . left the barracks and marched down Marietta Street toward the pond (Lynch's quarry). There were a large number of persons in the line and many more followed at a distance as spectators so that by the time the Army reached the scene probably five thousand people had found positions within the site upon which the exercises were conducted.
>
> While the eighteen converts were in a convenient building preparing for the ceremony, the religious exercises were begun.

> There was singing, praying and preaching in the regulation Salvation Army style, Captain Bruckner and Cracker Sam leading. A number of the members and other people made short addresses, the members telling in eloquent tones how they had been saved.
>
> Soon the converts appeared and shouts of delight went up from the soldiers.
>
> At their head came Colonel Light, attired in a blue gown with a broad white collar and red trimmings. After the converts had taken their position on the shore, the colonel conducted a religious exercise, which consisted of readings in the scripture, singing and praying. Then he and a lieutenant walked boldly in the water.
>
> At a distance of eight or ten feet the water had reached their arm pits and they stopped. Then, while the Army sang a verse of a hymn, the first of the class—a woman—walked into the pond. To her the colonel addressed some words which could not be heard by others and then he and the lieutenant ducked her under the water.
>
> The same ceremony was repeated with seven women and eleven men. All the time the Army was singing, "Happy in the Way" or some other appropriate hymn. Some of the converts became quite enthusiastic, shouting "Glory to God!" and similar expressions as they walked out of the water.

A little more than a month after this Colonel Light opened a training school. This school was for women only and could train up to fifteen at a time. (Men were trained in corps while married couples had no formal training at all.) The training sessions lasted about six weeks.

The Army planned a major celebration for July 4 in one of Atlanta's parks. The mayor of Atlanta steadfastly opposed this meeting and issued orders that the Salvationists be arrested if any attempt was made by the Army to meet. Colonel Light knew how to capitalize on controversy and went straight to the newspapers with an appeal for freedom of speech. Finally, on the eve of the scheduled celebration, the mayor backed down. The Army's right to hold open-air services in Atlanta was never again challenged.

In an effort to extend the Army's influence, Light formed a traveling brigade of Army officers known as Christian Crusaders. Holding meetings in tents and in friendly churches, the Salvationists crisscrossed the Deep South. In August, 1890 one such group held a meeting at the New Hope Methodist Church near Palmetto, Ga. Let by Scout Keith, who wore a buckskin uniform, the group was hosted by the Longino family. One of the Longino children, Ansel, an avid music lover, was deeply impressed by the message and lively music of the Salvationists.

Later, living in LaGrange, Ga. he often told his children of the Army. When, in 1919, The Salvation Army came to LaGrange, Longino, moved by the memory of his youth and the needs of the new opening, offered the help of his family band. Eventually three of his children would have distinguished careers as Salvation Army officers.

But, even with the victories in the South, all was not going well as the Moore forces marched into 1888. The Worldwide Salvation Army had gained the upper hand and was winning the wealthier and more populated cities of the East. Time and again Moore saw his soldiers and officers abandon him to join up with the parent movement. He was plagued by mounting financial troubles as evidenced by eviction from his Brooklyn headquarters because of nonpayment of rent. He became increasingly bitter toward the Worldwide Salvation Army, referring to the leaders in *The War Cry* as the "gaping bulls of Bashan" or "The British belchers."

Finally, to make matters worse, he was beset by family problems that were an embarrassment to him. His wife refused to wear a uniform and attend meetings. He had four sons who could, it was alleged, best be described as scoundrels. One, who was an officer, was reported to have had an adulterous affair and left his wife. Rather than disciplining this son, Moore assured the forces that his son had reformed.

His army also took a strange turn with its doctrine. At

first maintaining doctrines identical to the parent movement, there was a decided change in his view of backsliding and holiness: "We believe that the Scriptures teach that not only does continuance in the favor of God depend upon continued obedient faith in Christ, but that it is possible for those who have been truly pardoned to fall away and be eternally lost; but we do not believe in the backsliding of those who have made a complete surrender to God."

All of this brought growing discontent within his forces. Finally, on January 10, 1889, there was a split in the movement. The trustees felt that Moore had mismanaged the Army and demanded that he step down. He refused to do this. The trustees then approached Light, who by now had been promoted to the rank of Lt. General. Light chose to stay with Moore. The trustees then asked Colonel Richard Holz who first refused, but then accepted the title of Commander-in-Chief, turning down the promotion to General.

About twenty corps stayed with Moore, most of them in the South. This was about the same number that had stayed loyal to Booth four years before. But these soon began to falter. One by one they closed. In the South the work continued for a couple of years under Light's leadership.

When the Worldwide Salvation Army opened in Atlanta in 1890 Light left, and all remaining corps in the South closed. Just before leaving, the movement had changed its name from The Salvation Army of America to the Christian Crusaders. This organization lasted for a few more years in New England under Light's direction, but it too folded.

Moore resigned from the Christian Crusaders sometime in 1891 to become a Baptist minister. He died in the pulpit on January 7, 1898, in Harper, Kans.

Meanwhile, Holz named his splinter group The American Salvation Army and moved aggressively to open corps. There was particular success in opening corps in the Tidewater area of Virginia. He moved his headquarters to Mohawk, New York, not only supervising his movement and publishing *The American Salvation Army War Cry*, but pursuing the merger of his organization with the international Army.

He personally paid his passage to London to discuss this with International Headquarters, but was rebuffed. Finally he found a friend in the new National Commander for the United States, Ballington Booth. Ballington was quick to see the advantages of the merger. He cordially received Holz and convinced his father of the wisdom of this move and, together with Holz, the necessary plans were laid. In November 1889 at Saratoga, N.Y., Holz and about half of his officers, soldiers and corps were officially welcomed back to the Worldwide Salvation Army.

However, not everyone wanted back into the Worldwide Salvation Army. There was a split in the American Salvation Army when the merger with the international Army was announced. This splinter group also took the name of American Salvation Army and named Thomas Grattan to be their general. This set the stage for interesting future events between the two armies.

CHAPTER 4

THE GREAT SOUTHERN EXPEDITION (1884–1887)

IF WILLIAM BOOTH did not do something, and do it quickly, he could lose The Salvation Army's first foreign field. Without delay, he dispatched Major Frank Smith who arrived in America within two weeks of the mutiny. In trying to assess the wrecked remnants of The Salvation Army Smith asked the loyal corps to report. Only seventeen could be counted as faithful. His strategy for overcoming the damage was to hold on to what he had and then to advance. The primary task of the Army was to save souls and this great disaster could not change that. In his estimation, the dissenters were rebels, and, as such, deserved no further consideration.

In writing to his troops a month later, he voiced his optimism about the ultimate triumph of the Army in the face of adversity. "A hurricane of an unusual kind burst upon us lately, but, standing upon the lookout, faithful watchers, assisted by the flash of Heaven's lighthouse, saw the line of breakers ahead, gave the alarm, seized the helm in time to avoid the rocks, and faced the storm. A few ropes broke, a false light or two went out, but, my comrades, the winds are ceasing, the waters are calming, the rocks are getting well astern. My comrades, we do not fear . . ."

With the advent of 1885, Smith prepared to take the offensive, bolstered by the arrival of over fifty officers from the British field. He turned his eyes southward for a bold campaign that, if successful, would change not only the lives of individuals but of America as well.

Writing in *The War Cry* of July 11, 1885, Smith announced that "arrangements are being made for a great colored campaign and combined attack on the South." He went on to explain in the next issue of *The War Cry,* "Our colored brethren are supposed to occupy the same platform with the white, but we see by daily experience that the assertion is a benevolent fallacy. We desire to make that a living, practical reality . . . We of The Salvation Army have a holy ambition to be among the first Christian communities of America who will faithfully and wholly break down the wall of partition separating the white from the colored . . . We appeal to every Salvation soldier and every lover of Christ to set their face against any such distinction. Public opinion may not, at the present time, share in this conclusion, let The Salvation Army show the way; let it be the pioneer of this grand, social reform . . ."

What was the South's reaction to this invasion? The "color line" was an inviolable doctrine in the nineteenth century South. Writing thirty years after this initial Army effort, Leslie Hall, college professor at William and Mary College, wrote, "It is needless to say that this is white man's country . . . How preposterous for brethren of the Anglo-Saxon race to quarrel over a race so manifestly inferior, and so clearly intended by providence to occupy a position of inferiority."

While Smith intended to sweep through the South with the dark surge of Salvation Army uniforms, the newly formed White Knights of the Invisible Empire of the Ku Klux Klan were swarming across the land with a message of separation of the races.

The Salvation Army not only shocked the Southern mind with its efforts to reach the blacks, but also by using women as a major part of its invasion force. The Southern ideal of womanhood had persisted beyond the Civil War. A woman was to be beautiful, fashionably shy, but not necessarily a thinker.

If the Southern home had changed somewhat because of the war, the church had not. Women were to keep silent in the church. Imagine the shock to Southern sensibilities to not only see a woman preaching but doing so in a military-style uniform among the horses and dusty traffic of city streets!

As *The Birmingham Age Herald* records, "We have just found out that (there are) some members who are wonderfully strengthened in the religious faith . . . by seeing a woman beat the tambourine over her head, while a lot of trifling men were tooting brass horns and gyrating to the music of 'Possum up a gum stump, Raccoon in the Hollow' . . . If it's proper for young ladies to parade in the streets, enter saloons and dives, and herd together without regard to sex . . . in what they call 'barracks', then The Salvation Army is entitled to the respect and support of good people; but if womanly modesty and safety, as well as common decency, is required in religious matters, then they are not entitled to the respect . . . We have a great deal of sympathy for these poor girls, who have been induced to leave their homes and roam about the country in hope of serving God to a better advantage in The Salvation Army; and, just before a daughter of ours starts out on such a religious jaunt as this, we will send her to the insane asylum, where she can be properly cared for and treated for mental indigestion."

If these obstacles were considered by Smith, he did not let them bother him. Had The Salvation Army not thrived in the midst of controversy? Had they not found the difficult only another arena where God could bless the Army yet again and prove that the foolish things of the world could confound the wise? And if the Army was successful in reaching the nine million blacks of the South what good might be accomplished for eternity through their salvation? What good could be accomplished for America?

Smith only had to look at the efforts of the Army pioneer, Frederick Booth-Tucker, as he attacked the caste system of India. Was what existed in America that much different? Besides, all successful warfare involves taking risks with boldness, and this The Salvation Army intended to do.

Captain Braithwaite, a black Caribbean minister, offered himself for the Southern Expedition and was joined by three others: Captain Halliwell, Lt. Alice Evans and Cadet Ada Wade. These were the officers that spearheaded the invasion.

A corps in Washington, D.C. had just been opened in June when the expedition was announced. In typical Army fashion, the nation's capital was assaulted by an invasion force of three. It was here where the first effort of the Southern Expedition was launched.

In a visit soon after the opening of the first corps of the Southern Expedition, Commissioner Smith visited Washington, stating, "Never did we feel more convinced that salvation is the only missing link between the races; the golden link, which if we will only let it, will bind all men together in love and unity, irrespective of class, caste or color."

While the Southern Expedition advanced its efforts to win Southern blacks, Smith opened corps aimed at the white population as well. The first point of attack was Alexandria, Va. The pioneers there telegraphed the following enthusiastic report to headquarters: "Tremendous crowds. Hall packed from platform to door. Washington warriors to the front. Prospects grand."

From there Annapolis was attacked. It was here that the Army owned its first building in the south by the end of the year. Next followed Frederick, Md., which soon had both a black and a white corps. By November, the Army had reached the capital of the old Confederacy with the opening of Richmond.

When the Army opened cities with white corps, it was with the stated goal of reaching the blacks as soon as practical. Within months, Richmond, Annapolis, Alexandria, and Frederick had thriving black corps. The first difficulty of the Southern Expedition came when Captain Braithwaite, upon whom so many of the Army's hopes had rested, abandoned the Army and joined Moore's forces. Apparently, Moore's Army toyed with the idea of starting its own work among blacks but before this could be acted upon, Braithwaite left them as well.

Despite the setback of Braithwaite's departure, Commissioner Smith was encouraged by the success in the South. In early 1886, the Army opened another front, soon known as "village warfare" in the small towns of western Maryland. The Army quickly opened up in Frostburg, Westernport, Lonaconing and other small towns. Contrasted with the main arena of Army activity in the major cities, the village work was a new expression of Salvationism.

In the picturesque mountains the Army officers could stand outside the barracks and listen to the singing as Salvationists descended from the hills to the village, the only lights being the lanterns they carried. Here the coal miners came to the meetings with unwashed faces, their penitent tears making white streaks down their darkened cheeks. The Army brought a real religion to a people who knew nothing of pretense. Crossing from Maryland to West Virginia, the village work flourished as long as the coal mines did.

A jump to the deep South was attempted in the spring of 1886 with the opening of New Orleans. Accustomed to the polite indifference of Southern people, the Army was to find outright persecution here. When Captain Charles Miles took his first stand on the street, the roughs rioted. They took possession of the Army building, then in the French Quarter, where they destroyed all the seats.

An important aspect of corps work in these days was evangelizing and financing of the Army through the sale of *The War Cry*. Officers went with the magazines on their arm, tambourine in hand, to "boom the *Cry*." Collections were made at saloons, gambling houses, the streets, in surrounding villages, in open-air meetings—wherever people were and the opportunity to distribute *The War Cry* and collect presented itself. It was the only viable means of survival for the Army during this time. From this we have a couple of interesting tales from the South.

In Cumberland, Md. the officer reported that she came to a house where there lived a regular customer. In the conversation that followed the man told her that his goat was fond of eating *The War Cry*. "He said he would eat all the Crys he could get, or officer's account books, but would not eat the weekly papers of this town, especially *The Independent*."

She gave the goat an old one, which he quickly devoured. The next day as she was passing by the man reported, "That Cry gave new life in my goat. He just caught me between his horns and tossed me against the gate, and now he works splendidly." The officer noted, "If we can't get people saved, we can improve the goat."

In another incident *The War Cry* was credited with saving a man's life. He had put the paper in his inside coat pocket, having folded it several times. As he left the Army meeting, a man met him with a gun and shot him. The bullet hit *The War Cry*, saving the man from certain death. *The War Cry* was saved and used as evidence in the trial.

The sixth anniversary celebrations of the Army in America were held in three cities in 1886: Chicago, Boston and Washington. At the Washington celebration, Commissioner Frank Smith said, "If everybody was converted, there would be no need for laws. We would make the Senate chamber The Salvation Army Barracks."

The celebrations were crowned with a tremendous moral boost when Commissioner Smith and selected officers were received at the White House by President Grover Cleveland. Smith reported, "We were introduced to President Cleveland . . . by name, each receiving a hearty shake of the hand as he saluted with a robust 'God bless you!' and passed on. All, both colored and white, were greeted alike."

Later, when Smith went to Frederick, Md., he had the happy duty of enrolling twenty-five blacks as soldiers. But his exhilaration was dampened when he saw that the blacks were allowed to sit only in the balcony. Acknowledging the deeply rooted prejudice of the whites, he remarked dryly that they "stood it very well."

The end of 1886 brought the welcome news that General William Booth would be making his first visit to America. Included in his plans would be stops in Washington and a visit to Frederick #2 (Colored) Corps. Most of the Salvationists in America had seen only pictures of the Founder, read his messages in *The War Cry* and heard word-of-mouth stories about him. His coming to America was a long awaited dream come true for the Army in the United States.

As in other places, the visit of Booth to Washington was big news. Crowds of Salvationists and reporters, the curious and the seeking met him when he reached the capital. His meetings at the National Rifle Hall were crowded out with thousands turned away. His review of the "colored troops" in Frederick was the focus of national and international attention.

Writing to his son Bramwell, he said, "I like the 'South' so far better than the North. They told me I should, and the farther South I go the warmer-hearted they say the people are. Anyway, I like Washington people. Oh, what a splendid city this is and is going to be. I have no doubt but they will make it the finest city in the world."

Buoyed by the visit and obvious affection of their international leader, American Salvationists were more determined than ever to see the Army sweep through America, developments in the South making it a more fertile field of labor.

The Carolinas were especially promising as those states began to develop economically for the first time since the Civil War. Everywhere cotton mills were springing up, giving the South industrial muscle that had been so noticeably absent when needed during the war. Rather than sending their cotton to mills in the North or to foreign countries, the South was beginning to take its future into its own hands. With that advancement, the Army saw promise for its future with the emergence of the New South.

Opening shots were heard for the first time in North Carolina with the Army beginning operations in quick succession at Raleigh, Wilmington, New Bern and Goldsboro. When the Army opened in New Bern, the officer announced she would attack the devil in an open lot near the center of the city. The word spread, causing throngs of people to come, believing that she had somehow managed a face-to-face encounter with Lucifer himself. They were greatly relieved to find that the battle was a spiritual one.

The war was pushed over the state line to South Carolina when "Salvation guns" opened up in Spartanburg and Greenville. In the push further south, the Army avoided entering cities where Moore's corps were established. In this way Charlotte, N.C., Columbia and Charleston, S.C. and other cities were bypassed by the Worldwide Salvation Army.

But the further south the Army went, the further it drifted from the goal of the Southern Expedition to reach the blacks. Perhaps it was the realization that in these days, poor whites and blacks differed very little in need. It may have been that the ingrained prejudice of the region was too much even for the optimism of the Army. It may have been that the expected officer recruits from the black population did not come to fruition, not because blacks were not interested, but because most possessed only the most basic of skills and were hamstrung by widespread illiteracy.

The Army's financial resources were always near exhaustion and to expect the blacks to support this work when they could barely afford an impoverished existence was too much. In addition, the crusading abolitionists of a generation ago simply lost interest in the plight of Southern blacks, and so could not be depended upon for support of the Army's work.

The Army had also come at a time when the major denominations of the South were regrouping into all-white and all-black organizations. The black was given the opportunity to ascend into roles of leadership in his denomination but the Army could offer only such an opening in an organization which would continue to be dominated by whites. The Army did not completely grasp at that time a way to meet the needs of the black community in the South. Instead it would attempt again and again to reach the blacks in the same way it reached whites. So the first effort failed as the Southern Expedition slowed, and then sputtered to a halt.

Although seemingly indefatigable, Commissioner Frank Smith, at the point of exhaustion, asked to be relieved of command in the United States. The Founder honored his request, sending his son and daughter-in-law, Maud and Ballington Booth. The Army was to enter a new era.

CHAPTER 5

EDGING FORWARD
(1887–1896)

MAUD AND BALLINGTON BOOTH captured America's heart. Standing well over six feet tall, handsome, with commanding features, Ballington had the look and bearing of a military commander. He was arguably the most gifted among a family of eight exceptional children. He had come to America with his bride, Maud Charlesworth Booth, who barely cleared five feet.

She had been raised as a gentlewoman, the daughter of an important Anglican minister who had bitterly opposed her association with the Army. Her size and background could not hide her fighting spirit. She had been part of the pioneering party for the Army's invasion of France and Switzerland—particularly bitter campaigns in which she had been jailed and assaulted repeatedly. Their appointment to America would change the Army's direction and character forever.

Replacing the embattled Smith, the new national commander found an Army, with an explosion of growth in both new corps and American-born officers, which had made remarkable progress in the three years of his predecessor. There was every reason to look forward with new hope for the Army's future in America. Everywhere, that is, except in the South.

By the time the Ballington Booths arrived, the Southern

Expedition was a confirmed failure. The Worldwide Salvation Army found its way blocked by the advances of the Moore forces. It continued to take stands which made it odious to many Southerners. Among these was the Army's view on tobacco. In the South of the 1880's only cotton was a more important crop. Not only was tobacco a source of income, but many enjoyed both chewing and smoking it. It was a foregone conclusion that even children would use it. From the pages of its publication, the Army's position was clear. The Army proclaimed tobacco a narcotic poison. Beyond that, the Army considered the use of tobaccco degrading to the person.

One writer challenged, "God never created man to use his mouth as a chimney, or his nose as a dust-bin. How can you praise God with a clean heart and clean lips when you use dirty snuff? Can you smoke to the glory of God?" A divisional officer reported on a soldiers' meeting where "I asked the comrades whether any would like to meet Jesus Christ in person with his or her mouth full of snuff." This disregard of what Southerners saw as economic life itself must have made the Army viewpoint seem to many insensitive and uncaring.

Part of the Army's difficulty in the South was also linked to the depth of southern poverty. Cities of the South were plagued with slums whose filth bred disease and despair. Rural areas were giving birth to the infamous company stores, where sharecroppers traded their sweat for life's necessities. Many stores not only overpriced their goods but also charged interest rates from 40-80 percent—all charged against the unharvested crops of the farm workers.

The crops themselves, including the staple cash crop of cotton, warred against the farmer. King Cotton sucked the nourishment out of the ground, making each year's crop smaller. In the meantime, cotton prices were on a steady decline. The farmer was struggling in economic quicksand.

A song from the era testifies to forlorn hopes of the farmers:

My husband came from town last night
As sad as man could be,
His wagon empty, cotton gone,
And not a dime had he.

Huzzah, Huzzah,
'Tis queer I do declare:
We make the clothes for all the world
But few we have to wear.

In trying to get ahead, many Southerners began to have large families. The more children, the more farm hands there were. The more free farm hands, the more chance to somehow break out of the cycle. At the mills, the same principle applied to children as factory workers. Machines, with few safety features, were manned by children as young as age six. Over 23,000 children under twelve were thus employed in the South alone.

The mills, with their bright promise of economic security, began to take on the appearance of the old plantations. The mill replaced the plantation house, the mill village replaced the slave quarters, the paternal reign of the mill owners the plantation owners, all combining to strongly parallel the South of bygone days. The poor were now enslaved by debt and illiteracy.

Neither the federal government nor the churches, forces which should and could have made a difference in the South, really helped. Each institution failed it miserably. When Texas suffered from a drought, President Cleveland vetoed a bill appropriating $100,000 to farmers to buy seed even though there was a surplus in the treasury. The churches, most controlled by congregational governments, owed their buildings and financial security to the wealthy merchants and mill owners. It would have been economic suicide for them to speak out against the evils of exploitation. Security and silence walked hand in hand. Few Southern Protestants saw a connection between their business dealings and their abuse of fellow Southerners. The Army's message of personal holiness, with its ethical implications, was a direct challenge to the prevailing attitudes of both the churches and the wealthy.

Climate and tropical diseases further complicated Southern life. Yellow fever and malaria, both spread by mosquitoes, brought death and sickness. The heat was oppressive. This was keenly felt by Salvationists with their blue serge uniforms and poorly ventilated, but inexpensive, meeting places. This led to the view among many that being sent to the South was akin to missionary service.

Writing about his appointment to open the Army's work in Mobile, Ala. in 1887, Captain Edward J. Parker wrote, "Many times previously I had felt the urge to volunteer for missionary service . . . it seemed as though my desire for the mission field was at last to be realized. To be sure, Alabama was not far away India, but it was nearly as hot, I was given to understand."

Salvationists were certain God had raised up the Army to bring salvation to the entire world. Even the difficulties of the South could be overcome. Though swimming upstream, advances were made. The old battleground of Frederick, Md. was the scene of the erection of the first building built specifically for the Army in the South in 1887. The wood structure was appropriately painted in Salvation Army colors of yellow, red and blue.

When economic conditions forced the closing of most of the corps in the Carolinas and Virginia by 1889, the Army opened another attack further west. Target: The Lone Star State.

The Army's foray into Texas had already begun unofficially when Adam Janelli emigrated from Italy in 1888. Janelli, a former ship's captain, attended out of curiosity an

Army meeting in Calcutta, India. He was deeply impressed, traveled to England and offered himself for service as an officer. He served for a time as a corps officer in Italy but left officership to marry a young Methodist girl. With their emigration to the United States, Janelli sought in vain for his beloved Army in Dallas. Not finding it, he began his own work, conducting open-air meetings in front of the post office.

Amid scorn and persecution, he was the solitary Army figure in a town which found as much amusement with his strange uniform as his accent. He deluged headquarters with letters requesting that officers be sent to take over. But his own ministry did not end when the Army officially opened in Dallas. He *was* The Salvation Army in that city's eyes. Years later, when a divisional commander attempted to open a bank account in the Army's name he was forbidden to do so until Adam Janelli confirmed he was a Salvationist.

When Texas was opened in 1889, it was not only because it was a boom state but because the Moore forces had only begun to reach that far west. Staff-Captain Annie Rees headed up the four woman pioneer force which boasted a variety of accents from the "Yankee, English, Irish and Welsh warriors." Austin was the point of attack. Captain Rees victoriously reported that the Army hall was a wing in the temporary capitol. Three weeks later San Antonio was opened, followed by Houston three months later. Moore's forces did not venture into the cities occupied by the Worldwide Salvation Army, nor did the Army enter cities Moore occupied until that movement folded.

In late 1889, the reconciliation between the Worldwide Salvation Army and the American Salvation Army took place in Saratoga, New York. A small splinter group, still under Moore's direction, struggled on but found itself closing in city after city until it finally withdrew altogether from the South. The new year dawned with the Worldwide Salvation Army ready to fill the vacuum left by the collapse.

Following up on the opportunity, another thrust into the South was spearheaded by an attack on Nashville. When Major John Dale opened work in the city he was met by soldiers who had belonged to Moore's group and were only too willing to join up with the Army. But Dale was immediately bogged down in the reality of Southern poverty. In the pages of *The War Cry* he pleaded week after week with readers to send him money to buy a tent so work could commence.

The idea of using a tent was not new in the South. As early as 1887 the Army regularly had used a tent in Richmond. Tents were both good and bad. In the heat of summer, they were far more inviting than the stuffy buildings. The tents were also striking in appearance when erected in some prominent place. The problem was that they were subject to the evils of vandalism and inclement weather. Sudden and ferocious storms characteristic of the South could make short work of a tent which had taken hours to raise. In the fall, the cooler air drove the crowds indoors, away from the tents. Still, the tents were the mainstay of the Army's work for twenty years and were not entirely abandoned until well into the twentieth century.

Major Dale was able finally to purchase his tent. Having done that, he took his wife and made his way to Atlanta to open the work there. This is the only Southern city that the Worldwide Salvation Army occupied at the same time Moore maintained a corps. It was at the invitation of soldiers of the Moore contingent that Dale came to Atlanta. He was promised support but found instead things in a state of confusion. He was on his own. Soon the Moore forces withdrew from the city. The city's reception was cool, the public having lost confidence in the Army. No one seemed to realize that one Army had come and another one had left.

A cynic wrote in *The Atlanta Journal*, "The Salvation Army

seems to be on the wane. The last time I saw them on dress parade I counted only five warriors, three of whom were females. They were all making music and marching out Marietta Street in the direction of the sunset. Thus passes the glory of the world." The next May, the Atlanta corps was presented the first flag in the South. The officer at this time was Captain Emma Pigg, known to the people of Atlanta as "Pleading Minnie."

Further expansion came south with a flanking movement from Missouri. The land rush was on in the Oklahoma Territory. Over 1,900,000 acres of land taken from Indians was offered free to settlers. The Army swept in with the settlers, opening in little Oak Grove and then in Kingfisher.

Holding the first religious meeting on record in Kingfisher, we have this description: "In the afternoon we marched into a dive—a theatre in the back of a saloon kindly loaned to us by the proprietor. Here a crowd of tough looking men filled the place to suffocation—a churchless company of gamblers, drunkards, infidels and cowboys. How well I remember their singing! They not only sang, they listened and wept and finally pelted us with money on the stage—big stuff at that, and without asking—for they knew the real thing and appreciated it."

In the town of Hennessey the barracks "consisted of about thirty black jack trees and leaves, which served as a roof. Stakes driven into the ground, with rough lumber nailed on, served as seats. Outside the place was lighted by four large fires at night, and small lanterns lighted up the inside. In one meeting we counted 485 people."

Oklahoma warfare presented its own unique challenges, not the least of which was the wind. Reporting in *The War Cry*, an officer wrote: "Saturday night we had a terrible storm. It came while we were on the march. Brother Fletcher and Cadet Bernard had a tussle with the drums. And sometimes the drums would get the benefit of the winds and would swing the boys around at a lively gait."

The biggest news in 1890 for The Salvation Army in this country did not originate in the United States, but from London. General William Booth had published his landmark book, *In Darkest England and the Way Out.* The world had been thrilled by Stanley's account of his explorations of Africa. Taking his cue from Stanley's description of the jungles and life in the wild, Booth startled Victorian complacency by telling his countrymen life in the cities of England was as ferocious as life in the Dark Continent.

His timing could not have been better. In America, the Reverend Washington Gladding published a book with a similar theme entitled *Burning Questions.* This same year, Jacob A. Riis published *How the Other Half Lives.* The social gospel was being preached, advocating the abolishment of child labor, better working conditions for women and higher wages.

Booth went a step further than his American sympathizers by offering a solution to the problems he outlined. He proposed that The Salvation Army would address the needs of the neediest, those he described as "the submerged tenth." Avoiding claims to create a Utopia, Booth nonetheless spelled out plans to rescue those he saw awash in a sea of dispair.

Not everyone welcomed his plan. An editorial in *The Atlanta Constitution* carried a solemn warning: "If General Booth is like ordinary mortals he is the most dangerous reformer that has appeared in the present century. How long will he and his followers be satisfied with voluntary contributions? When they realize their power they will increase their demands. It will not be strange if they finally resort to violent methods to distribute property on a more equal scale. In the name of religion and reform blood has been shed in the past, and history may repeat itself."

Divisional and Territorial Headquarters and Early History

Southern Divisional Headquarters (1921–1927), 339 Luckie St., NW, Atlanta.

Territorial Headquarters (1927–1955), 54 Ellis St., Atlanta.

Territorial Headquarters (1955–1976) on Seminole Ave., Atlanta, with Temple Corps nearby (right).

Territorial Headquarters and Conference Center, 1424 Northeast Expressway, Atlanta, dedicated in 1976.

School for Officers Training on Stewart Ave., Atlanta.

An annual Memorial Day service is conducted at The Salvation Army plot, Westview Cemetery, Atlanta.

Commissioner George Scott Railton officially opened the work of The Salvation Army in the United States in 1880.

Major Thomas Moore, Commissioner of The Salvation Army for the United States and Canada, followed George Scott Railton.

Col. Richard Holz in the 1890s.

Col. Holz and his cavalry troops invaded the Kentucky mountains.

Ballington and Maud Booth, National Commander for the United States, later starting the Volunteers of America.

The first Atlanta Corps Band, 1891.

Adam Janelli, pioneer worker in Dallas.

Major M. Elizabeth Barter (left) with other Salvationist, distributing Christmas dinner in Baltimore, 1906.

Baltimore Day Nursery, 1925.

Girl Guards in the early days of the Southern Territory.

Ella Dean, early Girl Guard (later Mrs. Major Railton Sprake of the Southern Territory).

Dedication of the new territorial headquarters at 54 Ellis St., Atlanta, 1927, Commander Evangeline Booth and Lt.-Commissioner William McIntyre leading.

A Salvation Army parade in Atlanta during the early days of the territory.

Texas contingent at the opening of the new territorial headquarters, Atlanta, 1927.

Louisville, band marches down Peachtree Street in Atlanta at the opening of the Southern Territory in 1927.

Staff Band about 1927, still wearing the originally planned "Sam Brown" belts.

Sharing in a 1928 radio program with Commissioner Alexander Damon, territorial commander, are (seated) Mrs. Major Gordon MacGillivray, Major Sidney Cox, and Mrs. Major Cox; and (standing) Hal Ingoe, Gordon Swyers, Major MacGillivray, and Mr. Curran.

Dedication of The Salvation Army Industrial Home in Dallas by Commissioner McIntyre, 1928.

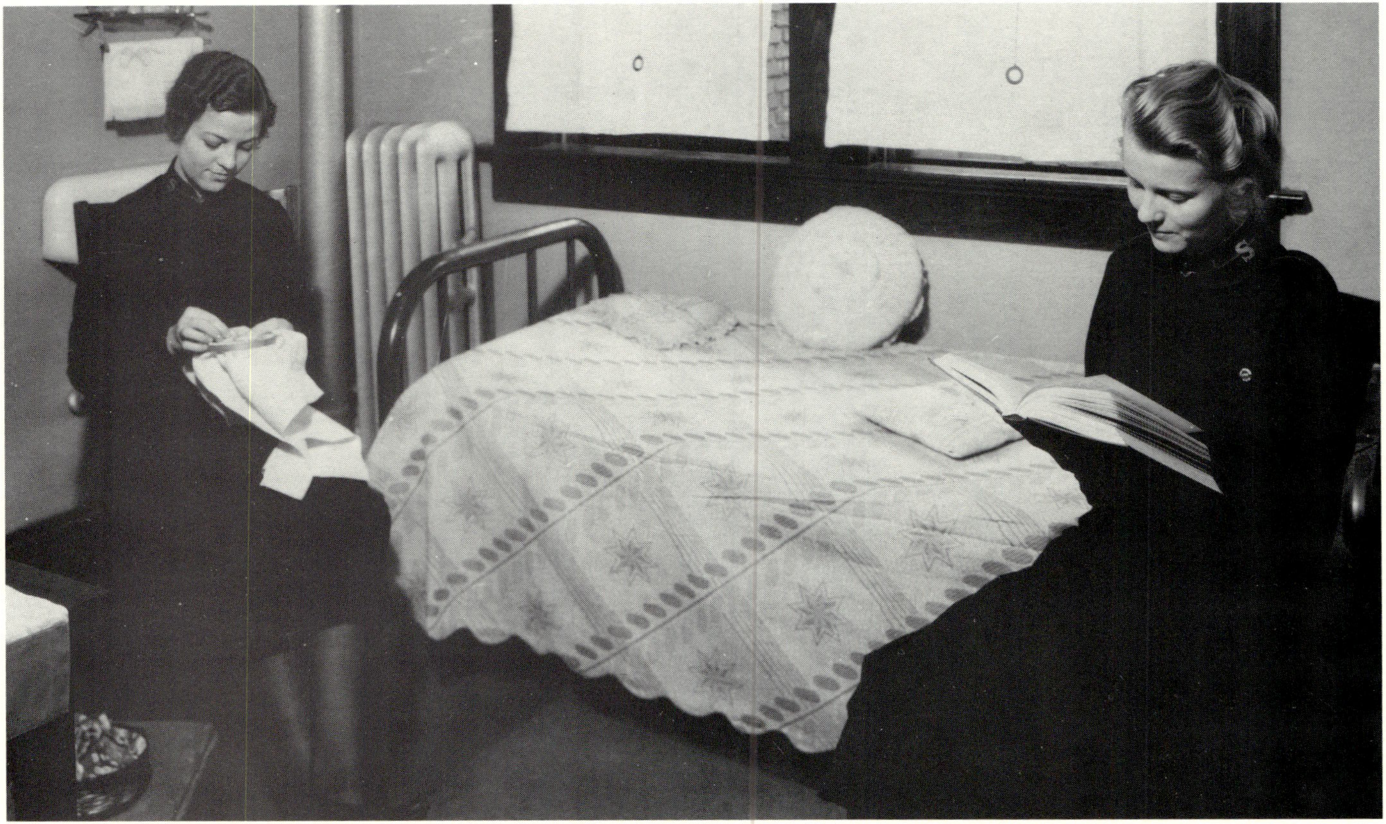

Cadets shared small bedrooms at the Training College at 339 Luckie Street, Atlanta, 1930s.

Cadets at Luckie Street, 1928, with Brigadier and Mrs. Harry Bayes and staff.

Southern Cadets String Band, 1934.

Colonel Alfred Tyler, with Carolinas divisional staff, 1937.

In a timely coincidence that December Maud Booth was the guest speaker of the Women's Christian Temperance Union convention in Atlanta. She won the hearts of the people with more than her gift of oratory. When the gas chandeliers could not be lit (the church janitor was on a picnic and returned late), she had the capacity crowd singing hymns interspersed with prayers until the lights could be turned on. After her visit the criticisms of the Army's social plans were hushed.

The Army's new emphasis did not abate its evangelistic fervor. This zeal encouraged creativity. In efforts to attract crowds to the buildings, efforts such as a "sash parade" graced Southern streets. The soldiers would go out after dark carrying torches and wearing sashes inscribed with Scripture verses or other mottoes.

In other places the Army held midnight open-air meetings. Elsewhere, "novelty meetings" were held when the soldiers dressed themselves in various costumes. Perhaps the Salvationists, who appeared odd to people in their uniforms anyway, looked even more so in costume. In an unusual twist a "Cavalry Corps" was formed in Havre de Grace, Md. composed of unsaved men who penalized those who left the services early.

The continued need for money gave birth to unusual fund-raising ideas, always combined with evangelistic efforts. In seashore towns such as Norfolk, oyster suppers were held. In Baltimore, coffee and cake suppers appeared. In Nashville, ice cream was served. The ice cream suppers caught on in the South by providing a delicacy and relief from the heat at the same time. In all these, evangelistic meetings were held as the customers dined.

Officer shortages further hamstrung the Army's progress in the South. The divisional officer from Texas tried to recruit help by appealing to the ascetic in his readers: "Salary chasers not wanted; those afraid of work can stay away; sleepy folks need not come; those who don't like hard 'go's' sit still; please, we don't want Y O U ; no dolls need apply."

The conditions in the South fought against the recruitment of quality officers. With oppressive heat, little money and poor attendances among the difficulties an officer faced, volunteers could go almost anywhere else in the country and find themselves happier. Because of this the South, although having many outstanding officers, became the repository of some of the poorer officers, further complicating its problems.

Often the officers were without buildings either because of a lack of funds or eviction. This left them with only the streets as a place for meetings. Even this became more difficult as persecution began to appear.

For the first time, Salvationists were arrested in the South. The first arrest came in Austin, Tex. In a pattern which would be repeated throughout the country, the city council had passed a law against public use of the drum, fondly referred to within the ranks as "the Army's church bell." The ordinance was only selectively enforced—circus parades and local militia bands were unmolested. Arrests came in Dallas, Oklahoma City, Galveston and other cities across the South.

Although the charges were usually dismissed, that was not always the case. The young corps in Salem, Va. was snuffed out when the corps officer, a man with frail health, was arrested for having conducted an open-air meeting and sentenced by the mayor to hard labor for 27 days, complete with a twenty pound ball chained to his leg.

Freelance efforts brought the Army unofficially to Florida as early as 1884 when a corps was opened in Apopka. Contemporary accounts tell of open-air meetings in Jacksonville as early as 1889. Neither the Worldwide Salvation Army nor the Moore forces laid claim to these operations. Finally, in

1891, the Army reached Florida officially with an opening in Jacksonville.

At one point in its early work the Army was in jail—this time renting the old unused city jail for a month while searching for another building. Later, when the Army entered its second Florida city of Tampa, the officer had to fight for control in the first meeting after a group of hoodlums announced they were taking over. Captain Wilbur Hall bodily ejected them, sustaining a gash across his nose in the process, but returning to the platform to finish the meeting.

Further north, the Army's work continued to prosper in Maryland, spurred on in 1891 by a mass meeting held at Glyndon Campground outside Baltimore. In what was to become an annual event for many years, Commander Ballington Booth held meetings attended by over 8,000 people.

Trains were chartered from Baltimore to carry the thousands who wanted to hear the oratory of this now famous Salvation Army leader. While in the area, the Commander gave approval of plans to open a food and shelter depot, the first effort at social work in the South. For some unknown reason the shelter was never opened.

It was left to Texas to lead the way in social service work. The first free public Thanksgiving dinner was held in Dallas in 1893. This was followed in Houston by the opening of a wood yard. At the wood yard the Army required men to chop wood for a night's lodging. The wood was then sold at discount prices to the poor, with the proceeds supporting the operation of the men's shelter.

In 1894 it was decided once again to attempt to reach the blacks of the South. At the same time, decided efforts were being made in the South to steal away every gain made by blacks since the Civil War. Starting in Mississippi in 1890, when the state constitution took away black suffrage, efforts expanded to form what became known as the Jim Crow laws. These laws were not only to keep the vote from blacks, but to keep every advantage of American citizenship from an entire race of people.

These moves only underscored the South's split personality of wanting to join the mainstream of progress on the one hand, and wanting to recapture the exaggerated romance of the old South on the other. If the laws were not enough, violence against blacks resulted in their being lynched at a rate of three to one over whites. The Army's effort to reach blacks at this time was feeble, withering in the face of this hostile climate.

A poignant example of the Army's attitude came in 1895 when two officers attempted to intercede in behalf of a black who was being lynched at Frederick, Md. The man had been accused of making an improper remark to a white woman. Captain Mott and Lt. Antrim stood outside the jail and pleaded for the man's life. The mob pushed forward, taking the man from the jail. The officers followed to see if there might not be another opportunity to intercede.

At the site of the hanging, another plea was made, only to be unheeded. As a last resort the officers asked if they might be allowed to pray with the man. The crowd consented, removing their hats and bowing their heads during the prayer, and then went on with the hanging.

Late in 1894, William Booth made his second visit to America. With the look of an Old Testament prophet, Booth was more popular than ever before, a world figure since publishing *In Darkest England and the Way Out.* He was greeted by more enthusiasm than ever, his every movement covered by the American press. But age was beginning to show on Booth. He missed his dear wife, Catherine, who had died four years earlier a painful death from cancer.

In constant pain because of a chronic stomach ailment,

Booth was further irritated by the nationalism in America, asking his son, Ballington, why the Americans were so addicted to flag waving. He disappointed Ballington by taking scant notice of what had developed in the years of his administration. When the Founder left America, he was thronged by well-wishers. He left behind a son and daughter-in-law deeply hurt. No one could then know how disastrous this breach would prove to be.

CHAPTER 6

RISING FROM THE RUINS

(1896–1900)

A GREAT CALAMITY in The Salvation Army's history in the United States occurred in 1896. Ballington and Maud Booth were issued "farewell" orders to leave the United States and to proceed to another as yet unannounced command. Instead of obeying, the Booths resigned. Events following this resignation would damage the Army for decades.

Salvationists would find out about the orders of their leaders, not through official channels, but from the newspapers. This only further complicated a confusing situation. Contradictory statements from the farewelling commanders did nothing to clarify the situation.

First it was announced that they would accept the Army discipline and proceed to their new command. Then, it was announced they would farewell but not accept the new appointment. It was next announced they would stay in New York and start a church similar to that Dwight L. Moody had founded in Chicago. It finally ended with the Booths beginning a rival movement.

There was more to the resignation than the hurt feelings engendered during William Booth's visit in 1894. The Ballington Booths felt that the Army's authoritarian leadership, though in the hands of the Booth family, was dangerous. In addition, General William Booth had decided, over Ballington's vehement objections, to place Montana, North Dakota and Washington under the command of Canada. The timing for these orders could not have been poorer.

In faraway Venezuela a long running border dispute between that country and Great Britain had grabbed American attention. The United States interceded in behalf of Venezuela, justifying its involvement by the Monroe Doctrine. Great Britain considered that this matter was none of America's business. As the dispute grew hotter, anti-British feeling grew until the United States was ready to declare war. Then from London, the focal point of the collective American hatred, came orders that would take away America's beloved Salvation Army commanders. When Ballington tried to point this out, his words were greeted with manifest deafness.

A rally was held at Madison Square Garden by leading citizens from New York and around the country with the declared purpose of persuading General Booth to change his mind. He could not. If he allowed one of his own children to be guided by a different discipline than other officers, the Army would be hopelessly compromised. The timing might not be the best but the orders would have to be obeyed. With this final word, Ballington and Maud Booth bid the Army farewell forever.

Immediately those more loyal to the Ballington Booths than to the Army flocked to them, offering any assistance possible. When the plans were laid to begin a new movement, two thirds of its first officers and soldiers were former Salvationists. The deserting Salvationists ripped the S's from their collars and sewed American flags in their place. The new organization named itself the Volunteers of America.

As had occurred when Moore split from the parent movement, the Volunteers quickly added the sacraments of the

Lord's Supper and baptism to their ritual. Although the Ballington Booths originally declared they had no intention of setting up a rival organization, the Volunteers initially were a nearly perfect copy of The Salvation Army. As time went on they would evolve differently but the likeness was so exact that the public would confuse the two organizations for years.

In a less dramatic fashion, another development in Philadelphia would affect the Army's work. James William Duffin, a former officer, had applied for reacceptance the previous year. For some reason now lost to us he did not reenter the ranks. What he did was call together a handful of people to resurrect the American Salvation Army.

A few of those rallying had been part of the splinter group which split from Richard Holz's leadership when reconciliation with the full Army was made in 1889. After struggling for two years, the original American Salvation Army had ceased to exist as an organization, although a couple of isolated corps called themselves by that name in Pennsylvania.

Duffin found that these corps were at the point of extinction. He succeeded in being elected their general, and under his leadership new life was breathed into the resurrected movement. With this action, The Salvation Army was to face two strong parallel and competing movements. The attitude toward each other was most often that of adversary. People were understandably confused when greeted by similarly uniformed evangelists, now representing three separate and distinct organizations.

Meeting these challenges saw Frederick and Emma Booth-Tucker as the new commanders for the United States.

Frederick de Latour Tucker had been a British civil servant in India when he read a *War Cry*. Convinced that what William Booth was doing in England would work in India, he offered his services to the Founder. The offer was accepted and Tucker became the first Salvation Army missionary. He immediately distinguished the Army's missionary effort by abandoning European dress, designing a uniform which matched the lowest caste dress of India, and changing names from European to Indian. In a land dominated by Hindu and Moslem sects, the Army was making inroads.

Tucker's life was marked by tragedy beginning in his service in India when he would lose his first wife to disease. Eventually he was appointed to London where he met and fell in love with Emma Booth, daughter of the Founder. Emma was perhaps the most mystical of the Booth children, and, like her other brothers and sisters, a gifted orator and insightful thinker. When they were married, Tucker incorporated the Booth name in his to form Booth-Tucker.

Receiving their orders to proceed to America in the wake of Ballington's resignation, the Booth-Tuckers left a sick child ashore, assured he was recovering from his illness. Emma herself was ill and, when word came that the child had taken a turn for the worse, only Frederick could return. By the time he reached the baby's side, the child was dead. Before he returned to England, Frederick would experience three more deaths in his immediate family. Nothing was easy about the appointment to America.

The Booth-Tuckers were greeted in America with a subdued welcome. The Army's heartache had given the press a heyday. Old enemies gathered like vultures to watch the last gasp of the Army in America. Confusion reigned as Salvationists saw their former commanders, loved and admired universally, now denounce the Army they had led. The first impressions of the Booth-Tuckers did little to quiet their fears. Samuel Logan Brengle described Frederick as a "stiff, cold, invigorating wind" and Emma as a "feminine, spiritual Bismarck."

With the fallout from Ballington's resignation, the Army suffered embarrassment and further financial hardship. Many of the Army's wealthiest financial supporters withdrew their funds from the Army and diverted their gifts to the Volunteers. The general public simply lost faith in the Army and with it, any desire to see its work prosper.

Rival corps of both the Volunteers of America and the American Salvation Army sprang up in city after city. Soldiers and officers left to join one of these "American" movements. The American Salvation Army, which traced its beginnings to the Moore split when Army social work was nonexistent, copied the features of The Salvation Army's social work introduced in 1890. Ballington Booth had complained that "the social work was being pushed to the detriment of the spiritual work."

Then the world watched as the Volunteers embarked on social work efforts which paralleled those of the Army. This emphasis foretold the trend which would mark the Volunteers of America as an organization that gave increasing attention to its social work with an eventual phasing out of its religious activities.

Meanwhile, Salvationists found themselves competing with their rivals. These were difficult days to be a Salvationist. Inspired by the struggles his troops faced, Booth-Tucker penned these words:

> They say the fighting is too hard,
> My strength of small avail,
> When foes beset and friends are fled,
> My faith must surely fail.
> But, O how can I quit my post
> While millions sin-bound lie?
> I cannot leave the dear old flag,
> 'Twere better far to die.

The troops began to rally, and more than that, to overcome. Booth-Tucker reminded them that, though they might be despised and forsaken, the treatment had been similar for the Savior they served. And God Himself had not left them. It was time to take up the battle anew, to reach the millions perishing in their sins.

The resignation of Ballington Booth did not adversely affect the work in the South as it did elsewhere. (The only corps harmed was Guthrie, Okla. where half the soldiers left the Army to form a Volunteers of America post.) Ballington Booth had virtually ignored the work in the Southern states.

In the eight years of his leadership, the South had netted only thirteen additional corps. There were half as many corps in Philadelphia as in all fifteen Southern states. The one effort to reach blacks which was made was the most anemic ever attempted. Any efforts made below the Mason-Dixon line were cursory at best.

Perhaps bolstered by his success with the poverty-stricken lower castes of India, Booth-Tucker seems to have viewed the South as a land to be conquered. The Southern work flourished under his leadership as it never had before. When failure came, as it did several times, it meant only it was time to regroup and attack again. The success of this tenacity is evident even today when so many corps can date their beginnings during the Booth-Tucker administration.

Booth-Tucker's first effort was yet another attempt to reach the blacks. This time the Army had the following endorsement:

> I am very glad to hear that The Salvation Army is going to undertake work among my people in the Southern states. I've always had the greatest respect for the work of The Salvation Army and especially because I have noted that it draws no color line in religion.
>
> I feel that there is a large class of colored people in the South, especially in the cities, who are not reached by the churches, but who will be reached by your work. In reaching the neglected, and I might say outcast, of our people, I feel that your methods and work have peculiar value. Certainly

there is plenty of room in the South for your ministry and others will give you a hearty welcome. There are thousands of my people in the cities who do not go to church. These as well as others I feel that you will reach and help in a permanent form.

God bless you in all your unselfish Christian work for our country!

Yours for the Master,

Booker T. Washington
Tuskegee Institute

Even with Mr. Washington's endorsement, the Army again found itself in the eye of the hurricane. The Supreme Court had just upheld the Jim Crow laws with a decision which accepted the "separate but equal" doctrine. This decision would plague minorities until its reversal in 1954. Segregation was now the law of the land as affirmed by the Supreme Court. The Army's work would be restricted by this.

Other historians have noted that the Army maintained segregated facilities in the South as its work progressed. It must be remembered that the Army was guided by what was then constitutional law; it had no choice but to segregate when local law dictated. The Army's work in the South cannot be faulted for segregation in those days.

Yet the Army extended work to the blacks when its donor base was almost entirely white. When desegregation was later ordered, the Army welcomed this change and was quick to comply. Like this effort in 1896, the Army's work among blacks was done with unselfish compassion in the best way available to it. This effort would fail, but it was far from the last time the Army would reach out.

The Army was encouraged by stories of its own success and influence. In Fort Smith, Ark., Salvation Army officers were admitted to a jail which housed the Buck gang, condemned to death for their crimes and awaiting execution. The officers went to their cell and pleaded with the men to seek forgiveness from a merciful God. After kneeling with them in prayer, the officers were permitted to walk behind them to the gallows and stand by their side as the death sentence was read.

Over in Norfolk, Va., a sailor named John Carlson heard two women singing in an upstairs room. Curiosity compelled him to climb the dingy stairs where he saw two lassies preaching and testifying to God's saving power. He was struck in his heart by the message and responded to the invitation to salvation. He became a faithful soldier, attending meetings and testifying in open-air meetings when he was in port. He left Norfolk when World War I was declared, giving such distinguished service that he was knighted by King Gustav V of Sweden. He was later appointed Swedish Consul in the United States, also serving on the advisory board in Norfolk.

As Army work was pressed in the South it was attended in places by dramatic revival. In the first four weeks of the Army's opening in Bristol, Tenn., there were 174 conversions, electrifying the whole city. Similar results were seen in Hot Springs, Ark., where the corps opening resulted in 140 souls won in ninety days. In a six week period following the reopening of New Orleans 316 people sought the Savior.

Even where numbers were smaller, the fruit was lasting. When Captain Olson came to Rogers, Ark., he paraded up and down the city streets alone, beating the drum and singing on a cold and rainy spring night. His zeal and dedication impressed a teenage boy who followed him back to the building for the meeting. There John Brown was, in Army terminology, "soundly converted." He followed Olson when he was transferred to Siloam Springs, Ark. to open the corps there. But the work was too difficult and the infant corps folded.

John Brown remained in the town, however, to found John Brown University. In later years, Brown sent his limousine each year to bring Mrs. Major Olson, now widowed, to the college's commencement. Seating her in an honored place on the front row, he would have her stand during the program and introduced her as "the woman who brought me to the Lord."

And the Army was not finished with unusual efforts to reach sinners. The Women's Calvary Brigade assaulted the Oklahoma Territory in 1897. Blanche Cox explained the wicked condition of this area because of "the isolation of the territory, the absence of restraint and the general abandonment to irreligion, forgetfulness, and ungodliness." She noted that these conditions "only more heighten the privilege of preaching to them." The potential danger to these unaccompanied women officers was perceived because "in such parts as these, both inside and out, (one can) see not one woman present."

In Mount Airy, Md., an officer reported the successful auction sale of children. Crowds came to bid on the children, one man offering the auctioneer a tip. The final bid was in, the deal was being closed by the third and last call. " 'Going, going, go-' A shriek was heard, and running down the aisle a youthful lass, arrayed in white, was seen crowding her way and holding a Bible. Catching her breath, she cried, 'For these children with a future before them, both in this world and the next, with a soul to love and save, I offer Christianity.' The people shouted and clapped. The auctioneer listened with moved heart and dropped his hammer in favor of the bidder."

Columbus, Ga., introduced the Army world to the "Ghost Meeting" when the soldiers whitened their faces and covered themselves with sheets. Thus attired, they marched the streets, bringing the desired crowd back to the building with them.

It was in 1898 that the social work of the Army was begun

in earnest. A shelter and a "workingman's hotel" opened in Louisville. Two other workingman's hotels opened later that same year in Houston and Atlanta. Heading up the Army's social efforts for the United States, Richard Holz realized the Army's challenge in the South to support such effforts when he observed, "(it) requires lots of thrusting and stirring about to make a success of the South."

The nation received a boost when William Booth announced his plans to make his third visit to America. The only place visited in the South this time was Washington, but it was here that the Founder received national attention when he opened the Senate in prayer. The visit of the beloved leader not only gave a moral lift to the Army in the United States, but the focus was off the competing movements. In his own grand fashion, William Booth held crowds spellbound as he propounded the Army's mission to the world. There were tremendous spiritual results in the meetings. The country which had cursed him two years before when the Ballington Booths left fell in love with him again.

But Booth would be crowded out of the headlines by news from Havana, Cuba. While in port, the battleship *Maine* was blown up. Americans were hankering for a fight and this incident was all it needed. Never mind that they were going to take on a second-rate power by fighting Spain. Never mind that there was a strong possibility that the battleship was blown up by Cuban insurrectionists who were seeking to draw the United States into the dispute by creating an incident.

Never mind that many in the United States had imperial designs of their own which included taking Cuba and other Spanish colonies as the spoils of war. Yellow journalism screamed glaring headlines that America had to be avenged. "Remember the *Maine*!" became a rallying cry for the nation. It would serve to unite a nation still smarting from the Civil War. It would be a time when people of the South would begin seeing themselves as Americans again.

The Booth-Tuckers heartily supported America's efforts to drive Spain out of Cuba. They also saw an opportunity for service when troops were mobilized for the invasion of the island. Brigadier Mary Lewis, accompanied by Ensign Annie Sands Anderson, was chosen to head up the Army's efforts to minister to the troops.

On the way to the troop encampments that dotted the South, the two women warriors were welcomed at the White House. While there the first lady, Mrs. William McKinley, personally donated the funds needed to buy a tent. As they headed to Tampa, and then Key West, they were welcomed by the camp commanders who were concerned for the moral and spiritual needs of the troops. The women set their tent up and immediately began to hold meetings. Each meeting was crowded with attendances that exceeded 700 at a time.

Brigadier Lewis could not forget the war if she wanted to. She reported that "the rostrum was skillfully built up with boxes of ammunition. Rather a unique sensation to preach from such a stand, with a novel feeling that if the oil lamps blew up it might blow up the pulpit and all, causing the occupiers to ascend to Glory after the fashion of Elijah (with) a chariot of fire."

The Salvation Army was the first organization (outside of the military) to start work so soon. It would work in camps which varied in size from 10,000 to 50,000 troops in Tampa, Key West, Falls Church, Va., and Chickamauga, Ga.

The Spanish-American War was quickly won, the Spanish suing for peace within a year. It had few major battles. When speaking about it later, Theodore Roosevelt said, "It wasn't much of a war, but it was the only one we had." The Army was thankful there wasn't substantial loss of life. Beyond that, it had introduced itself to America as an organization which cared for the service man. In the tragedy of world events that would occur fifteen years later, this introduction of the Army's concern would open the doors when its services were desperately needed.

Meanwhile, as the Army served its country in the war, Salvationists were being arrested in Galveston and San Antonio, Tex. Even in the victory of its war service it was clear that the Army's other battles were far from over.

CHAPTER 7

FANNING OUT
(1900–1904)

THE GALVESTON, TEX. weather report for September 8, 1900 called for sunny skies. What came instead was the greatest killer storm in United States history. Galveston is situated on a barrier island in the Gulf of Mexico, a short distance from Houston. Beautiful most of the time, the scenic location became deadly. Before the hurricane was over, it had carried 6,000 to 9,000 people into eternity. Estimates vary greatly because so many were swept out to sea and their bodies never recovered.

This tragedy became the platform for the first Salvation Army effort in behalf of those victimized by disaster. Across the channel at Texas City the Army set up a relief tent to feed and shelter the homeless. Ministering to those in shock from the sudden and totally unexpected calamity, the workers heard heartrending stories.

One woman described her mixture of despair and hope. As the flood waters began to rise she went with her husband and two little girls to the roof of her house. Still the waters rose, augmented by crashing waves. One wave swept her husband away, and she, holding her two daughters, could only watch in agony. As the storm's fury was unleashed, her smallest child, a toddler, was snatched from her arms. She held tightly to her remaining daughter, but she, too, fell victim to the storm. The woman herself was washed from the roof, only to be caught in a tree which somehow had not fallen. Sobbing, she decided to commit suicide by letting herself drop into the water.

Just as she did, another little girl, carried by the current, drifted by her. Instinctively she reached out for the child and held on, knowing that if she let go of the tree this little one would also die. She held on until the storm ended, and upon investigation discovered that the child had been orphaned. With the child standing at her side she told the Army workers she had found a reason to keep on living.

The Army corps had closed only months before the storm hit. When the stunned people reentered their devastated city the Army went back in, never to close its doors again. In later years the Army would again serve the area with relief for victims of another great disaster.

The work in the Galveston disaster underscores important advances being made by the Army in the area of social service work. While some of it was planned and directed from National Headquarters, other expressions were spontaneous. In Houston, Captain R. McKenzie hosted a children's outing in 1899. The city children were loaded on trolley cars and taken to a park for a day of games, fun and an abundance of food. These outings quickly spread across the South and later gave rise to the children's summer camps.

Booth-Tucker's passionate interest in the plight of the homeless in the next few years would bring additional shelters in the major cities of the South. The Salvation Army's most effective tool in dealing with the long term problems of the chronically homeless was the industrial home. Under the auspices of compassionate officers, men could learn trades while they worked for their lodging and meals, receive help to combat alcoholism, and hear the message of salvation. Opening originally in Baltimore, Washington and Dallas, the industrial homes would evolve into a widespread network of institutions, eventually renamed Men's Social Service Centers and later Adult Rehabilitation Centers. With the growth in numbers, the program became increasingly sophisticated, providing comprehensive services to those fighting the twin evil of homelessness and substance abuse.

Some of the Army's efforts to alleviate the suffering of the poor were the soul of simplicity. During the hot summer of 1902, Captain J.P. Sayers of Atlanta solicited barrels from the city and ice from the ice houses. He then placed barrels of ice water in the poverty-stricken areas of the city. As in any other successful effort, his success would be duplicated in other cities.

Booth-Tucker set his heart again on reaching the Southern blacks. In publicity for an upcoming campaign, it was announced "the opening of the colored work in the South, the establishment of our work in Cuba and in the Philippines will probably commemorate our Century Advance." The work in the South was obviously still considered akin to missionary efforts. This effort of 1899 was aborted.

It was followed by another announcement in *The War Cry* in 1900: "A new lifeboat for the rescue of our colored brethren of the South has just started out of harbor on her mission. Colored comrades throughout the land, this is an order for you. If fully consecrated and given up to God, apply at once."

An African Division was created under Ensign Smith, headquartered in a former Baltimore police station, opening the only black corps in America. The mantle of leadership was soon passed to Staff-Captain Widgery.

The Baltimore American reported: "Recent notice of plans of The Salvation Army, particularly the purchase of the old Southern Police Station, are only in part indicative of the aggressive campaign which will be carried on by this organization in Baltimore . . . plans include the general remembrance of the poor at Christmas time, the offering of industrial opportunities to poor colored people . . . it is proposed to establish a colored shelter and industrial institution to accommodate 200 men . . . also a wood yard."

But even a generation after the Civil War the attitude toward blacks was almost universally hostile. In the same year of this Army effort blacks were found enslaved in parts of South Carolina and Anderson County, Ga. Later in 1901, Booker T. Washington dined with President Theodore Roosevelt.

In an explosive reaction to the perceived violation of racial separation, scores of blacks were killed in a New Orleans race riot. The Army effort was still not strong enough to overcome the entrenched attitudes of many white Southerners. One black corps opened in Baltimore, closing within two years.

The further expansion of corps work brought the Army to Alabama with successive openings in Birmingham, Montgomery and the reopening of Mobile. In 1902, opening shots of the Salvation War were heard in Vicksburg, site of the great Civil War battle. Encouraged by early success there, Memphis, then known as the "Murder Capital of the World", was slated next. Here the work of the Army was suspended for a time, not because of violence, but because of an outbreak of smallpox.

These advances would be overshadowed by news from Texas. John Archbold, an executive with Standard Oil, told Patillo Higgins of Beaumont, "You'll never find oil here. I'll drink every gallon of oil found west of the Mississippi." On January 10, 1901 the "Spindletop" oil well started gushing—the greatest strike the world had ever seen. With the rush of fortune seekers came Army officers to establish the Beaumont corps. Within a year the rich community had built the Army a proper looking citadel, complete with battlements, two store spaces to provide rental income and a hotel upstairs that offered rooms for 15 cents a night.

William Booth returned to America in 1903. With this trip he made his only extensive visit in the South. In January and early February he stopped in Chattanooga, Nashville, Memphis, Dallas, New Orleans, Mobile, Birmingham, Atlanta, and Washington. In Mobile, Booth spoke to a large crowd at a black church. The visit to a black congregation was made even more notable by a spontaneous gesture Booth made as he traveled by train between cities. Seeing a black mother with her infant, he stopped to talk. Then he bent over and kissed the baby. Many Southerners were shocked by this violation of their racial standards. One newspaper trumpeted the headline, "William Booth Kisses a Coon." The Founder felt no apology or explanation need be made for his action. His love for all mankind was genuine and, besides, any attack the South leveled upon him was mild compared to the treatment he had received in his native Britain.

Traveling on to Nashville, he announced plans to open a fourth farm colony in Tennessee. The farm colony was part of the "Darkest England" scheme which had segments with more enthusiasm than practicality. The colony never materialized.

In New Orleans, crowds filled Tulane Hall to hear of the work of the Army by its now legendary Founder. At the close of a press interview, Booth told reporters that he would like to have a prayer meeting with the newspapermen as an audience, presumably to convert them.

While in Washington, Booth was hosted at a formal luncheon attended by President Theodore Roosevelt, several Cabinet members and high ranking members of Congress. The luncheon was nearly a disaster. The atmosphere was stiff with formality, the General tired and somewhat cranky.

When he rose to speak his voice was hoarse from speaking

at nonstop engagements for weeks. Finally, someone from the back yelled, "Louder!" The demand for volume seemed to breathe new life into the Army's aging founder. He gathered himself and gave a spirited talk which lasted over an hour.

While in the South the General admonished his troops to make additional efforts to reach Southern blacks. "There is indeed a great harvest to reap in the South among the colored population," he said. "True, at the moment our plans are not ready, but wait awhile, pray a little longer, have faith in God, and the advance will be sounded and we shall see mighty triumphs for our God and King."

After the General left, the Army was back in the headlines. This time Americans were fascinated with an expedition known as the Kentucky Mountain Brigade. As a provincial commander, Colonel Richard Holz had often discussed with Booth-Tucker his burden for the mountain people of eastern Kentucky and Tennessee and western Virginia. The area was infamous as a feuding area. In seven Kentucky feuds there had been 250 murders.

The foolishness of these fights elicited a definition of feuding from Mark Twain: "A man has a quarrel with another man and kills him; then that other man's brother kills him; then the other brothers on both sides go for one another; then the cousins take sides, and by-and-by everybody is killed off, and there isn't any more feud."

The bold experiment drew enough attention that the McClure newspaper chain sent a correspondent along. In an interview before leaving, Colonel Holz explained the Army's purpose in going: "An outbreak of feudal killing took place in Breatthit County, Ky . . . we felt we should get in touch with these mountain people. We are very hopeful that the methods of The Salvation Army will prove just the thing to awaken these peculiar people and bring them out of their ignorance and sin . . . Yes, there will be a degree of danger for us on this trip."

The newspapers considered the risks greater than Holz did. *The Philadelphia Sunday Press* wrote: "Preaching and singing, these Salvation Army men, less than a dozen in number, armed with hymn books and musical instruments, entered the very heart of the feudal district, utterly regardless of the dangers they were subject to in daring the displeasure of the people."

They invaded the mountains in a special khaki uniform which resembled the U.S. Army's field service uniform. Traveling most of the way on horseback, they brought two horse wagons to carry their supplies, blankets and musical instruments. Their first stop was Jackson, Ky. This was the same place where three people had been killed in recent weeks when men shot at the lanterns they were carrying to see if they could put out the lights.

There they made their first convert, Judge John L. Noble, known better by his colorful nickname "Rat Ankles." He had been involved with a gang that assassinated a young attorney only a short time before. At the meeting held in the courthouse he rose and said, "I will stop my evil ways and from this time be a better man."

The next stop was Salyersville, Ky., where the feeling was so bad between the feuding factions that they not only refused to be in the same building together but also on the same side of the street. The local judge noted with satisfaction that the closest either side had been to each other in memory was when they gathered around the Army open-air meeting.

Along the way the Salvationists had to reassure the mountaineers they were not Revenuers—their uniforms were almost identical. Having done that, they were allowed to have a meeting around a working moonshine still. In Wise

County, Va., Colonel Holz mounted the gallows to address 4,000 people gathered to watch a public execution.

When the expedition was completed the Kentucky Mountain Brigade had held 50 meetings in courthouses, jails and on mountainsides attended by over 15,000 people. They recorded 31 conversions while traveling over 200 miles on horseback. Having concluded the campaign, Holz decided the area was still too rural to support an Army corps.

Further advances in the South were being heralded. The Army forces that had numbered only 37 corps in 1896, ended the year of 1904 with 73 corps and 15 social service institutions. Colonel Richard Holz announced his hopes to make Birmingham the center for all Army operations in the South.

A great blow to the city which boasted the oldest Army work in the South came in February 1904. Topped only by the great Chicago fire of 1871, an inferno laid waste to Baltimore. Over 2,600 buildings were destroyed, including all three of the Army's shelters.

Staff-Captain Trudgeon was nearly killed when he tried to rescue men still in the burning buildings. "They (the men) fought me desperately, until the blood ran from the bruises in my hands, but after a time, having dragged some and carried others, I got them all out." Miraculously, not a single person perished in any of the Army shelters.

Sorrow had struck the worldwide Army when it was learned that, on October 28, 1903, Emma Booth-Tucker was the sole casualty in a train wreck at Dean Lake, Mo. Her husband, Frederick, was devastated. His grief prostrated him. The Booth-Tuckers had completely shared their American command.

Her loss was a severe blow not only to her husband but also to the administration of the Army. In addition to the loss of his wife, and the child who had died when they sailed to America, another child had died during their administration.

Booth-Tucker would struggle on but it became obvious that he alone was not as effective without the help of his wife.

Booth-Tucker, in spite of his grief, had testified magnificently at the funeral service in November 1903. Continuing alone without his wife in the American command, he took a delegation of officers to London for the 1904 Congress, being given a succeeding appointment in November, 1904.

As Booth-Tucker was recalled to London in 1904, Commissioner Eva Booth received orders to 'farewell' from Canada and come to the United States.

During the command of Eva Booth in the United States not only the world, but The Salvation Army itself would be dramatically changed forever.

CHAPTER 8

CONSOLIDATING THE GAINS
(1904–1917)

EVA BOOTH was as exciting as America's boom time. She was the picture of a leader. A talented dramatist, she could hold a crowd for hours, whether she portrayed characters such as a poor matchseller or preached with magnificent oratory. Crowds thronged to hear her. In Washington she outdrew evangelist Aimee Semple McPherson, while in Charleston, W.Va., her audiences dwarfed those for the president and evangelist Billy Sunday.

She was possessed with numerous idiosyncracies. When visiting Lakeland, Fla., she insisted on sleeping in the same hotel room which had been occupied by baseball great Ty Cobb. She was able to develop leaders while she seemed to dominate those under her. She was an incredible leader possessed with her father's charisma which inspired loyalty from her followers.

On November 2, 1904, Eva assumed command of the American forces—a single woman in a country which would let sixteen more years elapse before giving women the right to vote. To help his daughter administer the growing Army, General Booth divided the country. The Department of the West was formed in January 1905, still under Commander Evangeline Booth's direction, but with its own headquarters in Chicago. This department included from the South the states of Texas, Arkansas, and the Oklahoma Territory (which became a state that same year).

During the next thirty years, Evangeline Booth would direct the maturing Army along a course which dictated tremendous internal change. She would see her new country become a world power, watch it as it wavered between daring to face the future and falling back into the past. Her keen perception of events and their implications for the Army's mission permitted the Army to make brilliant adaptations. These adjustments catapulted the previously obscure organization to a major role on the national scene.

Change was the order of the day in the South. It could be no more clearly demonstrated than in the mass exodus from the farm to the city. Between the years of 1880 and 1900 the population of Birmingham jumped from 3,086 to 38,400; Atlanta tripled it population, growing from 37,400 to 90,000; Dallas mushroomed from 10,300 to 42,000. Similar growth occurred in other cities across the South.

The momentum set in the latter part of the Nineteenth Century has continued to the present. This change augured well for the future of the Army. Although it had limited success in some small towns and villages, it was, and continues to be, suited to urban environments.

The South continued to seek and develop its industrial base. With the strengthening of the labor union movement in the North, the abundant and cheap labor of the South looked more and more attractive to investors. This was greatly due to the foundering of the labor union movement in the South. Augmenting this was the continued surplus of laborers, dooming any attempts by workers to have wages raised. Southern workers consistently made one-third less than their Northern counterparts.

While the South rejoiced over the continued industrialization of the region, it was at the price of the individual. Whole families continued to work in order to make ends meet. With this, education was limited for children, leaving them to grow into adults with no choice but to work in menial, low-paying jobs. Industrialization was truly a two-edged sword. But, for the Army, it was also the promise of a better day. It had been most successful with the working class and now saw further opportunities as industrial progress reached deeper into the South.

Traditionally, many Southerners had shown little interest in social concerns. If you were poor you were no different from your father or his father or his father. Indeed, poverty had come to have a dignity of its own. Besides, even if you were considered "white trash", the black was considered to be one step lower on the ladder.

The Army had literally to educate some of the Southern population to the responsibility of reaching out to those in need. So it was that the Army found slow but steady progress in the continued opening of its industrial homes for alcoholic and homeless men.

The social work emphasis took a new turn in 1905 when a home for unwed mothers was opened in Birmingham. This was not the first expression of concern for women in the South. As early as 1895 it was reported that in Tampa, Fla., "one of our dear comrades being in much sympathy with this particular class (of fallen women) and having the work pressed upon her, has been working a little rescue home and a number of girls have been gotten hold of by this means." This free-lance effort was never reported on again. A permanent work was established in Baltimore with the opening of the Day Nursery in 1901. Although not directed at women specifically, the children were often from single parent homes.

It was the homes for unwed mothers which proved to be one of the Army's most important outreaches in the South.

The Southerner had always seen himself as the protector of a woman's honor and pronounced harsh judgment on any cad who had lowered this standard by taking advantage of a woman. The Army found immediate sympathy for this program.

The homes for unwed mothers were not always welcome. In 1910, when the officer, Captain Meridian, attempted to open a home in San Antonio on land donated by local philanthropist Colonel Breckenridge, she was at first refused a building permit. The divisional commander came down with an attorney, resulting in the city begrudgingly issuing the permit.

Before leaving town, the attorney pulled the officer aside and advised her to have someone stay at the site. With her assistant, the captain moved into the partially-finished building. Hearing noises outside during the night, the two women surprised a group of men who had materials to burn down the home. From that night on, the captain slept with a revolver under her pillow.

Upon finishing the building, it was discovered that the location was uncomfortably close to a club which engaged in illegal gambling and prostitution. The resistance from city hall was better understood when the captain discovered that the mayor owned and operated the club.

Stopping her later as she sold *The War Cry*, he said, "I have been the mayor of San Antonio for many years and have had fights with large and wealthy corporations but I never yet got licked by anyone but this measly Salvation Army and Captain Meridian. But you fought square, Captain. Let's shake hands on it." All opposition and hostility from the city government ceased from that moment on.

The interest in social work continued to grow among Army officers. The objecct of persecution in days past, they were now often seen as community leaders who somehow could address the problems that had been ignored or felt to be beyond solving. The effect was exhilarating as more and more officers rushed to find some service to offer the community. With each success came more praise, and wonder of wonders, money.

In his provincial brief of 1908, Richard Holz warned his successor that the Southern officers were tempted to ignore the Army's spiritual thrust by their involvement with social work. He reported that the Army was the entire welfare system in Savannah, Greenville, S.C., Mobile, Jacksonville and Montgomery.

Underscoring the spiritual concern, Holz reported that Jackson, Miss. had only four soldiers, Owensboro, Ky. had only two and Nashville had only one. The Army's spiritual influence was so weak in Charlotte that, when the officers arrived to take command, the police told them that they thought the work had closed, with the nearest corps 25 miles away.

Despite the warnings the social work rapidly expanded. In Cumberland, Md., the Army had a state-of-the-art steam wood chopper and, in addition, a six-acre farm. Montgomery offered the first "fresh air" camp for children in the South. A free medical dispensary opened in Houston. In Vicksburg, 107 poor mothers and children were taken on a paddle boat cruise on the Mississippi River. At Lynchburg, Va., the newly opened corps operated a night school for children who worked in the cotton mills during the day. A similar school had opened in Montgomery.

While it might have seemed wiser to the administration to slow down on the social work emphasis, the Army officers were seeing their work not only valued by the community but making a difference in the lives of the impoverished people around them. Once started, it was impossible to stop.

Not all the social work was permanent. A shortlived service provided what was described as "child rescue." It was reported from Charleston, S.C., that "the Army members go among the vicious and depraved, wherever they hear of children in circumstances too horrible to contemplate, and usually by persuasion, by the aid of the law if necessary, they snatch helpless babies from a certain life of misery and wrong, and place them where they have a chance to grow up among clean living surroundings . . .

"Through all sorts of channels do the children get into the hands of the Army. Some are brought to headquarters by tearful and disgraced mothers. One of them rescued in the past few months was left on the doorstep of the Army house in a basket." The Army carefully placed the children with childless couples.

In Greenville, S.C., the Army took over the Bruner Home, an orphanage which had been operating privately since 1906. During the years it was open the home saw hundreds of children pass through its doors. Funded partially by the Duke Endowment, the home could boast quality care at minimal cost—in 1931 it cost only 68 cents a day to keep a child. Before it closed during the Great Depression several of the children had found their way into the ranks as Army officers.

Even in the victories of the social work the Army faced problems in its daily existence. Yellow fever continued to plague the South, closing down whole cities. In 1905 the city of New Orleans sent out a plea to the United States government to help it in its fight against the deadly disease. As it spread, the officers in Natchez, Miss., were forced to close the corps temporarily when their city was ravaged.

Despite the diversions of the social work and the difficulties of Southern life, the Army continued to make progress with its spiritual work. In a spectacular move, the Army was aided by no less a figure than President Theodore Roosevelt.

The Army had requested permission to hold tent meetings in a vacant lot diagonally across from the White House.

When District of Columbia authorities turned down the request, Army friends reached the President and asked for his intercession. Since the lot was federal government property Roosevelt contacted the necessary people and the Army was allowed to conduct its services, with widespread press coverage prompted by the unusual action.

Meanwhile, in Mobile the officer jubilantly reported "one of the most remarkable captures made by The Salvation Army . . . is that of a landlady at one of the houses in the red light district here . . . she has given up her jewelry, sold her household effects, and is encouraging the girls who have been living a life of shame to return to their homes."

Other strides came when Major Elizabeth Barter became the first, and at that time the only woman to be a divisional commander in the South. Serving in two Southern divisions, she had to resign due to ill health. But that did not end her trailblazing. When she joined the police force in Birmingham she was the first policewoman in that city. She remained a faithful Salvationist all her life and, despite resigning for ill health, went on to live until she was 93 years old.

The first family to become soldiers of the newly-opened Miami Citadel Corps in 1913 gave two of the many outstanding pioneer officers of the Southern Territory: John and George Bivans.

John also became the first candidate to enter training from Miami. His evangelistic fervor on the street corners was highlighted by nearly 10,000 open air meetings conducted, resulting in hundreds of decisions for Christ. He skillfully commanded many of the large corps and city commands of the territory, always blessed of the Lord in additions to the soldiery, building of skilled bands and songster groups, as well as financial and proper facility acquisitions.

The second generation of Southern Salvationists had not lost its sense of humor. Captain McAfee of Anniston, Ala., reported on an open-air meeting attended by a large crowd. When two of the women soldiers were called on to sing, a family in a buggy pulled up to listen. As the singers reached the chorus of the song, the mule joined in. The mule continued to bray each time the women reached the chorus and quit when the song was over.

The Baltimore Industrial Home reported in with news of an unusual donation. A woman at a boarding house had an undesirable tenant. She tried without success to have him move. In an unguarded moment the tenant removed his wooden leg. The Army became an unwitting accomplice when she called the industrial home with word of a donation, offering the stolen leg.

When the discovery was made by the man, he demanded his leg back, only to learn that it was now property of the Army. The landlady told him to fetch it himself, but that she would be glad to provide the cab fare. Reaching the industrial home, he startled the unsuspecting officer by angrily insisting upon the return of this leg. Putting it on, he stomped off to find a new boarding house.

A bigger shock came when the salvage workers opened a long black box. In it was a skeleton. To the great relief of the shaken workers, it was revealed that the skeleton had been owned by a doctor who had recently passed away. When his daughter was clearing out his things she could think of no one to give it to save the Army.

On the serious side was the discovery of an important historical document. By chance the officer looked through the box of books. To his amazement he found the diary of the doctor who was with Lincoln immediately following the assassination at Ford's Theatre. In the diary, he described the injuries and the postmortem examination. The diary was turned over to the Smithsonian Institution in Washington.

The South is the only United States territory to be involved in the opening of the work in four foreign countries—Cuba, Mexico, Guatemala and Taiwan. The first foreign foray came in 1912 when the Army flag was unfurled in Havana, Cuba. Under the direction of divisional headquarters in Atlanta, the work was carried on for a little over a year before the solitary Cuban corps was closed.

An innovation in fund raising came the same year in Charleston, W. Va. The Army had been instrumental in the conversion of one of West Virginia's governors, the Honorable William A. McCorkle. The former governor became a Salvation Army Sunday school teacher, serving in that capacity for years. Early in his Army involvement he told the officers that with his contacts he could raise enough money to erect a building for the Army. With, for that time, a phenomenal goal of $30,000, ten days were set aside in April for the drive.

The War Cry reported, "Laying aside business and professional cares, the committee actually thought, talked and slept in the spirit of The Salvation Army . . ." When the ten days were finished $37,000 had been raised. Years later the Army would continue to benefit from the former governor when his beautiful 30 room stone mansion, known as "Sunrise", would be deeded to the Army.

On August 12, 1912 the world heard the sad news that the Army's founder, William Booth, was dead. In Army vernacular he had been "promoted to Glory." Memorial services were held across the South. In Charlottesville, Va. over 500 crowded into the Army hall to pay tribute to this man who had become a world figure. Even larger crowds were seen elsewhere, with Savannah reporting over 1,000 at its memorial service and Richmond relating the news of the largest crowd, in excess of 3,000.

The new general would be Bramwell Booth, the oldest son of the founder. An excellent administrator, he possessed the autocratic leadership nature which characterized the

Booth family. He was a sincere exponent of the doctrine of holiness, with a great love for young people, but little of his father's charisma. In contrast with the visits of his father, when he came to America he would scarcely be noticed. On these visits he was frequently upstaged by his sister, Evangeline.

When William Booth had begun his work in the east end of London there was little to suggest it would be more than another attempt to reach the destitute. Under his direction a unique organization was formed. The reorganization of the movement along military lines was a stroke of genius. It galvanized his followers, giving rise to a special concept in Christian work. When later the Army made a commitment to social work it further distinguished itself. With this came the principle that success will be imitated.

In the early part of the Twentieth Century the landscape was overrun with imitations and counterfeits of The Salvation Army. In this period when the Army itself was still obscure, unscrupulous imitators could pass themselves off, with relative ease, as the real thing. Some efforts were sincere but they nonetheless confused the public as to what army they were dealing with.

An exception to this was the Volunteers of America which had already sought to distance themselves from the parent movement by changing their uniforms to gray, dropping the use of the bass drum and phasing out street meetings. It was the other groups which caused the Army the greatest concern.

The largest was the American Salvation Army (ASA). Duffin's organization had continued to grow after its reorganization in 1896. The problem for The Salvation Army was more than the confusion with similar names. In Martinsburg, W. Va., and Athens, Ga., the corps closed when the ASA came to town. In Selma, Ala., all but three soldiers left the corps to join with the other movement, with similar problems encountered in Baton Rouge. But it was the confusion in the public's mind which forced the Army to initiate legal action against the ASA.

In 1910 the State of New York found that the ASA was guilty of imitating The Salvation Army so deliberately as to cause confusion in the public's mind. They were enjoined from using the term "Army" in their title, using the title of *War Cry* in connection with their publication, having bonnets or other uniform gear which closely resembled that of The Salvation Army.

Duffin then changed the name of his organization to the American Rescue Workers, an organization still operating in parts of the United States. The confusion did not end with this change. Their Knoxville 1916 Annual Report went to great lengths to show that it was the "real" Salvation Army. But when the report came out it used the logo of the American Salvation Army.

This New York injunction was more than a foregone conclusion. Thomas Moore had copyrighted many of the familiar symbols of the Army including the Army's logo and the title of its official publication, *The War Cry*. The Army had adjusted by replacing the crown on top of its logo, called the crest, with an eagle. It kept on using the title of *The War Cry*, though legally it had no right to. The American Salvation Army called their publication *The American Salvation Army War Cry*.

With Thomas Moore now dead, both organizations approached his widow and two sons to obtain rights to the use of the title. Though the Moores seemed to favor The Salvation Army over the American Salvation Army, they meant to have something tangible for what had now become a hot property. In something of a bidding war, The Salvation Army finally settled with the Moores by paying $200 for the rights to the title *The War Cry*. The positive effect of this was to fortify an already strong case.

This legal decision set a precedent for the Army to deal

with the other "armies" that it found. To their credit, the American Rescue Workers actively cooperated with the Army in this effort. In the years of 1913 and 1914 alone, Baltimore reported "armies" entitled the American Salvationists, the Samaritan Army, and the Salvation Army Church. In Knoxville and Louisville the Christian Army was operating.

Knoxville had the Colored Salvation Army, also named the Aultermane (translated Law and Gospel) Salvation Army. This latter group apparently was a sincere effort to help blacks. Some interviews were held with Commander Norris, the young man who directed the organization's efforts, to see if he could be brought into the Army and continue his outreach to blacks. Unfortunately, nothing came of this.

The Army's concern for blacks continued with yet another effort at reaching them. The usual *War Cry* announcement came: "The time seems right for the The Salvation Army to regularly organize work among the hundreds of thousands of colored people who, particularly in the Southern states, formed no inconsiderable part of the population." Since the last effort, blacks were asserting themselves more, aided in 1909 by the founding of the National Association for the Advancement of Colored People (NAACP).

A more important development came with the increased use of the automobile. Blacks were migrating to the North and West. This migration would increase in volume until the Depression. While this was happening the Army in the South had sought to further extend its social work to the black population. In Jacksonville, Fla., the Army placed a much appreciated ice water barrel in the black section of the city. In Atlanta a local paper reported on the Christmas distribution, saying, "Neither did the Army discriminate in color. The deserving negro was looked after . . ."

Still, the lot of blacks was usually far below that of the poorest whites. The migration of blacks and the continued efforts to organize themselves inspired fears in many whites who had assumed that blacks would always take only what was given to them. D.H. Chamberlain, former governor of South Carolina, wrote, "Regarding the negro problem, I am forced . . . to say that perhaps our first practical aim should be to undo, so far as possible, what we have heretofore done for the negro since his emancipation—namely the inspiring in him the hope and dream of sharing with the white race a social or political future . . ."

With white sentiment sometimes against blacks, the Army made progress. Opening the first permanent black corps in Washington, D.C., (#2), black corps were opened in Charleston, S.C., Richmond, Va., and Elizabeth City, N.C., Major James Roberts, a black officer, headed the Army efforts. Although some of these attempts were to eventually languish, Roberts continued to command Washington # 2 for many years.

Later, the first effort to reach Hispanics came with a notice in *The War Cry.* "Do you know of any good, well-saved Salvationists who can speak Spanish? Volunteers are wanted for the opening of work among the large Mexican population in the South and along the border." It was reported that work among the Mexican population in San Antonio and Houston was planned if workers could be secured. This early attempt with Hispanics would meet the same fate as the early attempts to reach blacks.

In 1914 Salvationists traveled to England for the International Congress. Saddened by news that many of their Canadian comrades had died in the sinking of the *Empress of Ireland,* they would find that tragedy eclipsed by the single shot of an assassin's gun in Yugoslavia. Through a series of complicated treaties Europe was plunged into a war which would claim 50 million lives.

The United States stayed aloof for a time, though deeply

sympathetic with the cause of the Allies. But America had already become a nation determined to influence world events. It was only a matter of time before Europe's battlefields would be watered with American blood.

CHAPTER 9

THE WAR TO END ALL WARS

(1917–1922)

AFTER WALKING the international tightwire for three years, on April 6, 1917, the United States entered World War I on the side of the Allies. Although it had proclaimed itself neutral from the outset of the conflict, the Americans had in fact been sympathetic all along with the Allies. America's entry into the war would turn the tide in favor of the Allies and assert once and for all the prominence of the United States in world affairs.

America's biggest contributions were her industrial might and manpower. Europe had been bled dry as she watched her men from both sides dying in the disease-infested trenches. It choked economically as surely as men choked on the dreaded mustard gas. When the United States entered the war, it brought fresh supplies and men to a deadly stalemate.

When the soldiers were activated, The Salvation Army immediately offered its services to the armed forces. At first it was turned down, but then a friend in the person of General John J. "Blackjack" Pershing, head of the American Expeditionary Force, interceded on the Army's behalf. He had tragically lost his family in a fire earlier and remembered well the Army's compassionate outreach to him. With the go-ahead given, Commander Evangeline Booth mobilized the Army's forces to give comfort and aid to the service man.

This service by the Army was to be remembered even in 1948 at the large state funeral for General Pershing. Twenty Salvation Army officers were seated in a prominent place in the amphitheater. General Evangeline Booth, though invited to a place of honor at the service, unable to attend, was represented at the impressive ceremony honoring the memory of this man, the only person other than George Washington to hold the position of General of the Armies of the United States.

When The Salvation Army arrived in Europe it took its place next to other service organizations such as the Red Cross and YMCA. While offering similar services, the Army workers became favorites because of their plain, but effective, Christian witness. It was the Army's desire to be of simple service that gave it its most enduring legacy from the war.

An example of this service came when a group of officers, headed by Adjutant Helen Purviance, were discussing what they could do for the doughboys. A young soldier, Private Braxton Zuber of Auburn, Ala., said, "Man, if I just had a doughnut like Mom used to make!" He later wrote about the experience:

> She (Adjutant Purviance) said that she would try the first one on me, and if that one killed me, it would not be wise to continue doughnut making. I ate that first doughnut made by The Salvation Army in France. The doughnut was delightful, and The Salvation Army accordingly embarked upon a doughnut making spree that has not ended until this good day. All the boys fell immediately for this new delicacy. Soon ambulances began stopping at our outfit to secure doughnuts for the wounded. All who ate them liked them. Our commander felt obligated to keep the ladies in sugar that the doughnuts might continue their fine work. In spite of all the limitations and the shortage of food, our commander managed to keep sugar on hand and the ladies kept the doughnuts rolling.

Not all the war work was done in Europe. Across the United States, military bases were enlarged and others sprang up. Always concerned about the temptations faced by young men in the military, the Army provided "huts" for the servicemen. These provided the serviceman wholesome fellowship with conveniences such as refreshments, recreation, and guest rooms for visiting family. The first hut in the United States was opened in Louisville at a base which housed 45,000 men. By the time the war ended in November 1918 there were thirty huts across the South. In Washington, a Colored Serviceman's Hostel was opened and operated for many years as part of the Washington #2 Corps.

A bit of intrigue came upon one of Evangeline Booth's visits to Washington. As she entered a hotel she was engaged in conversation with a doorman. He cheerfully asked about the Army's work among the troops, but when his questions became too specific about locations and battles, she became suspicious. She reported the incident, the man was apprehended and confessed to being a German spy.

An unusual White House endorsement of the Army's war effort came from President Wilson. As an example of commitment to the war effort, sheep were raised on the White House lawn. The president ordered that the sheep be clipped and the wool donated to the Army for its service to the military.

While the war was being fought in Europe, over 400,000 people died on the home front from a hardhitting flu epidemic. The scenes were frightful as whole families grew sick and died. People fell over dead as they walked down the street. Traffic police wore surgical masks to protect themselves from the disease.

The Army rushed to the aid of the afflicted families with food and care for those too weak to take care of themselves. The clinic operating in Charleston, W.Va., was overwhelmed with patients as it tried to render aid. The epidemic finally subsided in 1919, but in its wake millions were left with tuberculosis and heart problems. More died from this one epidemic than were casualties in the war.

With the end of the war, the returning troops found a country which had changed, but not as dramatically as had they. The blind optimism of the early Twentieth Century was shattered by the reality of war. The Utopian dreams of a society heading toward eventual perfection died on the No Man's Land of blighted battlefields. Still, America was more confident than ever. Had it not turned the tide of the war?

While Europe lay in ruins, America itself had escaped unscathed. The war had even brought some wealth to the South as it drove workers to the factories for the war effort. Families who had known only poverty found themselves with money in their pockets. These who had barely enough before to feed themselves now had even enough money to buy an automobile. The South had begun to believe it might at last emerge from its economic difficulties.

But sometimes it seemed as though God Himself did not smile upon the South for more than a moment. The factories which had belched smoke and welcomed workers began to close as the war ended. With the end of the war came surplus labor. Wages dropped steadily, until in 1925 Southerners were making half of what they had made in the war years. When the factory workers tried to return to the farms, they found that even King Cotton could not save them. Beginning in 1919, the boll weevil wreaked havoc on the cotton crop. The rest of America was entering the "roaring twenties" with optimism, but the people of the South could see only hard times ahead again.

The frustration of Southerners who had tasted the good life mingled with the frustration of the war veterans. Black veterans had found that Europeans did not usually share in the prejudices and race consciousness of American whites. They had been treated as equals, and, having served their country, they expected that treatment in their homeland. What they found was a nation which proclaimed its gratitude but denied the black any tangible proof of its thankfulness. Nothing had changed back home.

On the other hand, white veterans had assumed their superiority over blacks and chafed at the equal treatment accorded their fellow Americans in Europe. Whites wanted blacks to remember they were different and war had taught them how to deal with what was different. As W. J. Cash notes in his book, *Mind of the South*: "They (the veterans) were filled with hate for whatever differed from themselves and their ancient patterns . . . these men were superlatively ripe for hating. The organized propaganda of the war had drilled them in the habit of hate with a thoroughness and an intensity entirely without parallel in prior human history."

Such hatred breathed life into the reborn Ku Klux Klan. This time the violence was not just against blacks, but against Jews, Catholics or anyone else who varied from the ideal of white Protestantism. The Salvation Army had always officially stood against the very things the Klan had espoused, but there were times when the focus became clouded.

In Nashville, Klansmen would appear at a Saturday night open-air meeting, drop a roll of bills of $25 or $50, and then walk quietly away. In Lynchburg, Va., an officer gave permission for the Klan to use the corps building for meetings. This was promptly ended when word reached territorial headquarters.

The resurgence of the Klan was more than a nuisance—it was deadly. The city of Tulsa, which had heretofore enjoyed racial tranquility, became the scene of a pitched battle between blacks and whites when a race riot erupted on

June 1, 1921. Before it was ended, over 800 blacks and whites were dead and the entire black area of the city burned to the ground.

Other than the National Guard, The Salvation Army and the Red Cross were the only agencies allowed to operate in the devastated city. The Army was given responsibility of clothing those made homeless. Then a candidate for officership, Lt. Colonel Ruth Gibbs recalls feeding the black prisoners in leg irons who had been assigned to gravedigging detail. The news of the riot was quashed by the press, but this riot was a signal to the South that indiscriminate violence against blacks would not meet the passive acceptance of years past.

Contrasting the agony of the South, The Salvation Army found itself in the best position it had ever known. After the war, the Army was buoyed by the enthusiastic support of a grateful public. The doughboys had written home about the service of Army workers on the battlefield and, now that they were home, the Army was the object of their unending praise. The Army had been gaining respect all along with its practical social work and consistent Christian witness, but the groundswell of support following the war would change its character and place in national history. America had a love affair with The Salvation Army.

The popularity of the Army meant that it attracted the finances needed. Accustomed to abject poverty, Army workers found that money was flowing into their coffers. Being associated with the Army became honorable. Capitalizing on this, Evangeline Booth moved quickly to form advisory boards made up of leading citizens to help the Army as it entered this new age. The first such board in the South was formed in Knoxville, Tenn.

The end of the war also brought an influx of young people

into the training college to become officers. The Army had closed corps during the war because of the shortage of officers. In the session ending in 1919 only 37 officers were commissioned. By 1921 that number had jumped to 152. A number of these new officers were young men reached on the battlefields of Europe. Not only were there new officers made, but officers tied up on war service were now available for field appointments.

Perhaps the biggest change to the Army was that it now outdistanced similar agencies. When Ballington Booth offered the services of the Volunteers of America to President Wilson during the war he was turned down. The American Rescue Workers had made no attempt at any particular war service. Both these works watched their steady decline as the Army continued to advance. Indeed, its popularity not only overshadowed these two works but other social service agencies as well. The Salvation Army was a national force.

This could be no more clearly seen than in the fascination with a Southern girl, Rheba Crawford. Originally from Atlanta where she had been a newspaper reporter, Crawford was commissioned as an officer in 1919. Her first appointment was to St. Petersburg, Fla. Then she was sent to National Headquarters in New York as part of the editorial department. While there, she heard about the Army's early attempts to have a corps in the theater district of Broadway. Previous ventures had met with dismal failure. Captain Crawford was moved by the people of Broadway—both those who attended the theaters and those who worked in them.

She asked to be allowed to start the corps again but was turned down because of past failures. Finally she succeeded in convincing the administration to allow her to try. The first night she met with total failure. It was contemptible enough to be a young lady in unfashionable uniform among all that glamor, but her Southern accent made her the object of ridicule. She went home and sobbed, wondering why she didn't listen to her leaders.

But Captain Crawford went back the next night to her open-air stand. This time the ridicule lessened. A few stopped and then more, touched by her earnestness. The newspapers began praising her "soft, yet clear Southern voice." Her own sense of drama appealed to the crowds. "When she reached a climax and lifted her face to pray—the audience began to applaud." She counted among her converts a young reporter named Walter Winchell. She now had the attention not just of Broadway, but of America as newspaper after newspaper ran stories of the one they called "Sunshine Rheba", the "Angel of Broadway" or "Broadway's own Billy Sunday."

She was made the only honorary life member of the National Vaudeville Association although she never attended the theater. Along with other offers, George M. Cohan approached her to star her in her own musical. Efforts were made to coax her into the movies, but all were refused. Meanwhile, the nightly meetings choked the street and sidewalks with crowds estimated at 4,000. The very success of her ministry ended it.

Finally, in 1922, without warning the police ordered her to stop the meetings because of traffic congestion. When she refused, she was arrested. Though quickly discharged, the arrest shook her confidence. The Army did not want any further problems with the police, so all meetings ended. Captain Crawford resigned from the Army, first becoming an independent evangelist and later joining with Aimee Semple McPherson. She ultimately became an official in California state government. But her story was memorialized when Damon Runyon wrote the short story, *"The Idyll of Miss Sarah*

Browne." Broadway adapted it for the stage and Hollywood for the screen in the famous musical, "*Guys and Dolls.*"

The popularity of this one officer parallelled that of the Army. Things were better than satisfactory, brighter than good, more promising than hopeful. And in the South, The Salvation Army was sweeping through the land.

CHAPTER 10

ROARING INTO THE TWENTIES
(1920–1926)

THE 1920s was a time of turbulence and opulence, of cowardice and courage, of fact and fanaticism. In this span of time, the Ku Klux Klan would march its tens of thousands in Washington and organized crime would rule the streets of Chicago. Lindbergh would fly the Atlantic and radio would make the world smaller. A schoolteacher named Scopes would be tried for teaching evolution and Wall Street would be brought to its knees on Black Monday. The United States began the noble experiment of Prohibition while morals sank to an all time low. Movies added sound as Henry Ford made the Model T automobile within range of the common people's income. Women were allowed to vote and the disenfranchisement of blacks started to crumble. For good or ill, it was an exciting time to be alive in America.

The Salvation Army in the South saw more development in the 1920s than in the previous forty years. Following its success in the war, every problem looked like an opportunity. After being on the front lines, it could no longer settle for the store front. When the last battlefield of Europe was deserted the Army was ready to take to the field in the South.

A young doctor entered the New York Training College from Louisville, Ky., following his overseas service in World

War I. Before William Noble could finish his period of training, International Headquarters requested that he come to serve in India. He, with a God-honoring dedication to missionary service, was quick to obey.

In a one-of-a-kind ceremony on December 21, 1919, he was commissioned, married to fellow-cadet Etna Dodd, and farewelled for India. During the ceremony, his mother spoke of her efforts to raise him in the fear and knowledge of God. Having read of the need for officers in Korea and India, she had prayed that God would make her willing to give him up should that be His future purpose for William. At the same time, while William was at medical school at Emory University in Atlanta and a soldier of the Atlanta Temple Corps, he felt God speak to his heart about devoting his life to the service of The Salvation Army in India. His service at Catherine Booth Hospital in Nagercoil would be legendary.

In the selfless spirit of Christ, Colonel Noble would labor in often primitive, especially at first, circumstances. He would also further develop his skills as a surgeon by adding to his name the status of F.A.C.S. and F.I.C.S. Noble would experience sacrifice through the years, as part of his devotion facing the death while in India of his oldest son, Charlie, and the amputation of his arm as a result of radiation cancer.

With the fees Noble received as physician on call to the Maharajah of Travancore and inspector of government hospitals, he would devote every penny to the building of a huge and effective hospital complex from the comparatively small institution he found when he arrived. He also established branch hospitals including a 200 bed leprosy hospital in Puthencruz. His service in India would be recognized by the Kaisar-I-Hind medal for public service in India and The Salvation Army's highest award, the Order of the Founder, bestowed by General Wilfred Kitching.

The fires of revival were sweeping across The Salvation

Army in the South. In Norfolk, a sailor who was an inveterate gambler was wonderfully saved. An accomplished musician, Chief Petty Officer Everett H. Lynch stayed at his spiritual birthplace to form a band and serve as a dedicated local officer for over thirty years.

Envoy "Pop" Harrigan, born in Ireland and raised in the streets of New York, was a drifter. A veteran of the Spanish-American war and the Boxer Rebellion, he had been in and out of jail most of his adult life, including a stint for killing a man in a street fight. While wandering around the country, he met an old friend in Birmingham who had been converted at the Army. Out of curiosity he went there and was himself saved. A skilled pickpocket, he tracked down many of his former victims over the years and paid them back $1,800 from his meager salary. He eventually made his way to the Atlanta Industrial Home to live the rest of his days in service to men who had lived a life like his.

In Brunswick, Ga., a condemned man requested that, following his execution, his funeral be at the Army hall. He wanted his death to be a warning to others. Hundreds crowded the building in an emotional service attended by the dead man's family. A teenage girl closed the service by singing "Softly and Tenderly" which was interrupted by a rush to the penitent form, led by members of the criminal's family. The front was filled, and then the aisles as men and women knelt to cry for mercy.

In 1921, Lt. Colonel Wood reinstated John Early as a soldier. That in itself would not seem to be noteworthy except for the fact that Early was the most famous leper in the world. A former Salvation Army officer from outside Washington, DC, he was diagnosed with leprosy in 1909. He was promptly quarantined to his home, where a brick wall was built dividing the house and armed guards were posted to keep him away from his family. At night he would put his ear to the wall to listen to his family sing old Salvation Army songs. Eventually he was forced to enter the leper colony in Carville, La. The patients pleaded with federal authorities to take over the institution but ran into bureaucratic stalling.

During a congressional committee meeting the door opened and a man announced, "I am John Early, a patient at the leper colony in Carville, La."

"What are you doing here?" a shaken Congressman asked.

"I escaped from Carville and came here to tell you gentlemen about how much we patients need to have that colony made into a U.S. hospital."

No one dared touch Early and he refused to leave until he was certain the bill would receive favorable consideration. He then submitted to the authorities and was sent back to Carville. He was later rewarded with news that the bill had passed.

The flames of revival reached the Blue Ridge mountains of Virginia. In Roanoke, the corps building was crowded with standing-room-only crowds. Inspired by this success, Major Ellis, the corps officer, opened three more corps in the city, one in the neighboring city of Salem and another one in the next county at Radford. In Richmond, a similar condition initiated the opening of three additional corps there. In Norfolk, two more corps were opened as well. In fact, with the exception of the cotton states which were hard pressed in their fight with the boll weevil, corps were springing up everywhere. In the year of 1920 twenty-five corps were opened, topped the next year when thirty-five were opened. Although the number of corps slowed down in the years that followed, the momentum continued.

Corps were opened in Florida, now experiencing a land boom. Corps opened in the oil towns of the west, in the growing cities of the Carolinas, and in the coal towns of West

Virginia. Anywhere it seemed remotely possible for a corps to open, the Army flag was planted. In a span of less than a decade, the Army effectively doubled the number of corps in the South. Not all these corps survived but over half of them were in existence fifty years later. Every officer was a pioneer, every soldier a recruiter.

One of the most unusual corps to be opened was in McAlester, Okla. The prison warden gave permission for the Army to open a corps inside the state penitentiary. On May 6, 1921, fifty-four men dressed in white were enrolled as soldiers. Before their meeting each Sunday at 1:30, they gathered at the library to march, complete with drum and flags, to the chapel. Later these same men would build and donate a truck to be used for evangelistic outreach for the McAlester corps outside its walls.

The enthusiasm for the Army was not just within its ranks. In West Palm Beach, sixty union carpenters donated time and material to erect a corps building. This feat was accomplished in half a day.

When Captain Ruth Gibbs was in Bristow, Okla., she was invited upstairs to a ballroom. Explaining that Salvationists did not dance nor attend such things, she was finally persuaded to go up for a moment. There on the wall was a sign that read "Dance for The Salvation Army." Money had been raised to purchase the Army a new car and the overwhelmed captain gratefully accepted the keys.

The Salvationist spirit could be seen no more clearly than in the still largely unsettled state of Oklahoma. The oil fields were booming, bringing both quick wealth and heartbreak. Around the derricks, the fields were cluttered with tent cities built on muddy streets. Disease and hunger were rampant, as desperate people hoped that they might somehow strike it rich. The human cost was horrendous. A poignant illustration of this misery came as an officer was called to a tent on a cold and blustery winter day. As she entered, she found a newborn nursing at her dead mother's breast.

There were picturesque heroes in Salvation Army uniform. Major and Mrs. Leo Thronburg rode the oil fields on horseback. They preached and prayed, fed and sang, accompanied by their mandolin and guitar. But even the good work of the Army in Oklahoma was too much for some. In Muskogee, the city manager campaigned vigorously to stop the Army's street meetings. Public sympathy and constitutional law frustrated his attempts.

When Prohibition became law, the Army cheered. The "dry" conditions also dried up the former clientele of the Industrial Homes, now renamed the Men's Social. But, if that phase of the Army's program suffered, it was the kind of suffering the Army had longed to see. And there was an occasional unexpected benefit from Prohibition. In Savannah, Ga., five thousand bottles of bootleg liquor were discovered hidden in a train carload of sweet potatoes. The Army officers were called, gleefully entering into the task of smashing the bottles of booze. That completed, the Army collected its prize, the illicit sweet potatoes.

The work on behalf of women and children continued to grow. Under the auspices of the Women's Social Service Department, homes for unwed mothers became even more important in an age of declining morals, a condition blamed on the automobile. The Southern Presbyterian Church condemned the "unchaperoned automobile riding at night," quoting the matron of a home for unwed mothers as saying "that a considerable majority of the inmates of her home ascribe their fall to this habit."

Along with the homes for unwed mothers, the Army expanded its medical facilities with the addition of the Emma Moss Booth Memorial Hospital in Greenville, S.C. What the Army was not prepared for in the working of full scale hospital was the cost. This same facility was closed, at least as far as Salvation Army operations were concerned, ten years later after a loss during its whole history.

The Army was ready to try anything new which would help it spread the good news of salvation. When the Southern Congress of 1924 was held in Atlanta, it was attended by not only over 4,000 delegates but portions of it were broadcast by WSB Radio. The radio station estimated that the Army meeting was heard in 50,000 homes. The strength of the signal was confirmed when the Army received word that the broadcast had been received in Halifax, England.

In Texas, work began once more among Hispanics of the transplanted Mexican population. The work was led, in spirit and example, by Major Milton Atkins in Laredo, Tex. He started one day school for Mexican children and then was urged to begin another. At Galveston, an outpost for the Hispanic population was opened, led by the Workmans. This couple had been actively involved in the Mexican Revolution where Mr. Workman operated, covertly disguised as a saloon keeper. Mrs. Workman had actually been the private secretary of one of the Revolution's leaders.

The First Lady was impressed with the work of the Army and offered her help with the Washington Christmas distribution. Mrs. Calvin Coolidge continued to help each Christmas while her husband was president, and was followed by Mrs. Herbert Hoover and Mrs. Franklin D. Roosevelt.

In Florida, a devastating hurricane brought widespread destruction on Septemer 19, 1926. Over 5,000 homes were destroyed, leaving 18,000 people homeless. Over 1,000 were dead. A Salvationist reported in *The War Cry*: "They are a charnel of death and human woe. Sixteen thousand people without a change of clothing; 95 percent of property damaged. The situation in Lake Okeechobee area beggars description. Bodies piled in decomposing masses are being buried as quickly as possible to prevent plague. In one huge trench on the outskirts of this city, 600 victims were laid away near midnight . . . Salvation Army women visited the melancholy field and ministered . . . to the staggering diggers . . ."

A different kind of storm was brewing in Wichita Falls, Tex. Under the pen name of W. L. Atwood, a series of manifestos appeared at Army headquarters and corps. Heaping criticism on General Bramwell Booth, the papers demanded, among other things, that the Army government become more democratic, railed about "the General's refusal to appoint American officers to high places," and suggested that the Army in America split from the international movement and make Evangeline Booth its General.

The manifestos caused quite a stir with efforts being made to discover the identity of the writer. It was later felt by some that W. L. Atwood was none other than the former National Commander, Commissioner Frederick Booth-Tucker, who only recently had been forced into retirement by General Booth. But, as much as the Army leaders denounced the charges of Atwood, later events would prove that he was not alone in many of his sentiments.

The trends in the South during this time would directly affect the Army's work. The cities continued to grow. Through this decade, their population swelled by 25 percent. The Army's work was seen as more and more vital to the community, and cities invited the Army to come and establish its work. The attraction of the Army was its effective social work. Community leaders were sympathetic, if not sometimes puzzled by the Army's religious work.

It would be in the area of religion that the Army would find itself in a strange position between two diverging movements among Protestants. On the one hand were the fundamentalists, chiefly the Southern Baptists, Southern Methodists and Southern Presbyterians. They believed in the inerrancy of Scripture and the need for a definite salvation experience and had a strong sense of evangelism. In these areas the Army in America agreed.

Departures came on several issues. The Army believed in the equality of men and women, including in the ministry. Fundamentalists generally held women were to be silent in the church and exercise no spiritual authority over men. The Army further held to the interpretation of its Christian mission through social action and concern. Fundamentalists usually saw little correlation between their beliefs and social action. That is, they felt their efforts should be channeled only through pure evangelism.

The Army's doctrinal position further alienated these brethren. Although the fundamentalists did not hold that the sacraments were essential to salvation, they still felt they were important. The Army's belief that all God has to give His children can come independently of sacramental forms, leading to its wholesale abandonment of their observance, confused them. The Army's loyalty to the teaching of Wesleyan holiness also separated them from the mainstream. And when the controversy over evolution arose, the Army took no active part in the debate. The Army was too pragmatic for that. Dealing with the reality of original sin left little time to argue about how the sinful creatures got here. Still, the Salvationists sympathized with the fundamentalists on this issue.

On the other side was the rise in the pentecostal movement. Begun a few years earlier, the pentecostals held that all the gifts of the New Testament were operative today, most notably the gifts of healing and tongues. Their preaching insisted upon an experience beyond salvation, the baptism of the Holy Spirit. Their services were characterized by great display of emotion—a contrast to the quieter and more formal services of the fundamentalists.

Again, the Army found itself in sympathy with parts of the pentecostal movement. It, too, believed in a further work of grace in the life of the believer. Most pentecostals agreed with the Army that anyone, including women, should be allowed to exercise their spiritual gifts. The Army had also long believed that emotion was a valid part of the Christian experience.

But the Army also parted roads with the pentecostals. The Army never attempted to enter debate about which spiritual gifts were operative in this time. Nonetheless, it also did not see the necessity for, nor the desirability of, seeking more sensational spiritual gifts, especially the gift of tongues. When pentecostals said that the gift of tongues was a vital evidence of the filling of the Spirit, the Army simply said this was not its experience. The Army was as frustrating to the pentecostals in this respect as it had been to the rest of Christendom over the sacraments.

Meanwhile, both fundamentalism and pentecostalism gained their own momentum and became an integral part of Southern life. The Army remained between the two, not fundamental enough for the fundamentalists and not pentecostal enough for the Pentecostals. But it had found its niche in Southern life.

Now the unique character of the South, which had long been recognized within America, was seen in England, along with the acknowledgment that the Army's strength had greatly increased in the South. Accordingly, the following announcement appeared in the October 9, 1926, edition of *The War Cry*:

> Here's to the South!
>
> The General, after conference with the Commander, has decided to create a new territory within the United States command. This, in general, will embrace the Southern states and will be known as the Southern Territory.
>
> This development for a long time past has been upon the hearts of our leaders and we predict for the new territory a vigorous and triumphant experience in all things pertaining to the Army's welfare.

CHAPTER 11

THE SOUTHERN TERRITORY

(1927–1930)

WHEN IT was announced that the Southern Territory was being formed, very little was in place but the concept. General Bramwell Booth was an accomplished organizer. As he looked over the ever growing international Army, he saw advantage to breaking down large Army operations into smaller and more manageable units. Not only did this make good management sense, but he was aware that diversification lessened the chances for disastrous splits as had occurred in the United States and other countries.

This process had begun while his father was still alive and was now further implemented. In 1920, the United States was divided into three territories: the Eastern with headquarters in New York, the Western with headquarters in San Francisco and the Central with headquarters in Chicago.

This division of the United States command did not sit well with his sister, Commander Evangeline Booth. A leader who loved to lead, she found it somewhat frustrating to deal with the individual territorial commanders. Perhaps this was a reason the formation of the Southern Territory was delayed after having originally been discussed as early as 1922. The decision to formulate the Southern Territory was firm by mid-1926. As it was, the timing proved to be poor. If things could have jelled two years earlier, the territory's beginning would have been much less painful.

At the beginning, the only thing sure about the Southern Territory was that it would be in existence in the area which had been the old Confederacy. If Evangeline Booth was reluctant to see another territory formed, she did not show it in making the early decisions about its leadership. The first decision was the astute selection of Lt. Commissioner William McIntyre to be the South's territorial commander.

If The Salvation Army published its own illustrated dictionary, William McIntyre would be the picture next to the word "innovator." He loved to challenge those under him with ideas he called "hat stretchers." He admonished them with sayings such as, "the best way to lift the top is to lift the bottom." He was a creative genius, conceiving his own great ideas and treasuring those of others around him.

In 1909, he had created the "Boozer's Convention" while stationed in New York. This effort was his idea for reaching the alcoholics. Complete with bands, a marching whiskey bottle and a dinner for the honored guests (skid row alcoholics), it was a tremendous success. It continued for several years and spread to other cities.

In constant movement, McIntyre was called "an apostle of the best brand of hustle." When his wife wanted to start the women's Home League program in the South, she had to lock him in a room and refuse to give him a key until he listened to what she had to say. Thereafter, he became an enthusiastic supporter. In his first six months as territorial commander, he traveled 55,000 miles over largely unpaved roads to visit every corps in the South except Shawnee, Okla. One wonders how he missed Shawnee.

McIntyre possessed lightning wit. While Provincial Commander for the New England Province he had been the guest in a large church. The pastor introduced him in glowing terms and was especially complimentary about his fine head of hair. When McIntyre stood, he thanked the pastor, reached up and lifted his toupee and said, "You can get the same head of hair for $25."

Another example of his wit came when introducing the Southern Staff Band at a concert. He presented each band member to the audience and then asked the officer if there were a band in his corps. If the officer replied in the negative, McIntyre responded, "Go right back and start one!" When he came to the honeymooning Captain James Klaas, he said, "Oh, you're the young fellow who just got married!" With a twinkle in his eye he said, "You go back and start your band!"

McIntyre, a man of great compassion known as the "man of the second chance", reinstated over 30 officers his first year as territorial commander. This compassion also showed itself in a love for souls. When his car broke down in rural Alabama, his staff could not find him when repairs were completed. They finally discovered him in a field on his knees praying with a farm hand.

When McIntyre received word of his appointment to the South he was Provincial Commander in New England. Immediately he went to the Boston Public Library and checked out every book he could find on the South. At the same time he began to settle some of the details regarding his new command.

The exact boundaries were still up in the air. Neither the Central nor Eastern territories relished losing hundreds of officers and large chunks of their commands. The East regretted losing Maryland and West Virginia. When McIntyre attempted to have Delaware added to the South, he pointed out that the East would lose only one more corps. Besides, he added, it would look better on the map to be able to draw a straight line across the northern boundary of Maryland to the ocean. He lost that battle.

The Central wanted to keep the "panhandle" areas of Oklahoma and Texas. In typical McIntyre fashion he pleaded, "protect me from the selfish grasping hands" of the Central administrative officers. He won that battle. The only Southern city not included in the new territory was El Paso, which had always been administered from headquarters in California. Because of its distance from any other major Texas city there was no dispute that this arrangement would be continued.

One boundary issue had to be settled several months after the territory had begun functioning. Covington, Ky., had a hospital which at the time was operating at a loss. McIntyre already had financial difficulties without the burden of the hospital. Intercession was made and thirty counties including the cities of Covington, Frankfort and Lexington were reattached to the Eastern Territory. With this last matter settled, the boundaries were set. Over sixty years later, plans would be announced to reattach first Frankfort and then other parts of Kentucky to the Southern Territory.

The next question to be settled was the location of the new territorial headquarters. Several cities under consideration were visited by McIntyre, including Memphis, Baltimore, Washington, Birmingham and Atlanta. The search was narrowed to Atlanta and Birmingham because of the centrality of their location. Birmingham had always been a strong center for Army activity while Atlanta had been cooler toward the Army's presence over the years.

A strong pitch from Atlanta was made by the divisional commander, Brigadier Bertram Rodda, supported by the Chamber of Commerce and a very influential advisory board. Finally, Atlanta was settled on and arrangements were made through Brigadier Rodda to begin legal procedures to form The Salvation Army, a Georgia Corporation.

Finally, it was time for the new territory to begin functioning. McIntyre headed south from Boston on a night train, keeping two secretaries fully occupied with dictation. The Southern Territory was then officially born January 1, 1927. The building selected for the new headquarters was not ready, so the territorial command was in cramped quarters of the third floor of divisional headquarters in Atlanta. The new building acquired for territorial headquarters had been the Elks building, distinguished by the fact that it was located on the spot where the first artillery shell landed from Sherman's army in the Civil War Battle of Atlanta.

The opening ceremonies for the territory would have to wait until Commander Evangeline Booth, then suffering from a prolonged illness, could come. The date selected was April 10—William Booth's birthday.

In the inaugural issue of the Southern *War Cry*, the Commander wrote, "The people of the Southland have made for themselves a distinctive place in the life of the nation. Hospitable and generous to a fault, ardent advocates of their ideals, courageous and loyal in sunshine or in shadow, devoted to fundamental religion, ready in philanthropy, understanding and warm in support of those who give themselves to solving problems of the underprivileged and unfortunate, the erring and the down but not out—we have in the South a great community, deserving the best service The Salvation Army can give."

Evangeline Booth drew tremendous crowds wherever she went, and her coming alone would have been a stellar event. She also dedicated the new territorial headquarters, reviewed the troops and charmed the media. With her coming, opening ceremonies were attended by the brightest dignitaries of Atlanta.

During a parade of review, she was greeted by Texan cowboys complete with sombreros, husky miners from West Virginia, a giant peanut from Virginia, bales of cotton from

Southern Salvationists

Brigadier Elmer Capp, Order of Exceptional Service.

A/Captain and Mrs. John Jones, Order of Exceptional Service.

Colonel Ernest Pickering, charter Southern officer, who in retirement conducted many funeral services for fellow officers promoted to glory.

Mrs. Colonel Ernest Pickering.

Brigadier Louis Amberger and Major Louise Baldry, instructed cadets at the School for Officers Training.

Southern trained officers, Louise and Ted Morris, now Lt. Colonel and Chief Secretary, Japan.

Brigadier Leslie Hall leads singing at Southern Bible Conference

Lt. Colonel Frank Longino, artist extraordinaire with both pen and ink and the baton.

Colonel and Mrs. George Marshall, pioneer officers, with their children: then S/Captain and Mrs. George Marshall (later territorial commander, Mexico and Central), and Dr. Don Marshall.

Colonel James Longino, pioneer Southern officer and long-time Chief Secretary and Territorial Home League Secretary.

Mrs. Colonel James Longino.

Commissioner and Mrs. W.R.H. Goodier, Southern trained officers, later territorial leaders in the U.S.A. East.

Commissioner Inez Newberry, Southern trained officer who served as Territorial Commander in India.

Commissioner and Mrs. John D. Needham, Southern trained officer who served as National Commander.

Parents of Major Norma Roberts, Brigadier and Mrs. James Roberts, who served in the Washington, D.C. area.

Mrs. Florence Moyer is recognized by Mrs. Colonel Gus A. Stephan for her outstanding service as Corps Cadet Guardian in the Miami Citadel Corps.

Brigadier Walter Swyers, with great friends of the Army, Colonel and Mrs. Harland Sanders.

Brigadier Douglas Eldredge spent many years shaping the lives of boys through the Boys' Clubs of Baltimore and Camp Puh'tok.

Lt. Colonel and Mrs. Wesley Bouterse served as Territorial Education Secretary, divisional commander, and founder of the Southern Bible Conference.

Mrs. Franklin D. (Eleanor) Roosevelt, with Brigadier James Longino, receives salute from Girl Guard in Washington, D.C.

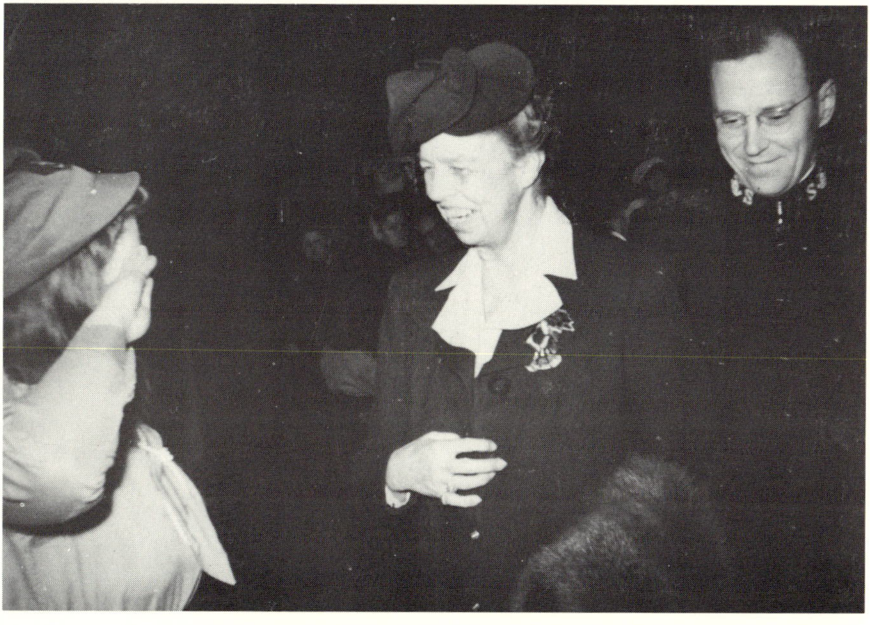

Order of the

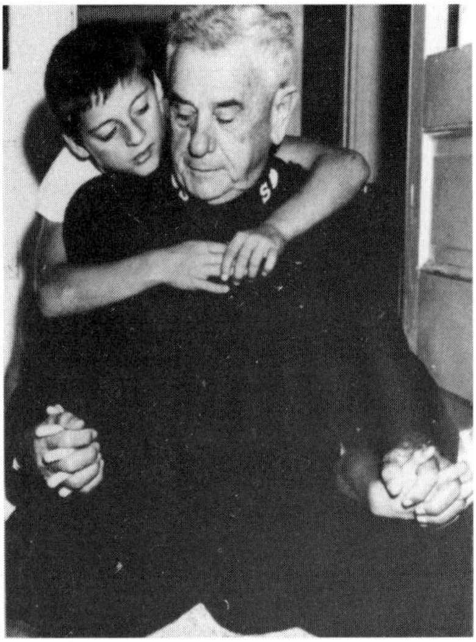

Brigadier Julius Satterfield

Mrs. Brigadier Keitha Holz is presented Order of the Founder by Commissioner James Osborne, as her children, Commissioner Ernst Holz, Lt. Colonel David Holz, son Edwy, and daughter Nancy look on.

Colonel (Dr.) and Mrs. William Noble with a group of youngsters at a missionary rally. Colonel Noble, a member of the first graduating class of Emory Medical School in Atlanta, served at the Catherine Booth Hospital in Nagercoil, India.

Founder

Mrs. Ruby Ferraez Laudun, "Mother to the Needy."

YPSM Clara Paige of the Norfolk Corps.

Major Cecil Brown, Shepherdess of the Hills.

Alabama and Mississippi, giant peaches from Georgia, super-sized oysters from Maryland, a miniature Washington monument from the nation's capital, a Daniel Boone from Kentucky, and from the Carolinas, colonial men complete with powdered wigs, knickerbockers and lace blouses. The strength of the South was found in its 11 divisions of 220 corps, 49 social institutions and 672 officers.

At the same time the Southern Staff Band was introduced, wearing gray uniforms. The band was to have a short but colorful history. Following the opening ceremonies, the band went on tour in a battered bus. At every stop they were served fried chicken, until Captain Albert E. Baldwin, the bandmaster, wired ahead with the message, "Please! No chicken!"

On their way to Gainesville, Ga., for a concert they found themselves on narrow roads of red clay, when it began to rain. The bandsmen had to get out of the bus and walk beside it, holding its sides to help keep it on the road. When they arrived an hour late for the concert, they were covered with red clay. The crowd was leaving but they cheered the bandsmen when they arrived and returned to hear the full program. Soon after the band would conduct a weekly radio broadcast at WSB Radio in Atlanta.

At the opening of the territory, the new training college for officers was initiated. Located in the former Argonne Hotel which had previously served as the Men's Social Service Center, Major Harry Bayes was appointed as the first principal. A total of forty cadets, originally from the South, were brought back from the training colleges in New York and Chicago. They completed their last two months of training and were commissioned the following June.

No sooner had the opening ceremonies ended than McIntyre was made aware of the immensity of his challenge in the South. Though economically improving, it was still the poorest section of the country. In 1926 the number of Southerners who made enough money to file income tax returns was only one-third that of the rest of the country. Though the South was becoming more urban, 80% of Southerners still lived on farms.

There were notable exceptions, but McIntyre had in his command some officers who were considered generally inferior to those in the rest of the country. Being appointed to the South was referred to as "being thrown over the garden wall," reserved too often for those being disciplined or who failed to succeed in Northern corps. Indeed, there were some officers who were practically illiterate. When the opening ceremonies were being conducted, McIntyre had to endure some officers who came in homemade uniforms ranging in color from regulation dark blue to purple. In response to all this, always a student himself, he announced a training program for officers which included Bible study and sermon preparation. Included for some were more basic instructions in handwriting and mathematics.

He also found himself saddled with operations across the South that were not only poor, but losing money fast. The Men's Social Service Centers, which were supposed to help finance the territory, were instead losing money in every location except Washington. The socials struggled more in the South because of the practice of used clothing and furniture often being used as "in kind" payments in lieu of, or part of, the salary of laborers. The idea of giving items away to an institution was thus totally foreign.

If Lt. Commissioner McIntyre had any illusions about the difficulty of his work in the South, they were quickly dispelled by an enormous disaster. No sooner had the ceremonies ended than news reached Atlanta that the Mississippi River had flooded, leaving over 200,000 people homeless, several hundred dead and over 30 million acres submerged.

Property damage exceeded $300 million dollars, making this calamity greater than all previous disasters combined.

The Salvation Army was first on the scene, setting up relief operations in Vicksburg, Greenville and Jackson, Miss. When levees had to be cut outside New Orleans, a riot almost erupted when residents refused to believe the authorities who had insisted they would be cared for when forced to abandon their property. It was agreed that the Army would deliver the aid, resulting in all parties being satisfied.

McIntyre pleaded for funds for the relief effort to whomever would listen. International Headquarters sent money, while over $1,000 was raised at a tag day in Orlando, Fla. When confronted with the needs of 700 families in Greenville, Miss., he asked for crated chickens to be sent for victims of the flood. In characteristic McIntyre fashion, he added, "If you have no chickens to give to a worthy cause, please put wings on a ten dollar bill and send it along . . . Remember, the cackle of a dozen hens will sound like the whisper of Heaven to hundreds of stricken folk in the flood area."

When the flood relief was finishing up, McIntyre turned his attention to building the territory. He had the firm conviction that the Army could not operate properly in inadequate buildings. His concern for the housing of the Army was not misplaced. For example, the corps building in Salisbury, Md., was a log cabin. It was most gratifying then for him to see the second issue of *The War Cry* featuring the dedication of an excellent four story building in St. Petersburg, Fla. This progress was the exception.

On his many trips across the territory, he would consistently find buildings in places where corps officers had sworn none were available. Believing that prosperity had come to stay and that it was heading southward, he committed the Army to long-term mortgages.

McIntyre handled the acquisition of buildings with the same flair he used to conduct other business. In Macon, Ga., he bought a four story building in the middle of town. Giving the owner $100, he told the divisional commander to find the money to pay the rest of it.

Although his spending was later criticized, it should be remembered that, in the optimism of the 1920s, no one thought the good times would ever end. And, though there was risk involved in the investment in property, it is doubtful that some corps would have been able to raise themselves up had it not been for his vision. The spiritual benefits were manifest when it was revealed that 70% of all new soldiers during McIntyre's administration were enrolled in buildings bought since the territory opened.

The acquisition of buildings was only part of McIntyre's overall strategy. Soon after the territory began, an executive officers' councils was held in Bryson City, N.C., to consider plans for the next five years. Composed of the top administrative officers, what was originally slated to be a councils focused on the administrative issues facing the new territory, became in addition a landmark spiritual experience for the participants.

McIntyre had the foresight to invite his close friend, Commissioner Samuel Logan Brengle, as a guest. Brengle, the Army's leading exponent of holiness, brought with him a benediction upon the gathering. The presence of the Holy Spirit was so apparent that even the least emotional among the participants was moved to tears as they prayed for wisdom and strength to meet the challenge before them. When it was over a five year plan was introduced:

100 more corps
10,000 more soldiers
1,000 more candidates for officership
150 more halls (buildings)

75 more bands
10,000 increase in young people's activities
100 new young people's outposts
12,500 more junior soldiers
1,000 net increase in Corps Cadets
100 new Girl Guard troops
100 Young People's Bands and Singing Companies

Meanwhile, the news was more good than bad. Before the year was out, Mrs. McIntyre had begun organizing the League of Mercy and the women's Home League in the South. From the Roanoke, Va., Home and Hospital the territory sent its first missionary, Captain Katherine Lord. A nurse, she was sent to Nagercoil to work with fellow Southerner, technically from the Eastern Territory, Major Dr. William Noble. As is customary with officers sent to India, she adopted an Indian name: Captain Arulammal, meaning "gifted".

The federal government approached the Army about providing a Protestant chaplain at what was then the nation's largest penitentiary, located in Atlanta. Staff-Captain Fred Ladlow was appointed. In his first year, he reported attendances at his chapel meetings exceeded 60,000. The Brighter Day League, an Army club for convicts looking forward to the brighter day of their release, boasted a membership of over 1,000 of the 3,026 inmates incarcerated.

In April 1928 the men cadets were marching back from an open-air meeting. There were no street lights and the men in their dark uniforms were almost impossible for the driver of a car to see. Before the car could stop, Captain Kenneth Howarth, Cadets William Powell, Clarence Trimbath and Thomas Hayes lay in the road seriously injured. Fortunately, all four recovered from their injuries.

In December 1928 an ominous announcement appeared in *The War Cry*. Lt. Commisioner William McIntyre and other international leaders were called to London to meet in the first High Council. The action was necessitated by General Bramwell Booth's poor health and a corresponding degeneration of relations with other Army leaders.

When William Booth had organized the Army initially, it was with the idea that each General would announce his successor. The only exception would be if the General had been rendered incompetent by declining physical or mental health, or if the General died without naming a successor. Upon William Booth's death, a sealed envelope was opened and his son Bramwell was named the next General, to no one's surprise. In fact, his succession to the office of General was not only expected but welcomed.

In the intervening years, however, he had continued to alienate some Army leaders. Still, the decision to remove him from office represented the greatest crisis the international Army faced.

When it was announced that the High Council would meet, the officers there gathered approached the General about retiring voluntarily. Though bedridden by what would be a fatal illness, he refused. The High Council felt it had no choice but to proceed to remove him and elect a new General. General Booth's family started court proceedings to halt the actions of the High Council. They obtained a temporary injunction but it was lifted when the court determined that the High Council was meeting properly to perform its function.

Consequently, Edward Higgins, then the Army's second-in-command, was elected the third General. Although the Bramwell Booth family continued to make efforts to overturn the decision, it was allowed to stand. The envelope naming Bramwell's successor was destroyed by the Army attorneys, the contents never revealed.

Soon after the High Council adjourned General Bramwell

Booth died, or as Salvationists call it, was promoted to Glory. Memorial meetings were held worldwide. In the South every single corps and social institution held a memorial meeting on the Sunday following his death.

Back in the South, McIntyre surveyed the progress since announcing the five-year plan. In little more than two years the fighting force was increased by 200%. One of the most remarkable areas of achievement came in the Army's girls' activity known as Girl Guards. The number of troops had jumped from 13 to 89. The largest program in the entire country, in Logan, W.Va., had over 70 girls in uniform.

Elsewhere, the Army was voted the most popular religious and welfare organization in Charleston, W. Va., and awarded a $1,000 grand piano as a prize. In Corpus Christi, Tex., the corps officer was given a check in the amount of $655.50, proceeds from the sale of the first bale of cotton sold in the 1929 season. When no cotton boat was available to ship it, the bale was sent by airplane to New York—the first time cotton had ever been transported by air. Having attracted national attention, it was auctioned there with half the proceeds going to a New York charity and half going to the Army in Corpus Christi.

As 1929 was winding down, Commissioner McIntyre was able to report that the Army had already acquired 135 new buildings. But even with this worthy acomplishment, he went on to note: "(This) is the greatest period of commercial depression that the South has known since the War Between the States. The coal regions have seen the hardest times in a generation. The oil fields have been hard hit. Thousands of people have moved away. Agriculture has not been good . . ." In *The Salvation Army Year Book—1930* it was further stated: "The territory was opened on a commercial and financial ebb tide and the condition has grown worse every year. Money raising has been difficult. The financial problems have been unusually heavy . . ." At this time the South had over half of the country's 150,000,000 eroded acres.

The difficult times led to the dissolving of the South Carolina Division, combining it with North Carolina, and later a further realignment of corps to cut the division number from 13 to 11. The South was in a depression.

While McIntyre was preaching one night at the Atlanta Temple corps, he stopped in the middle of his message and called on Brigadier Robert Young to pray, saying, "Come up here and lead us in prayer. You know we need money. Just pray to the Lord that if a man of influence dies tonight, he will have included the organization in his will."

The hard times were only beginning. October 24, 1929, would be known for all time as Black Thursday. The stock market crashed, after being fueled by wild and foolish speculation for years. The rest of the country could now join the South in its misery. The night of despair was just starting.

At the time no one could know how serious the crash was. Many thought it was only a temporary setback; the good times were bound to return. But the Army knew differently. It began to see the effects of the collapse immediately. In 1929 alone, the Army in the South served 50,000 families and 200,000 transients through relief efforts.

The Army was aided by its friends in often unusual ways. At Wichita Falls, Tex., the officer was called by a rancher from the neighboring city of Goodnight. He donated a dressed buffalo weighing out at 857 pounds which provided enough meat for 300 Christmas baskets. And, hoping for better times, the Army pushed ahead with plans to open an orphanage in Sumter, S.C.

In 1930, the Army was celebrating its fiftieth year in the United States. Evangeline Booth planned the first national congress to be held in New York. For this event the Southern Staff Band was resurrected—it had been disbanded for economic reasons. The gray uniforms gone, it was attired in distinctive light blue uniforms. When it traveled with the rest of the delegates to the congress in March, it joined other musicians from across the country in a massed band led by famed march king, John Philip Sousa. At that time he introduced a new composition, "The Salvation Army March" which incorporated the well-known Salvation Army song "O Boundless Salvation."

The jubilee year also saw the first Home League rally in the South held in Atlanta. In Lake Charles, La., an outpost was opened in neighboring Goosport. When it was discovered that some of the population were unable to speak anything other than French, the first French-speaking meetings in the United States were begun.

The year brought administrative changes. The Chief Secretary, Colonel Arthur Chandler, was replaced by Netherlands native Lt. Colonel E. Marpurg. More startling was the announcement that Lt. Commissioner and Mrs. William McIntyre were farewelling to take charge of the Central Territory. The progress of the South had been amazing in their short stay.

In their place, Commissioner and Mrs. Alexander Damon were appointed as territorial leaders. Few could know how near the territory was to extinction.

CHAPTER 12

SURVIVING

(1930–1934)

IN HIS 1932 inaugural speech, Franklin D. Roosevelt said, "The only thing we have to fear is fear itself—nameless, unreasoning, unjustified terror which paralyzes needed efforts to convert retreat into advance. In every dark hour of our national life a leadership of frankness and vigor has met with that understanding and support of the people themselves which is essential to victory."

His comments on the Great Depression continued, "Values have shrunk to fantastic levels; taxes have risen; our ability to pay has fallen; government of all kinds is faced by serious curtailment of income; the means of exchange are frozen in the currents of trade; the withered leaves of industrial enterprise lie on every side; farmers find no markets for their produce; the savings of many years in thousands of families are gone. More important, a host of unemployed citizens face the grim problem of existence and an equally great number toil with little return. Only a foolish optimist can deny the dark realities of this moment."

Against this dark backdrop of the Great Depression, the Southern Territory was gasping for its next breath.

The man appointed to lead the South through its darkest hour was Lt. Commissioner Alexander Damon. Hard times were nothing new to Damon. Born in Lowell, Mass., three months after his father died, he began working when he was six years old selling fruit and newspapers, doing odd jobs and running errands to help support his family. At sixteen he owned his own grocery store in Boston. After an initial contact with the Army in his hometown of Lowell, he was reintroduced to the Army in Boston when two lassies came to the Damon home selling *The War Cry*. This time he became interested and was enrolled as a soldier of the Boston #3 corps.

Following his training for officership he served in several corps and administrative appointments, culminating in his appointment as territorial commander to the South in June 1930, the first native American to be a territorial commander with the rank of Commissioner. His wife, the former Annie Barrow, had joined the Army in Kendall, England. Approved to serve as a missionary to India, her appointment was changed at the last minute for her to go to New York. There she met and married Alexander in 1895.

Damon was the picture of a businessman. With a trim figure and a neat mustache, he had a keen mind for analysis. He had a reputation through the years as an exceptional speaker whose increasing expertise in business matters never dimmed his love for soul-saving work. A meticulous organizer, he even indexed his diaries. If McIntyre was the perfect choice as the pioneer of the South, the appointment of Damon was as inspired to keep the new territory alive.

Aware that Damon was to follow him, McIntyre warned about the financial condition of the territory, saying, "We're having to jiggle and juggle mortgages and notes around to take care of our indebtedness." The mortgages on all the new buildings purchased in the promising prosperity of the late twenties now placed an overwhelming burden on the back of the corps and headquarters budgets alike.

Damon never felt the buildings purchased were a mistake—no one could have foreseen how extensive the depression would be. But donations were dropping while demand for social services was rising. Hanging over everything else were the monthly mortgage notes which demanded payment.

The total crisis was more serious than the mortgage situation. Commander Evangeline Booth was having second thoughts about the wisdom of continuing the operation of the Southern Territory. Already it was hopelessly behind on payments; it owed International Headquarters $16,000 and National Headquarters $8,000, substantial amounts in depression dollars, especially when the indebtedness was growing daily. The Eastern and Central territories both saw hope for easing their own financial woes if they could recover the divisions lost three years earlier when the Southern Territory was formed.

By the time Damon arrived, one plan being considered was to divide the South into five "chief" divisions and to dissolve headquarters in Atlanta. Also under consideration, if the territory closed, was a move to Philadelphia where Southern work would be overseen. Strong consideration was given to moving THQ from Atlanta to Washington if the territory was allowed to continue. Atlanta was still only lukewarm toward the Army. In addition, the railroads out of Washington were willing to provide headquarters officers with free rail passes—a major consideration in those hard times.

But Damon was resolute. In his diary he wrote, "If any attempt (is made) to reduce territory, we'll fight it hard." By this time a growing number of officers at both national and territorial levels were advocating the dismantling of the territory. The Commander told Damon to dissolve the trade department, close the school (sending the cadets to Chicago and New York for training), stop publication of *The War Cry* and close an unspecified number of corps and social institutions. She pressed him for his consent to close the territory.

General Higgins awaited word from Damon that he would go along with the feelings of the others. But Damon stood firm, believing that to dissolve the territory would "effect very little savings and the morale of officers and forces of the South would be ruined." With this confrontation over, talk of eliminating the Southern territory died away.

A veiled reference to the crisis appeared in *The War Cry*: "The Salvation Army is not an experimental organization. It is tested by years. It has seen wars, pestilences, famine, panic and the whole range of economic change. In all that time it has given a good account of itself . . ." Passing this internal crisis was only the first test the Army in the South was facing.

Back on the home front, Damon had little to encourage him. The hospital in Greenville, S.C., while receiving the highest marks for its medical work, was $39,000 in debt and sinking further in at the rate of $10,000 a year. The Men's Social Service Department reported an annual loss of over $30,000. In Norfolk, Va., the Army maintained a Navy and Military Home which had lost $110,000 in fourteen years. The Army struggled just to make the interest payments on the Norfolk property. In a major cutback, the South would join the other territories in 1932 in closing the training college for a year.

During Damon's administration, two divisional headquarters were dissolved and their corps absorbed by other divisions. The territorial headquarters staff was slashed, the officers who remained pulling double duty as they headed two or more departments. At the corps level the Army facilities were being overrun by the poor as the shadow of the Depression night deepened.

Despair increased as factories and mills closed down or severely cut their hours. Men left their homes early in the morning to look for work, with the cries of their hungry children sounding in their ears. Returning late at night following a fruitless job search, they heard the cries again. Professional men deserted their vocations to find work as taxi drivers, cooks, laborers—anything that would let them keep their home and feed their family. But the bottom was crowded with poor families, white and black alike, who had never lived more than a hand to mouth existence. Farmers left their worthless farms for work in the fabled cities, only to find soup lines and emptiness.

At times the frustration boiled over into violence, as in Harlan County, Ky., where coal miners warred against the mine operators, leaving over a dozen dead. Later a textile strike, centered in Gastonia, N.C., spread across the state to take 325,000 workers out of the mills. The strike turned violent as strikebreakers and carloads of strikers, called "flying squadrons", turned mills into battlegrounds. On the street and in the labor halls, Communists and Socialists alike called for the end of capitalism. Southerners nursed their longtime distrust for the Yankee.

The federal government, elected during the halcyon days of prosperity, found it could not cope with a disaster this large. As always, it was worse in the South. When help finally came through the government-sponsored WPA, the wages paid in the South were at best half of what they were for the same job in the East. Things were bad, then they got worse, and then they degenerated from there.

Answers were sought everywhere. Even the Southern Baptists, usually seemingly aloof on matters of social concern, spoke out as witnessed by a Sunday sermon of J. Frank Norris in Ft. Worth. "Why, somebody cries, 'socialism, socialism!' To hell with your socialism or whatever you want to call it! People are starving!"

The answer of the common man was more direct. If you can't find work at home, go where work is. The problem was that there wasn't any work anywhere. "Stay at Home this Winter," sounded *The War Cry,* going on to reason that the jobless stood a better chance of finding work at home than on the road. Nonetheless, hundreds of thousands took to the roads looking for work. In Texas alone it was estimated that there were over 75,000 men at one time wandering through the state looking for work. Sadly, many of these were young people.

Commissioner Damon reported that in one place he visited there were 1,455 transient men cared for—all of them under 21. One of the homeless men in the Army center in Memphis expressed his concern about the young, saying that they are "starting themselves in the company of derelicts like myself—seeing life at its worst. The public would be appalled it if knew what was happening . . ."

The Army moved quickly to aid the homeless. Wild game and livestock were donated to feed the poor. Wood yards across the South were maintained which served a dual purpose—the homeless man was required to chop wood for a night's lodging. Then the wood was distributed to the poor of the area for fuel. In Baltimore, the divisional commander, Major George Rose, obtained the use of an idle showboat to be used as a temporary rest and recreation center for the homeless during the day. Contrasting that was Ensign Ernest Pickering, in St. Petersburg, who asked for the three-masted sailing ship "Wallace A. McDonald", which had been abandoned and washed ashore. Using the labor of homeless men that winter, the boat was chopped up and the wood distributed to the poor.

More conventional services came with the housing programs for the transients. An old school was turned over to the Army in Charlotte and promptly opened to house 300. A series of shelters in Washington could house close to 1,000 a night. But even these large facilities and others like them across the South, were inadequate to house all those who needed their protection.

Little public welfare other than child welfare existed in most Southern towns and cities, including Dothan, Ala. There Captain and Mrs. Victor Tidman headed, in addition to a full corps program, what was almost the only assistance during this time of great physical need.

Transients and homeless, fleeing the bleak cold and slim work opportunities further north, piled off railroad cars in droves almost like animals, heading for The Salvation Army Shelter.

Collins Baking Co. kept load after load of bread coming to the corps to help feed both local destitute and transient needy. Grocers and produce wholesalers kept canned goods, vegetables and fruit coming to the Army to help these people.

Captain Tidman provided needy families with plots of ground, together with seed, so they could grow their own much-needed food.

In addition, the local corps building was used regularly as a clinic where doctors performed minor surgery for children. And the Army officers, with a group of volunteers, gave emergency disaster service for many weeks following floods in nearby Elba and Geneva.

The Men's Social Service Centers fought a two-sided battle. On the one hand every bed was taken by men who wanted to work. On the other hand donations, which had always been poor, dried up altogether. Later, when the Federal Emergency Relief Administration (FERA) opened to house transients, it used the Men's Socials as feeder hostels into its larger camps. For this the Army received 30 to 50 cents per day—admittedly a pittance, but an income that the troubled program had not had before. Even with this help, many centers did not survive. A number were turned over to the local corps for operation with little or no notice of the changeover.

The Women's Social Service Department, with its network of homes and hospitals for unwed mothers, had been growing steadily since the territory opened. Although also hurt financially by the depression, it suffered less than other services. Women's auxiliaries were formed to aid this work. The first one formed since the territory began, which boasted 50 charter members, was in San Antonio.

Elsewhere, the Army grappled with feeding both the homeless and the area residents. Soup kitchens sprang up everywhere, with almost no means of paying for the food. Captain Edward Laity, in Roanoke, Va., made rounds to the local restaurants to ask for any food he could use to make soup. In Ft. Smith, Ark., the Army served what was donated—almost always cabbage and beans.

In other places, the Army did not wait for donations of food. It grew its own. Major Julius Satterfield had a ten acre farm in Lakeland, Fla., worked by the poor, where they were paid in food. Surplus food was sold to finance other Army operations. An even more ambitious program was run by Adjutant Harry McDonald in Cumberland, Md., where the Army ran a 40 acre farm.

Arranging for free water, plowing and using the labor of the unemployed, the farm produced potatoes, corn, tomatoes, beans, cabbage and cucumbers—all given to the workers in exchange for their labor. All of this was taken even one step further by Major Albert B. Figgins of Columbus, Ga., who opened a canning plant, enabling the Army to preserve both the food it had grown and the surpluses donated by neighboring farms.

In the spring of 1932, desperate World War I veterans marched on Washington to demand early payment of promised bonuses they earned for serving in the military. Soon dubbed the "Bonus Army", veterans marched from all points in the United States, swelling their numbers to over 17,000. They vowed to stay until Congress authorized payment of their bonuses. Most of the marchers stayed in a tent city they erected near the Capitol. Over a thousand sought refuge at Salvation Army shelters.

The District police asked for the Army's help in feeding the marchers. Over 4,500 meals a day were served. Tragically, the demonstration was broken up by the military with tanks, machine guns and tear gas. The tent city was set on fire and the marchers driven out of Washington. The only clear winners in the whole incident were the Salvationists who reached out to serve.

Unique opportunity for service came in Waycross, Ga., when a deaf mute youth named Francis Roberts came to Lieutenant Harakel with an unusual request. He was convinced that if he could ride in an airplane his speech and hearing would be restored. He had been injured the year before in a fall from a two-story window. The doctors considered his case hopeless. Lieutenant Harakel finally found a sympathetic pilot who would take the boy at no charge. At 10,000 feet something popped in his head, he heard the plane engine and was overjoyed to find his speech and hearing restored.

In Vicksburg, Miss., the police confiscated huge amounts of bootleg liquor. After emptying the bottles, they decided to give them to the Army. The bottles were sold and bought food for 500 people. In Williamson, W.Va., the officers were overjoyed when the local Maytag dealer decided to lend them the use of a washing machine. This luxury resulted in Captain Virginia Bolton giving an almost scripted endorsement: "The Maytag washers are efficient, economical, and can be depended upon at all times to wash and wring clothes properly."

In neighboring Welch, W.Va., a fruit peddler was arrested

for selling oranges without a license. He had no money to pay the $2.80 fine. "Do you have a local Salvation Army?" he asked. Answered in the affirmative, he then proposed to give 50 bushels of oranges for the Army to share with the poor. His sentence was suspended upon delivery of the fruit at the Army's door.

In Atlanta, the Christmas relief efforts included the first Christmas Toy Shop in the South. The toys were displayed as they would be in a store and parents were allowed to choose the toy they wanted for their child.

The intrepid Major Satterfield of Lakeland, Fla., discovered that 125 children scheduled to go to summer camp needed their tonsils out. With the help of donated anesthetic and the free services of 13 doctors and a free night at the hospital, the operations were performed. Afterwards, the children recuperated for a week at the camp.

As if things were not difficult enough, when officers in Paducah, Ky., and Nashville conducted their open-air meetings, they were arrested—a practice which had died down after the turn of the century. In both cities charges were dismissed by the judges the next day. On a more positive note, the Army's ministry in the Sunday School, then known as company meeting, was growing. In Ft. Worth, the officer reported 868 at its 1930 Rally Day. Colonel Smeeton, the Chief Secretary after 1931, suggested that the Army move the company meetings from Sunday afternoon to Sunday morning to help revive sagging morning worship attendance.

Despite the poor conditions, the Army held a congress in Atlanta in May 1931. The special guest was the first elected General of The Salvation Army, Edward Higgins. The General and 900 delegates were received by the Georgia governor, L. G. Hardman. In a press conference, General Higgins praised the territory as the fastest growing territory in the Army world—an ironic announcement in view of the efforts to dismantle it the previous year.

Elsewhere, while Clarksburg, W.Va., commissioned its first harmonica band, Envoy Albert Bartlett was in Savannah, Ga., organizing his 65th brass band in twenty-five years. But the big news in Southern music was not a what but a who.

Serving first as head of the education bureau, then as territorial youth secretary and finally as training school principal, was the Southern Territory's most prolific song writer, Sidney Cox. Cox had started writing songs in 1914, but many of his best known songs were written while he was an officer in the South.

He had the amazing ability to write songs almost anywhere at anytime. On a thirteen week tour of Texas, he wrote a new song for each corps he visited, including "My Lord Knows the Way through the Wilderness." While on the platform at the close of a meeting during a youth councils held at the corps in Orlando, Fla., he penned what is perhaps his most meaningful chorus:

All there is of me, Lord,
All there is of me.
Time and talents, day by day,
All I bring to thee;
All there is of me, Lord,
All there is of me,
On thine altar, here I lay
All there is of me.

Although Cox eventually left the Army over doctrinal issues and a desire for full-time Bible teaching, he remained a close friend and a frequent guest at Army meetings. Both Cox and his wife, Violet, are buried in The Salvation Army plot at Westview Cemetery in Atlanta.

With the inauguration of Franklin D. Roosevelt in 1932, Prohibition came to an end. What also came to an end was the worst of the Great Depression. In his first one hundred days in office, the new President initiated extensive social programs. The South was immediately benefited by the establishment of the Tennessee Valley Authority (TVA). The TVA took over the dam at Muscle Shoals, Ala., while starting work on a series of new dams to provide inexpensive electricity, fertilizer production and protection against the devastating floods which had ravaged the areas along the Tennessee River. The work meant jobs for the unemployed and progress for tens of thousands of rural homes where people had only dreamed of electricity. Other programs brought additional jobs and hope to the South.

Private industry picked up as government workers used their paychecks to patronize stores which had long been financially off-limits to them. *The War Cry* gleefully published a long list of factories and mills which recalled workers or had raised the wages of their employees. The comeback was not overnight. In fact, it was agonizingly slow, but a sense of optimism was felt for the first time in years.

Even in these difficult days, the Army was looking for new ways to serve those in need. The city of Charlotte was confronted by the problem of dealing with delinquent youths. After several meetings were held with the leading businessmen of the community, the only tangible suggestion that could be agreed upon was that the Army be asked to begin a boys' club. The Army, from the start, asked that the boys not be labeled delinquents. It had seen the potential with the problem. The boys' club work continued to spread in the Carolinas and into the rest of the South. Because work among girls was also included, most of the facilities would become known as community centers.

The Army was further encouraged by fund-raisers on its behalf. Famed radio broadcaster and cowboy philosopher Will Rogers decided to do seven broadcasts for the Army and donate part of the proceeds to the Army.

In a telegram to Commander Eva Booth introducing the

idea, he said, "Here is how this rough and tumble broadcastin' thing come about: the Gulf Oil Company kept wantin' me to litter up the microphone wth some Oklahoma grammar. Now, Amos and Andy and others have never had any cause to be jealous of me in their industry, but I did want to make a donation to a couple of good causes . . . but I didn't have the dough."

During a fund-raising effort in Miami, a Goodyear Tire Company blimp made flights over the city with a streamer that read, "The Salvation Army Needs Help Now" while 100 teams of volunteer campaign workers collected donations.

The War Cry of August 28, 1934, contained the announcement that the High Council would convene to elect a new general to replace the retiring Edward Higgins, who pleased Southerners by announcing his plans to live in Sebring, Fla. When the High Council finished its work, it had elected American national commander Evangeline Booth as its first woman general. That election set in motion a series of moves which culminated in October with the announcement that Lt. Commissioner and Mrs. Damon would leave the South to assume command of the United States Eastern Territory.

When Damon farewelled, he could see both that the Army and the South had experienced subtle, if not decisive, changes. With the desperation of depression days, the Army was lauded far and wide for its social work. Though Salvationists still felt their primary mission of reaching the lost was paramount, the country came to look to the Army for its practical helping ability.

The Army had mobilized more quickly and effectively than had the government itself. It continued to comfort and to reach those in direst circumstances, as it had with the famous doughnuts during the Great War. The public tolerated the Army's religious message, while wholeheartedly supporting its charitable activities. The organization's identity as an evangelistic movement was obscured in the chaos of the nation's economic collapse. Fifty years later it would still be reminding the nation it was more than a social service agency.

The South had changed as well. The other sections of the country had lorded their supposed superiority over the South since the Civil War. The South responded by insisting on its separateness and the evil of outsiders. But the Great Depression had placed all people on equal, if not lower, footing. Consequently the sectional distinctions lost some of their meaning.

When the rest of the country joined the South in its economic misery, the South responded by starting to join America's mainstream. As uncertain and ambivalent as the farmers leaving their dirt floor houses, the South was beginning to leave its self-imposed isolation. It would struggle with its heritage, deciding what was good, and what was better left behind. In this sifting, the South would writhe in agony. The Great Depression began the process.

To this changing scene the Army appointed a new territorial commander and chief secretary. Neither would serve a single hour in their new positions.

CHAPTER 13

MEXICO, MOUNTAIN MISSION AND MOMENTUM

(1935–1939)

COLONEL ARTHUR SMEETON, Southern Territory Chief Secretary under Commissioner Damon, was announced to be the new territorial commander for the South. He was to be assisted by Colonel George H. Davis from the Western Territory. Between the time of this announcement and taking the office of territorial commander, Smeeton suffered a serious heart attack while packing his things to move. Upon examination by physicians in Atlanta, it was determined that he was not able to fulfill the demands of his new appointment. Smeeton fought this, asserting his own ability to function. Unheeded, he found that he was instead forced into a period of recovery, that was terminated a year later by his retirement. With Smeeton's illness, Davis' orders were cancelled.

In place of Colonel Smeeton came Lt. Commissioner Ernest I. Pugmire. He had been preceded in the South by his father, a pioneer of one of the Army's illfated campaigns to reach blacks. Trained in Canada, Pugmire had served in Canada, Japan, China and the United States, though never serving as a corps officer. In his youth he was one of the

Army's premiere euphonium players—one of the few from the Canadian Staff Band who survived the sinking of the *Empress of Ireland* in 1914.

With his appointment as territorial commander, he was the youngest commissioner in the world at age forty-seven. Although not considered by some to be particularly creative he was able to see opportunity and to know when to make a needed move. This ability advanced the Army work in the South even in a time when caution was the order of the day.

Coming to the South for Pugmire was infinitely better than it had been for Damon. While Damon's administration watched the country sink deeper into the malaise of the Depression, by the time Pugmire took the reins, the worst was over. Still, things in the South were far from secure. During the Pugmire administration President Roosevelt would say, "It is my conviction that the South represents right now the nation's number one economic problem—the nation's problem, not merely the South's."

Evidence of this economic plight could still be found in the disparity of wages for Southerners and workers in the rest of the country. In the South the average income per worker was $314 per year compared to the national average of $604. As Pugmire took office, Oklahoma was suffering a severe drought, creating a huge dust bowl. This natural disaster ruined farm families who had already suffered from the Depression. Many chose to leave, heading out west where they felt they would have a better chance.

Despite these conditions, the new territorial commander was ready to try a new venture. His opportunity came from a single woman officer who wanted to go home.

Captain Cecil Brown was raised in the Smoky Mountains of North Carolina. The area was sparsely settled, little changed over the last century. Electricity and modern plumbing were virtually unknown. The preferred method of transportation over the steep mountains was mule or horse. Cecil's education was halted at the seventh grade because her teacher herself had gone only that far. Cecil went through the seventh grade three times, until her books were worn out. Finding that there was little for her to do on the family farm, she asked permission in 1924 to go stay with her brother who had moved to Asheville. Leaving the mountains, she was taken by the sights and sounds of the city.

She soon found a job at a department store and through that met The Salvation Army. Eventually she became a soldier during the administration of Captain Dorothy Guice, who saw Cecil's potential. She was soon sent to the training college in Atlanta. Talking about the training experience years later, she said, "The training college kinda oiled my brain. I felt I could never get through . . . I had to spread my books out on my bed and pray over every subject."

Following her training, she had several corps appointments, including opening the corps in Reidsville, N.C. But she had not found her place in regular Army work. In fact, in many respects she was considered to be a failure. No one knew this more than Cecil herself. Her mind was elsewhere as she yearned to return to the mountains to bring the Gospel there.

Years before, the last of the circuit riders had abandoned the hills due to lack of financial support, leaving whole communities with no access to a church. In the communities where she served, she could see not only the Army corps but many other churches carrying on their work, while her people back home were left spiritually abandoned.

Finally word reached her divisional commander, Major William Gilks. In January 1935, with the promise of a four month trial, Captain Cecil Brown was sent back to the mountains to open a mission work, her first officer home being a mere shed built for her by her brother, Fletcher. Beginning in Waynesville, she then opened work in Shelton Laurel with a hay loft as her headquarters.

She labored long and hard to open mission stations in remote mountain areas with such picturesque names as Little Creek, White Oak, Cold Springs, Spring Creek, Max Patch, Fines Creek, Big Bend and Maple Springs. Some of these areas were so remote that she could travel by car only part of the way, then by horse and finally on foot. One day she walked twenty-three miles over muddied roads and swollen creeks to conduct a meeting.

The following is an example of what she faced when she started her work:

> Big Bend was a feuding center that had claimed the life of many men including several sheriffs. The law was of no effect here. Not only was it a hostile place but the approach to it was a nine mile footpath cutting it off effectively from the outside world. Cecil Brown had to reach these people. Song books were useless since only one person could read. The men sat in the back smoking during the services. The only songs they knew were country ballads that spoke of unrequited love or melodies suitable for drinking bouts.
>
> After finishing one of these meetings in Big Bend, she reached for her bag for the long trip home when it was picked up by a young man, who at twenty-three had already killed three men. During the nine mile walk he spoke only three times and that in answer to her questions. At the end of the journey he shook her hand, thanked her for the meetings and promised her protection whenever she was in Big Bend.

Not only did she have to face difficult surroundings, but prejudice of the people. If Southerners as a whole did not care for women preachers, the feelings on this subject were especially strong in the Smoky Mountains. The curiosity and controversy surrounding her ministry brought crowds in that otherwise might have ignored another preacher's work. In mission after mission revivals broke out, beginning at times with the conversions of the most skeptical.

Word of the success of the Mountain Mission spread. Brown was invited to a meeting of officers who were discussing various problems they faced, including how to attract more people to Army meetings. Brown responded to this by saying, "My problem is not getting people in my halls, but how to get halls for my people." In a spontaneous collection that followed her talk, enough money was raised to construct a building in Maple Springs.

Later she would appear on the CBS radio program, "We the People", to tell her story to ten million listeners. In addition, uncounted newspaper and magazine articles chronicled her work. For her efforts she was awarded The Salvation Army's highest award, the Order of the Founder.

Brigadier Douglas Eldredge, together with his wife Dorothy, carried on a unique ministry in the specialized work of the Boys' Clubs of Baltimore which he set up in a small way in 1936. The program grew and expanded, with the Brigadier serving as national liaison for The Salvation Army with Boys' Clubs of America.

A friend and student of Ernest Thompson Seton, author and naturalist, Brigadier Eldredge used the knowledge derived from this association both in the club programs and in developing and carrying on the activities of famed Camp Puh'tok. The Indian village and Top Bar Ranch of the camp were so skillfully built and carried out that often photographers from the Department of the Interior in Washington would come to the camp to take pictures to use in their publications.

Other outreaches included that of Sgt-Major J.S. Butler of Welch, W.Va. In the largest coal producing area of the state, he visited each mine to carry on a ministry of witness and relief. By walking, hitchhiking, bus, train or whatever means available, he worked the mines until the cool reception he was first greeted with changed to open arms of welcome.

Further south the corps in Montgomery, Ala., could report the most unusual choir in the country. In Kilby Prison, Salvationists conducted meetings among the twenty men on death row. Each one was given his own song book. Every man sang so heartily the music from death row was heard throughout the prison.

Good news was coming from all over the territory. A record attendance of 1,056 was set at the Carolina Division youth councils. From Augusta, Ga., came the first open-air meeting ever broadcast, courtesy of Radio Station WGPC. Meanwhile, in Atlanta the first Vacation Bible School was run more like a college than a youth program. At the Washington Georgetown Corps, a forerunner of the Men's Club, known as the "Better Husband's Club", started meeting at the same time as the women's Home League.

The library of the city of Houston became the beneficiary of a donation of books and materials which had belonged to Army pioneer John Milsaps. With a grandfather who had died in the Alamo and a father who had fought for the Confederates in the Civil War, Milsaps was raised in poverty, despite his rich heritage. His only entertainment as a boy had come from the small collection of books at the Houston Lyceum, the library of his day. He grew up and left Texas, heading west and meeting the Army there.

He was to have a distinguished career as an Army officer, becoming the first Salvationist to be a United States military chaplain, serving in the Philippines during the Spanish-American War. He became editor of the Western *War Cry*, and counted among his converts Captain Joseph Garabed, better known as Joe the Turk. In his gift to the library he left over 12,000 books and other materials which the library has designated the Circle M Collection.

Other developments included the purchase of a plot at Westview Cemetery in Atlanta for the burial of officers, soldiers and their families. During the dedication, Major Sam Pearce was the soloist. In an unusual coincidence, he was the first person to be buried there a month later.

A pioneering work among parolees began in Texas in 1937. Monitoring the ex-offender's progress following his release, the Army had a success rate of 95%. All of this work was done with no payment from the government and in addition to the other responsibilities officers carried.

Not all the changes were welcomed by the Army. Commissioner Pugmire noted the decline in open-air meetings due to "traffic, noise, and restricted parking making it increasingly difficult to hold on to the customary downtown open-air stand. The tendency of some corps is to give up in despair."

Other things that should have been changed but couldn't be included living conditions of officers. Since the depression began, all officers had been requested to give back 10 percent of their meager salaries to be shared with officers who could not draw money at all from their appointments. Nor were they to be encouraged by living conditions in some of the quarters.

Mrs. Lt. Colonel C. William Jaynes has related the conditions she found at Washington Southeast in 1936: "Our first quarters was rat-infested. Drunken wharf rats big as cats, literally. They would come up from the wharf, stop off at the beer joint, imbibing of the mash, and by the time they got into the quarters they just sauntered around the house."

The need for money made for a strange compromise in Wilson, N.C. The Army had always taken a stand against the use of tobacco but economic necessity forced the officers to accept donations of tobacco from farmers who wanted to help them. The tobacco was graded and sold through tobacco auctions.

Ten years after the great Mississippi flood that hit soon after the inauguration of the territory, the river again terrorized the South. All along the river, cities were flooded, leaving 230,000 homes under water. The Army set up disaster relief stations in Louisville, Ky., Wheeling, W.Va., Memphis, Tenn., Hattiesburg, Miss., Wellsburg, W.Va., Parkersburg, W.Va., Huntington, W.Va., and Little Rock, Ark.

During the crisis in Louisville, 10,000 persons a day were fed. At Huntington, Salvationists built boats from scrap lumber to aid in the rescue work. Over three hundred officers, cadets and employees were involved in the rescue work. Later, the Army was called upon to serve again when a school in New London, Tex., exploded, leaving 500 dead. The Army was the first relief organization on the scene, arriving 45 minutes after the explosion.

A more positive celebration of the tenth anniversary of the territory came with the announcement that General Evangeline Booth would be in Atlanta to conduct a congress on her first visit back since being elected General. The congress was the largest gathering of Salvationists in the South since the territory began. Delegates streamed in from all points to celebrate. Features included a Gospel quartet from the Mountain Mission and a novelty band of ten cornets and ten accordions. Then followed the surprise introduction of a delegation from Mexico who came to the platform to sing a song in Spanish. It was announced that the Army was opening its work in Mexico under the auspices of the Texas divisional commander, Major William Gilks.

The idea of the Army's work in Mexico was nothing new. In the international Army publication, *All the World*, in 1904 it was announced, "One of our future battlefields will, we hope, be Mexico . . ." An actual attempt was made in 1909 when Colonel Wright from International Headquarters went to Mexico City, meeting with the president, General Porfirio Diaz. Following an explanation of the Army's work and purposes, the president encouraged Wright to open the work.

After reports of Wright's visits to a couple of cities, no more reports came from Mexico. What looked like a promising opening simply disappeared. Work along the border was carried on by the corps in El Paso and Laredo. In Laredo, Brigadier Milton Atkins had opened an outpost in neighboring Nuevo Laredo, Mexico. This was made a corps in 1930 when Commissioner Damon visited there to dedicate the building.

The real work of the Army would be begun by Mexicans themselves who had absolutely no knowledge that The Salvation Army existed. The key figure was a man named Alejandro Guzmán. A born leader, as a youth he had been secretary of the Communist Union in his hometown of Mexico City. Converted through a Methodist youth group, he soon was the recognized leader because of the enthusiasm of his witness and the zeal he had for outreach. He became disillusioned with his home church when he saw a drunkard thrown out during a service.

Feeling God speak to his heart about reaching those unwanted by the church, in 1934 he gathered a group of friends around him to begin *La Patrulla Salvacionista,* or The Salvation Patrol. The group went through the streets, witnessing in slums, bars and bordellos. This was in violation of Mexican law which allowed freedom of religion within church walls but which prohibited any exercise of religion in the streets. Members of The Salvation Patrol were arrested, but unrepentant, they returned to the streets to carry on their work. Eventually they got enough money to rent a house to use for sheltering the poor.

One day at a religious convention, Guzmán was asked to talk about the work of The Salvation Patrol. At the end of the meeting a minister said to him, "Listen, brother, your group is doing the same kind of work as done by The Salvation Army." Guzmán replied, "The Salvation Army? What is that?" Soon after that, he came across a copy of Hugh Redwood's book, *God in the Slums,* which included descriptions of the Army's work in England.

Fascinated, Guzmán was determined to meet someone with the Army. Through an acquaintance, he made arrangements to travel to San Antonio on his first trip outside of Mexico. There he met the corps officer, Adjutant William Stevenson. When Stevenson heard Guzmán's story, he immediately phoned his divisional commander, Major William Gilks, the same man who had been in the Carolinas at the beginning of the Mountain Mission. Gilks arranged for an interview, speaking with Guzmán for three hours. He contacted Commissioner Pugmire about the exciting development.

Arrangements were made for Gilks to accompany Guzmán to Atlanta where he was shown Army facilities and more of the Army's operations were explained to him. Guzmán returned to Mexico to present what he had learned to other Patrol members and to an advisory group which had been formed to aid them in their mission. Pugmire asked Gilks to travel to Mexico City to get a closer look at the Patrol's work. Gilks reported enthusiastically of the Patrol's efforts to reach the very lowest, of their faithfulness to the Gospel message, and of his own hope that, through the Patrol, the Army might at last have access to the millions of Mexico.

Following this visit, members of The Salvation Patrol were invited to the meetings in Atlanta conducted by General Evangeline Booth. Pugmire had explained the developments to the General who joined the Southerners' joy at the prospect of this providential opening. At the congress meeting, eight members of the Patrol were called forward to receive an Army flag with the General's charge: "Be true to its colors and to its teachings. Fight the good fight of faith, and we shall meet again in Heaven, if not on earth." With that, The Salvation Patrol became The Salvation Army. When they returned to Mexico the women handmade the first uniforms. Gilks came within a month and enrolled twenty five former Patrol members as soldiers.

Guzmán's work was not to be made any easier by affiliation with The Salvation Army, or, as translated in Spanish, *Ejército de Salvación*. In addition to the restrictions on street meetings, no one was allowed to wear clerical garb outside the church. The state had the power to assign the number of priests in each locality and to declare which churches could be opened. Nor did The Salvation Army have the legal status of a church, instead being considered a cult.

Guzmán warned about the danger of evangelical work in his country, citing the machete killing by a mob of a man outside his church in Pueblo. "I do not fear the mobs in their efforts to stop the development of the Gospel in Mexico, but I do think they will continue and many of our group will be murdered. Therefore, we must be prepared to meet the difficulties . . . even (if they) burn our truck and kill our men."

Complicating the Army's outreach in Mexico were deteriorating relations between the two countries. The United States had been guilty of periodic interference in Mexican affairs for nearly a century, resulting in strong anti-American sentiment. This was further escalated by Mexico's desperation as it faced the Depression. In 1938, Mexico raised the tariff on American made goods by 100-200% followed by the nationalization of the oil fields owned by American companies. But the Army remained above the controversy as money and supplies poured in for the new work. Within a year of the opening the Army the first new building in Mexico City was dedicated.

When another opportunity presented itself in Atlanta, Pugmire was quick to seize upon it. A man who had heard Evangeline Booth speak at the congress was impressed with what she said regarding the Army's needs for a better training facility for its cadets. Commissioner Damon had originally been offered the property at 1032 Stewart Avenue, S.W., but no money was available at that time with which to even consider it. The gentleman again approached Commissioner Pugmire about making available to the Army this location, the old Atlanta Theological Seminary.

The property originally had been a farm owned by Josiah Sherman, with the building erected three years after the Civil War. It had served for years as one of the few Southern seminaries which had admitted women. It had been vacant for some time, and was offered to the Army at an extremely low price. The purchase was completed, renovations completed and the property dedicated on June 5, 1938, by retired General Edward Higgins.

Brigadier Ernest Richard Holz was to be the first principal of the School for Officers' Training at 1032 Stewart Avenue, S.W. With his wife, the former Captain Keitha White, he had served successfully in corps appointments in the Eastern Territory before entering the U.S. Army Chaplain Corps in 1918. After the war the Holzes had been appointed as divisional leaders in the Washington and Potomac Division and the Oklahoma Division.

His appointment as principal of the Southern Territory's Training College in Atlanta was to be his last major appointment prior to his untimely promotion to Glory in December, 1938. During this time he had trained 163 cadets and saw the school through its move from 339 Luckie Street to 1032 Stewart Avenue, S.W. At the dedication of the new campus in

1938 he had raised the cornet to his lips to play *"Call to the Colors"* while the flag was being raised for the first time. The same year he was promoted to Glory, with the sound of the trumpet as certain as ever.

Meanwhile, the Great Depression was winding down, signaled by at least one very positive sign. The Army rejoiced to see that the Men's Social Service Department finally was breaking even, after operating at a loss since the territory began. Related to this was the uniquely Southern development of corps-operated thrift stores.

Elsewhere in the world, thrift stores were the exclusive province of the Men's Social Centers. But in the South, the desperate needs of the corps forced them into finding money wherever they could. With the donation of so much materials when money was needed, the creation of thrift stores was inevitable. The South today has the largest number of corps-operated thrift stores in the world.

As 1939 opened, it was with the notice that Lt. Commissioner and Mrs. Pugmire were to proceed to New York to assume command of the Eastern Territory. The turnaround in the Southern Territory had been phenomenal during the dangerous days of the Great Depression. But even as the light seemed to be dawning, distant thunder forewarned a coming fury.

CHAPTER 14

VYING FOR VICTORY

(1939–1947)

UNITED STATES reaction to world events was to withdraw into isolationism with the archaic notion that the Atlantic and Pacific served as moats for Fortress America. It barely winced when Mussolini rolled his Italian army through backward Ethiopia. When Hitler annexed the Rhineland, Austria and Czechoslovakia, the country was content to know that no shot had been fired. When Japan bloodied the Chinese landscape with a preview of worldwide atrocities, the government lamely cut off some exports while still selling the oil that fueled the Japanese war machine. With incredible blindness it failed to recognize its place in the worldwide community. The United States would believe it could profit from a revitalized war industry but never directly confront those who sought to subdue the world. By exposure to such brutality it was time for America's ideals to be tested. With the rest of the world The Salvation Army would be tested as well.

The man chosen to lead the Army in the South through this time was Lt. Commissioner William Arnold. Born in Germany, as a child he had emigrated to the United States to live in Spokane, Wash. He eventually entered officer training from Helena, Mont. while that section of the country was still under the Canadian command. During his early officership the West was still largely unsettled. Similar to the methods of Army officers in the early days of Oklahoma, Arnold was involved in what was called outriding work. Done largely on horseback, officers visited far flung outposts and conducted meetings in towns that had no other religious influence.

When it was decided to form a Prairie Schooner Brigade, Arnold was included. He not only proved he could withstand the rigors of this type of work but demonstrated musical talents evidenced in a magnificent tenor voice and mastery of the violin. The Brigade worked its way through Montana and Idaho in its trademark prairie schooner. From this ministry he was appointed to finance work at headquarters.

Here he met his wife, Irena, a Canadian, who had served as a corps officer and editor of The Salvation Army children's magazine, *The Young Soldier*. She was also an accomplished poet, her works finally collected in two volumes. Together they ascended to increasingly responsible positions of leadership. As territorial commander, Arnold would not only command the forces through the greatest international crisis in the world's history, but would serve the longest term of anyone in that office in the South.

Soon after Arnold's taking office in March 1939, the territory was part of an international religious assembly. The Baptist World Alliance was meeting in Atlanta, with over 50,000 delegates. The Army was requested to provide the music. This resulted in the resurrection of the now defunct Southern Territorial Staff Band. With Adjutant Albert E. Baldwin as bandmaster, 38 bandsmen came from all points in the South for the special function.

Even though they had not played together for years, the band in its short rehearsal time functioned as if there had never been a break, marching in a parade and playing for the major meetings of the Alliance. Although territorial bands would be assembled again, when these bandsmen left to go home the Southern Staff Band never functioned again.

When summer ended, the unthinkable happened. On September 1, German and Soviet forces poured across the Polish border. England and France quickly declared war on Germany. World War II had begun.

Against this backdrop, the Training College began a weekly radio broadcast on WSB in Atlanta. *"Hymns from the Fireside,"* featuring the music of the cadets and their principal, Major Sidney Cox, was literally heard around the war-torn world, with letters coming from as far away as 15,000 miles in the South Pacific.

Music provided comfort to a future enemy at Christmas in Ft. Lauderdale. A German tanker, the *Arauca*, had sought refuge in the Florida port, trying to escape British warships. The crew was held captive in their ship, barbed wire strung across the dock to keep the prisoners in and the curious out. Captain James Klaas took the soldiers of the corps to the docks where they sang Christmas carols to the crew. In response, the sailors sang back in their native tongue. For a short moment in time, hostilities were put on hold.

As bad as things were on the international scene, the war did put an end to the Great Depression. Officially a neutral, the United States found that its factories were filled with orders for not only war supplies but every other imaginable material. Farm prices rose as countries availed themselves of America's plenty. The South prospered relatively more than the rest of the country. While the per capita income for the rest of the country rose by 109 percent in the period of 1940 to 1946, in the South it rose by 112 percent in Virginia and 170 percent in Alabama.

In 1940 the Selective Service Act came into effect as America began to mobilize in the event of war. With that came military bases and the South received a considerable number of these. Sleepy little towns of yesteryear became bustling centers. Laborers were used not only to construct the new bases but to build housing for the families of servicemen. Women were in demand to fill jobs formerly occupied only by men. At a time when no Americans were dying on foreign fields, it was hard not to smile about what was happening at home.

One result of this was that the Army found itself with money again. Forging ahead, Arnold initiated the first Territorial Music Institute, held at the Training College, and followed by the first Territorial Youth Institute held at Shocco Springs, Ala.

The finances sometimes came in interesting ways. In New Orleans, Major Walter Needham was stopped on the street by a soldier who handed him a "cuss bucket", explaining that, when a soldier in his barracks used profanity, his buddies made him contribute to the fund. Later, more conventional means allowed Commissioner Arnold to swing through Oklahoma to celebrate the burning of mortgages in Oklahoma City, Clinton, Duncan, Enid, Muskogee, Okmulgee, Bartlesville, Bristow, Sand Springs, and Chickasha.

The Army was conscious not only of its own needs but of the suffering caused by the war. Mrs. Lt. Commissioner Arnold activated the Home League across the South to provide clothing, knitted goods and blankets for the refugees streaming into Great Britain. As the war dragged on, the help would be extended to Scandinavia as well.

On February 4, 1941, the Army joined with the YMCA, YWCA, Catholic Community Services, Jewish Welfare Board and Traveler's Aid to form the United Service Organizations, better known as USO. The USO was aimed at providing a wholesome alternative to soldiers besides the brothels and bars that sprang up around military bases. Commissioner

Arnold spelled out to the Army the parameters of its involvement:

> 1st—to provide a wholesome home environment for the men of the armed forces.
>
> 2nd—to continue, and, if possible, intensify the spiritual influences of the family group, the home, and the church. "Righteousness Exalteth a Nation."
>
> 3rd—by this means to protect the men from the baleful and injurious influences so often present in the vicinity of the training camps.

Arnold wrote elsewhere: "The soldier of today will find provided by the Army comfortably furnished clubrooms, reception lounges where he may meet friends and relatives, refreshments from a modern snack bar, washroom facilities, and writing rooms with desks and stationery . . . for entertainment the soldiers will have amateur dramatics, quiz programs, illustrated movie travelogues, groups games, and stunt nights. There will be good books, lectures, newspapers and magazines, and when music is wanted, there will be the piano, radio, recorded music, songfests and vocal soloists." Also included were recreation rooms, athletic events, religious counseling, classes and services. The biggest help was relieving the overwhelming loneliness experienced by the men at the camps.

Although the USO was the biggest wartime program of the Army, it also maintained a similar program separate from this called the Red Shield Club. The first Red Shield Club was opened in Fayetteville, N.C., at the end of 1940 when Captain Charles Collins was the commanding officer and Lt. Colonel Alfred Tyler the divisional commander. This was soon followed by one opened in Lawton, Okla., which included rooms for visiting mothers and wives. Typical of these grassroot efforts, Major Leonard Van Egmond opened a large downtown Red Shield Club with adequate housing for service personnel in Montgomery, Ala.; while Brigadier Richard Bergren took over the Howell Elementary School in Dothan, Ala., for a similar purpose.

The first Salvation Army USO opened in the South was at Eunice, La. The USO buildings were built by the government and then leased back to the agencies which ran the programs. As the work spread, the Army branched out to open one USO exclusively for women in New Bern, N.C. It also opened two USOs for blacks in Smyrna, Tenn., and Frederick, Md. The largest of the 3000 USOs in the country, operated by Major C. Langley Andrews—Salvation Army and other agencies included—was in New Orleans, having over 550 beds and a total attendance in its existence of 2,954,200.

Captain Walter Swyers ran one of the busiest USOs in the country in Alexandria, La., near Fort Brantley, a base commanded by future great, Major Omar Bradley. Once the club was opened, the door was never locked. With a strictly enforced curfew in town, the men crowded into the USO. One night Swyers went by to check on things and found the club so crowded he couldn't get in the door. Over 700 men had jammed the building, many of them sleeping as they were, standing up. The club also included the first U.S. Military Symphony which regularly gave classical music concerts.

The USO in Lawton operated a school of math, art and music which aided the men trying to pass the examinations to become commissioned officers. The Salvation Army officer hired three college professors who, with the staff of the club, graduated 1,200 men during the war. The importance of this work was in evidence later when these same men helped engineer the breakout from the hedgerow country following the Normandy invasion.

The USO became a major thrust of Army effort through the next six years, especially following the United States' involvement in the war. At its peak in 1945, the USOs of the

South were serving 1,500,000 service personnel per month in 78 USOs and 30 Red Shield clubs. The South contained more of these clubs than the other three United States territories combined. By the end of the war, 47,821,795 service personnel had passed through the Army's doors. Salvation Army operations of USO Clubs continued until 1974 when The Salvation Army, for policy reasons, severed its relationship with USO nationally.

Colonel John Allan, a Salvation Army officer (later Chief of the Staff), head of the U.S. Army Chaplain Department in Washington, was in Cumberland, Md., to dedicate an outpost building. On the Sunday afternoon of the dedication, a messenger came to the platform and the program concluded hastily. It was December 7, 1941. Rear Admiral Bellinger had telegraphed a message which stabbed the heart of isolationist America, "AIR RAID, PEARL HARBOR—THIS IS NO DRILL."

When the Japanese attacked, the U.S. Pacific fleet was docked in the harbor. In the surprise strike, 18 ships were either sunk or damaged along with the destruction of 349 aircraft, resulting in about 3,700 deaths. The same day, the Japanese attacked American outposts at Guam, Wake Island and the Philippines.

In his address to a joint session of Congress the next day, Roosevelt referred to it as a "day that would live in infamy." War was then declared on Japan. Germany and Italy responded by declaring war on the United States. The war that America thought it could sidestep was now on its door step.

The effect of the war on The Salvation Army varied from program to program. Officers were already being diverted to USO work; at its peak over a hundred Southern officers would be involved. A number of younger men officers resigned to join the military. Male candidates for officership were either drafted or, feeling an obligation to their country, enlisted. At one time there were 2,523 Southern Salvationists in the armed forces.

In its recruitment efforts for badly needed officers The Salvation Army sometimes gave scant details. In Eustis, Fla., a young musician was advised by his Methodist minister that, with his dedication and talent, he should join The Salvation Army. Accordingly, Oscar Eckstein contacted the nearest corps in Sanford, Fla. The officer, Captain Ralph Rose, came to Eustis weekly where he collected money and sold *The War Cry*. When in town he visited Eckstein and assured him that the Army had ample opportunities for a dedicated Christian and gifted cornet player. Convinced that this was the place for him, Eckstein agreed to enter the school. What he did not know about was the strict discipline at the school which required cadets to live virtually in their uniforms, perform countless work details, and do evangelistic outreach in addition to their class work.

He arrived in Atlanta wearing his best suit; he didn't even own a uniform. Seeing the officers in the dining room eating breakfast, he introduced himself, telling them he had come to major in music. He was quickly informed how wrong his concept was. Under these circumstances he should not have lasted 24 hours. Instead, he went on to become an extremely successful officer known for his Bible teaching—he was able also to play his cornet for the glory of God.

The war affected no program more drastically than the Men's Social Service Centers. Having just attained a firm financial footing, the war years would be a time of leanness. First, the centers, which had been overflowing with men before the war, were emptied by the combined forces of higher paying jobs in industry and the Selective Service Act.

The centers were hit with the same shortages all Americans faced. Gasoline was rationed as was food. Tires were next to impossible to replace, wire for baling virtually non-existent, replacement vehicles only a dream. Finally, the shortages faced by the American people meant that they were not willing to give away what they might not be able to replace. Donations slowed to a trickle. Even with the shortages, the last relic of the past did not survive. The last horse cart still in use in the South was retired from Louisville.

On the other hand, the Women's Social Service Department found itself in a boom time. The maternity homes were full of girls who had succumbed to wartime romances. Fortunately, financing was not difficult and the drain of personnel did not adversely affect the all-female forces of the Women's Social.

The reality of the war was brought home in many ways. In Parkersburg, W.Va., the band became the first all woman corps band in the South when all the men left to join the war effort. At the Training College, Lt. Colonel Alfred Tyler had much of the school's eleven acres planted with crops, known in wartime as "Victory Gardens." In Greenwood, S.C., children were brought to Vacation Bible School in horse and wagon because of the gasoline shortage. Among the tragedies of war, Army officers in both Welch, W.Va., and Montgomery, Ala., were called upon to conduct mass funerals for young men killed in training exercises.

Meanwhile, in Mexico the work forged ahead. At the end of 1941 the Army allied itself with other Protestant churches in a Gospel Crusade whose goal was to place a Bible in every Mexican home. Obtaining a motor launch to reach the seaports, the Army also had a sound truck for open-air work to take to the less settled areas of the republic.

Joining his brother, Alejandro, was Adolfo Guzmán. Having a military background, he was specially suited to carry the crusade to the back country of Mexico. With a few companions he went into areas he knew were hostile to outsiders.

Some areas were so remote that even Spanish was a foreign language. When the Crusaders reached one of these areas they used recordings provided by Wycliffe Bible Translators in the villagers' native tongue.

Some of those reached had never seen an automobile and were stunned to see one that could "talk." In one village large baskets of rocks were gathered to stone the Salvationists when they finished their presentation. Fortunately they were able to calm the villagers with what they said. In other places they were unable to eat—the villagers refused even to sell them the most basic foods.

Mexico entered the war on the side of the allies in mid-1942. Mexico's primary contribution to the war effort was oil from its vast reserves. Circumstances in Mexico improved for The Salvation Army. Encouraging to the Army was a friendlier attitude from the government regarding religious work. Church persecution disappeared as clerics were permitted to wear their collars outside of church, following a prolonged absence of this privilege. The Army was allowed for the first time to parade occasionally on the streets of Mexico City. Complete with police escort, they marched to the "Heroes of Independence" monument to lay a wreath.

Bolstered by these victories, the Army extended its work to Monterrey in 1944. The corps occupied one of the few buildings in town that had running water. To serve the community, public baths were installed and access was given to the water for drinking purposes. A small medical clinic was opened to serve the poor.

Back home in the United States, Commissioner Arnold became enamored with the work of the Mountain Mission carried on by Major Cecil Brown. A day school had been started at Miller's Gap. In addition, there was the erection of a new building at Little Creek, replacing a hay loft which had served as the Army's meeting place. During Arnold's administration, Brown would receive the designation of District Officer—the only position of its kind in the South.

In another development, the Army International Headquarters created the Distinguished Auxiliary Service Award to recognize outstanding volunteer service on the Army's behalf by a non-Salvationist. The first recipient in the South was Preston S. Arkwright. As advisory board chairman in Atlanta, Arkwright had been instrumental in influencing the Army to locate territorial headquarters there. Wielding considerable influence as head of Georgia Power Company, he served the Army faithfully for twenty years as an advisory board member. In Birmingham, the Home and Hospital honored Dr. J. E. Garrison who attended the births of 2,975 babies, all at no charge.

In 1943, General Carpenter made a brief visit to the South. He was greatly handicapped during his administration by the restrictions on wartime travel. The trip to the United States was the first time he had been able to leave Great Britain since the war broke out. Visiting Atlanta and coming to Washington for a congress, the meetings were decidedly more subdued than those to which the Army was accustomed.

A more joyous occasion was commemorated in Sebring, Fla., when retired General Edward Higgins celebrated his eightieth birthday. To mark the event the corps was presented a stained glass window featuring Army symbols and William Booth.

As 1944 dawned, the fortunes of war were clearly in favor of the Allies. Key victories were being recorded in both the European and Pacific theaters. The line of defense which Hitler called Fortress Europe was breached following the Allied invasion at Normandy. This, coupled with the Soviet Union advancing from the east, caught Germany in an inescapable vise. The Japanese Empire was shrinking under the island-hopping strategy of the American forces in the Pacific.

Though the war was far from over, it was more favorable to talk of an Allied victory.

At the same time, honors were coming to Salvationist military chaplains. Both Major William T. Powell and Captain Allen Dillon were awarded the Bronze Star, with Captains James H. Cranford and James Neighbors also being among Salvationists who gave distinguished service during this period. Major C. Langley Andrews was honored by the government of the Netherlands. Queen Wilhelmina appointed him a knight of the Order of Orange-Nassau for his USO work in New Orleans where he had hosted seamen from the Netherlands, a kindness reported to the royal family.

Following Germany's surrender on May 7, 1945, the Army shared in the victory parades across the nation. When General Courtney Hodges of the American First Army, together with five other generals and men from the "Fighting First", returned to Atlanta, Commissioner Arnold was invited to ride in the parade. The Army band also participated. In Washington, the Army band was a part of the reception for General Dwight D. Eisenhower who saluted the band as he passed by.

But the war was not over yet. It took the unprecedented fury of two atomic bombs to bring Japan to its knees. With the surrender of Japan, hostilities ceased. The reaction to this news is best seen through the eyes of a worker at the USO club in Washington:

> On Tuesday, August 14, 1945, came the news of the Japanese surrender. Tenseness was as tangible as a brick wall just before the word was flashed out, and had been for days. So was a great hope disguised as cynicism. You could reach out and touch the "Oh, yeah! You'll have to show me!" attitude. And then came the news—official news! There was a moment of absorbing, adjusting silence, and then a spontaneous outburst of joyous release. Outside 801 (was) the sound of a few car horns blowing. In a matter of minutes (it) had grown to a steady

> crescendo which was to be the accompaniment for a celebration all during that hilarious night, and the streets were suddenly obliterated with people. People laughed, and shouted, and hugged each other; people shot off a few long-hoarded fire crackers; and scattered any kind of paper—from windows and doorways; people cried. People had a common purpose—to get within sight of The White House and within sound of the President. Those were the symbols which would transform a wonderful dream into reality and bring it within reach of their minds as well as their hearts. Women stood, backs to the Executive Mansion, holding compact mirrors in order to see over the heads of the throng. Traffic crawled or stopped altogether, human bodies sandbagged the stalled streetcars; policemen smiled or shrugged off the snarls. There may have been grass at Lafayette Square that night, it could not be seen for the feet of all the human beings who stood there. But the lighted Capitol at the end of Pennsylvania Avenue could be seen and its light was reflected in the faces and hearts of a sometimes grumbling but always courageous people. And in Potomac Park, west of the Washington Monument, a little of the sadness seemed to have lifted from the face of Abraham Lincoln.

With the end of the war the Army was able to press forward on several fronts. The Men's Social Service was the first to see the positive effects of peace.

Americans had long been saddled with shortages and ration books. Now this was changed. These restraints were removed. The Men's Social found itself overwhelmed with donations as people happily parted with their wartime clothing, applicances and furniture. At the same time, the centers were beginning to fill with veterans returning from active service.

Many of these men were not able to make a successful return to their former life or were not sure what they wanted to do. The Men's Social was a welcome option. When they went to the centers, they would find a new approach to helping the men with their problems called "Service to Man."

The programs of the centers were decidedly centered on the man, with efforts being made to understand the individual needs he brought with him. Aiding this was a shift in the Army's priorities as income from the centers allowed the construction of new facilities.

Setting an example of this new thought among the Men's Social officers was Sr. Captain Sven Ruthstrom. His center in Houston was considered to be the finest in the South to exemplify the goals of the Social for the men's spiritual needs and rehabilitation. For the longsuffering Men's Social, the changes were welcome. As noted in Edward McKinley's book *Somebody's Brother*, "These were the golden years (of the Men's Social) in the Southern Territory."

Following the war, General Albert Orsborn was elected General. He was immediately invited to come to the South. Beginning with a congress in Atlanta, he proceeded on to Washington where he was accorded the greatest international honor ever given to an Army leader.

General Orsborn was the guest of honor at a dinner which had representatives from thirty-three nations, most of them ambassadors. Also included among the dignitaries were two Supreme Court justices. Music was furnished by the United States Navy Band. This visit to the South also involved a reception at the White House by President Harry Truman.

The General was pleased with what he saw in the South and for the progress being made. An example of this progress was in Mexico which had only recently become a division under the leadership of Brigadier and Mrs. Ray Gearing. The creation of the division took Mexico from under the control of the Texas division, which up until then had been paying most of the expenses associated with the Army's work there. It also made the Mexico Division the largest division in the world with respect to land mass. The work was developing well and it was felt that closer direct supervision would allow for more expansion.

Probably the most urgent reason for the change was found in the personality of Alejandro Guzmán. Although no one would question his evangelistic zeal, he was finding the Army's structure difficult to handle. The Gearings diplomatically worked with a man who did not welcome their coming.

Among the changes the Gearings brought was the beginning of *La Escuela de Cadetes,* the Training College. With ten cadets in the first session, the Gearings served not only as divisional commander but also as training officers. Their only help came from Adjutant Verna Davis who functioned as divisional finance officer, training officer and the divisional commander's secretary. All of this was conducted under one roof that also served as quarters for the Gearings and Davis. When the cadets were commissioned the following year, they received their first officers' uniforms, paid for by the Home Leagues of the Southern Territory, and Bibles as gifts from General and Mrs. Higgins (R).

The Army continued to render disaster aid when the need arose. Along the Gulf coast of Florida, Mississippi and Louisiana, a hurricane brought widespread devastation. In Atlanta, the worst hotel fire to date claimed 127 lives at the Winecoff Hotel. The Army served in these emergencies as well as serving over 10,000 meals in Woodward, Okla., following a tornado. These disasters would be eclipsed at Texas City, Tex.

On the morning of April 16, 1947 a crew was at the docks loading the ship *The Grand Camp*. Inside its hold was a mixed cargo, mostly fertilizer. In one of the other compartments was a load of ammunition. A fire of unknown origin sent an orange cloud up through the deck. Curious about the smoke and attracted by the sirens of the fire trucks, a crowd gathered to see what was happening. At about 8:30 the ship exploded, sending a mushroom cloud 3,000 feet in the air. A second explosion soon followed, scattering debris. Later at an oil refinery over two miles away, a 2,850 pound anchor was dug up that had been buried sixteen feet underground by the blast.

The two explosions not only destroyed the ship but killed most of the onlookers and wiped out all the fire fighting equipment in the area. The force of the explosions flattened nearby empty oil tanks, ruptured full ones and set fires across the city. The Monsanto chemical plant was an inferno. As the flames spread, refineries in the area began to catch fire and explode. The explosions caused a small tidal wave which killed even more people. The blasts had been heard one hundred miles away.

The scene was that of a nightmare. An eyewitness recalled seeing the victims in the street: "Grotesque figures they were; black with fuel oil and smoke, and red with their own comrades' blood, walking with arms broken and dangling, or crawling with mangled legs and feet. One man was seen to pause just three blocks from medical aid to lean against a pole for rest, only to slump to the ground dead."

The Army had been on the scene within two hours of the first explosion. Army workers helped look for survivors and aided in the search for bodies. Some bodies were so badly burned that the only determination that could be made that they were human was when a melted ring or coin was found among the charred remains. Canteens were in service to help the victims and the rescue workers. J.C. Smith of Beaumont, Tex. was serving in one of the canteens the next day when another ship, the freighter *High Flyer,* exploded. A piece of debris pierced the canteen where Smith was serving, amputating his foot and destroying the canteen.

When the Texas City disaster was over, 500 were known dead. Over sixty bodies were never identified. It was the largest man-made disaster in the history of the United States.

People who had seen the destruction at Hiroshima and Nagasaki following the detonation of the atomic bomb said that, while not as widespread, the devastation was more complete. During the disaster, the Army served over 27,000 meals and distributed 60,000 pieces of clothing.

The Army had more heroes than those who served in disasters. Following their discharge from the armed services, young men were making their way to the Training College. Among these was Cadet William Schmieder. Serving as a member of the 373rd bombardment squadron in Okinawa, he was standing at the edge of a field when a bomber without lights and carrying five 2,500 pound bombs made a crash landing on the field. When the plane burst into flames, Schmieder jumped into a nearby ambulance, rushed to the crash site and lifted the captain out of the plane. As he headed back, the plane exploded. For this action he was awarded the Soldier Medal at a ceremony at the Training College by US Army Colonel G.M. Halloran.

The postwar period also provided the Army with two permanent developments. The Army, seeking to extend its influence in towns too small to sustain a corps, devised in 1947 the service unit. With a group of local citizens, Army work was carried on to benefit the poor and needy in smaller areas. Service Units have spread across the South and many of these have developed into corps.

Another development came from the Carolinas. Spearheaded by Captain Fred Boyette in Greenville, S.C., and joined by Captain James Henry in Kinston, N.C., local men's clubs began meeting to provide Christian fellowship. Encouraged by the divisional commander, Brigadier Gus Stephan, the idea began to spread. The officers in the Carolinas formulated a manual, and the movement expanded until it became international. The South remains the leader, having the largest Men's Club membership in the world.

The War Cry of September 20, 1947, brought word that

Commissioner and Mrs. Arnold would retire in January. Their retirement would mark the end of the longest appointment held by a territorial commander in the South. They also became the first to retire from that position in the South. During their administration, America and the world as a whole had changed dramatically. The full impact of those changes would be felt by the next territorial leaders.

CHAPTER 15

ADVANCES ON CHANGING TERRAIN (1948–1952)

WHEN BRITISH born Lt. Commissioner Albert E. Chesham came from Chicago to the South it was in a state of flux. Not everyone knew exactly what was happening or why, but there were unmistakable signs that the changes wrought by the war were permanent. The center of Southern economic activity was now decidedly in the cities where manufacturing was finally outstripping agriculture in importance. Even in agriculture, the mechanization of the farm and the diversification of crops insured that there would be no return to life as it was a generation ago.

Southerners were enjoying the fact that their wealth did not evaporate with the ratification of peace treaties as it had following World War I. The per capita income in the South continued to outstrip the rise in other areas of the country. It was still so woefully behind as to leave the South with almost half of the nation's poverty while it had but one fourth of the national population. Still, most Southerners could reach in their pockets and find something besides a hole.

An indication of the prosperity of the South was the rise in the Women's Auxiliaries. The largest and most notable was formed in Washington in February 1948 when, with Mrs. Lt. Colonel Wesley Bouterse, four women met to initiate the organization. The auxiliary soon distinguished itself by fund raising efforts which included a yearly fashion show and garden party. Hosted by different embassies each spring, the garden party has had as many as 4,000 in attendance, becoming one of the premiere charitable social events in Washington society.

Later, the Women's Auxiliary Manual was presented and accepted by the territorial administration during the time Mrs. Lt. Colonel Gordon (Eunice) Swyers was stationed with her husband in Washington. Mrs. Rowland F. Kirks and Mrs. Harold Hitz Burton, wife of a United States Supreme Court justice, assisted in this project.

Other differences left the Army wondering. The Army officers continued to march their bands out to the street corners to publish the news of salvation, but discovered they had to contend with more than increased traffic noises. People stood around to listen for shorter lengths of time. When it came time to march to the building for the evening service fewer people were following them back. On the other hand, indoor services were being better attended, a trend seen in other Protestant denominations as well in the early fifties.

The most far-reaching changes in the South affected blacks. In case after case, the Supreme Court struck down laws on voting rights, transportation, education and labor unions aimed at discriminating against blacks. President Truman ordered the integration of the armed forces, while baseball became the first major league sport to break through the color barrier when Jackie Robinson took up the bat for the Brooklyn Dodgers.

More blacks were leaving the farm for the city. By 1950, 48 percent of Southern blacks lived in urban areas. Even those who were attempting to hold back inevitable adjustments in the name of an Old South which had already begun to die could not change the face of things to come.

The Army saw the change among blacks to be the opening of a door of opportunity. Led by its editor, Adjutant Vincent Cunningham, *The War Cry* announced, "The Salvation Army Launches a Program for the Southern Negro." Published with the announcement were letters from five Southern governors, the mayor of Atlanta and Senator Strom Thurmond.

The campaign to reach blacks was kicked off on Saturday, April 3, 1948 in an open-air meeting on Auburn Avenue led by Lt. Commissioner Chesham. It was noted that "the event occurred on the same day that Atlanta, breaking the tradition of a century, sent uniformed Negro policemen into the area, supplanting the white officers who had previously patrolled the section."

A key to the Army's plans for reaching blacks was the use of a gifted black woman, Norma Roberts. The daughter of officers who had commanded the black corps in Washington, she felt that the Lord wanted her to labor in the South. Because of race restrictions in Atlanta, Roberts was trained for officership in the Eastern Territory. It was planned that she would operate a Home and Hospital in Tulsa to be built for blacks—the first such institution in the South. While receiving enthusiastic support in both the black and white community, this plan was scrapped when a campaign to raise the necessary funds failed. Commissioner Chesham asked the East to give Roberts an appointment for eighteen months until plans could be made to send her somewhere else in the South. Accordingly, she was stationed at the Home and Hospital in New York City.

Despite these delays, Roberts remained firm in her desire to return to the South. She was uncompromising in her belief that the Army was backing its principle with practice. She also knew that few religious organizations would allow a woman the opportunity of service afforded by the Army. She was fully aware that, like her father a generation before, she was breaking new ground.

As part of the campaign to reach Southern blacks, it was decided to send Lieutenant Roberts to Little Rock to take charge of an outpost recently opened by Lieutenant Margaret Moore. The building was so decrepit that women refused to enter it for Home League meetings. Despite this, it was valuable because it was located where needed in a poverty-stricken area of East Little Rock.

Encouraged by her commanding officers in Little Rock, Major and Mrs. Wilbur Young, she was assured that the Army had plans to build a new building when a proposed housing project was completed. The new building eventually was constructed, and Roberts served a thriving outpost in a city that would soon become known for an epic civil rights struggle.

Elsewhere similar work was opened in Memphis, Birmingham and Lawton, Okla. Other work included the Jackie Robinson Boys' Club opened in Johnson City, Tenn., as well as a boys' club for blacks in Concord, N.C. In Montgomery, Booker T. Washington Center was opened under the direction of Corps Sergeant-Major Jimmy Maiden. It soon boasted one of the largest Home Leagues in the South and Maiden was commissioned the Home League Secretary, the only male to ever occupy that position in the Army's history.

The hills of northern Georgia were the backdrop for another advance. Envoy Mary Peacock had been pressed into service during the war to command the corps in Athens, Ga. A turn came in her life when Mrs. Bess Truman forwarded a letter to the Army which had been written by a mountain woman in tiny Robertstown, Ga. Outlining the poverty in that section of the country, she asked that something be done for the children of the area for Christmas. Following a visit there, Peacock gave a party the very next day.

She had already reopened the corps in Gainesville, Ga., after obtaining a ninety-nine year lease on a building for $1. The work there was so successful that Judge Sam Harben reported, "Since the inauguration of the Salvation Army program here, there has been a steady decrease in cases of delinquency reported to the Juvenile Court. Cases in 1949 have averaged about half those of 1948, especially in that area covered by The Salvation Army."

Turning the corps over to other officers, she proceeded to Cleveland, Ga., located in what was then the poorest county in the state. She secured an old schoolhouse in Union Grove for one of her mission stations and then built another one at Sals Mountain. Here she was called one night to a log cabin where she found a baby not an hour old, wrapped in an old newspaper, with the drunken parents passed out on the bed.

Another time she went to the electric chair with a mountain boy who maintained that he killed in self-defense. She was there with the people when she needed to be, doing what needed to be done. As her work progressed, she opened two additional corps in Toccoa and Elberton, Ga.

Even the outbreak of the Korean War in June 1950 did not slow the Army's progress. The USO program was resurrected but was not nearly as widespread as during the previous war. The Men's Social Centers again saw their numbers to be served decline, but they were not as adversely affected. Elsewhere, in 1949 the Territorial Music Department was created, headed by Major and Mrs. Frank Longino. Meanwhile, in the Carolinas the growing boys' clubs had their first conference while in the same division the Men's Club had its first camp when 100 men gathered near New Bern, N.C.

Important trends were seen in finance in the territory. The Army had enthusiastically joined Community Chest organizations as they had formed across the South a score of years earlier. The Chest seemed to be the perfect answer to one of the corps officer's dilemmas. The traditional tambourine collections and Home Service Campaigns were time consuming and difficult. By affiliating with the Chest, the Army joined other organizations in a united fund raising campaign to achieve needed money.

As these campaigns gained success, the individual Community Chest organizations had a tendency to exert more control over the programs conducted by participating agencies. Later, when most of these Community Chest organizations converted to the United Way, the member agencies would be subject to close review of their programs, budgeting and fiscal practices. These actions were interpreted, often correctly, as efforts to "control" the Army, and were met with stiff resistance as Army officers insisted upon the autonomy of the organization and its freedom of program service based upon its close contact with those in need.

To further complicate this, some of the Community Chest organizations were having difficulty meeting their fund raising goals. When this happened, they logically sought to set priories on services in order to fund what they felt was most important. The first real problem along this line was noted in Washington where the Army's fund raising continued to escalate and the Chest's contribution to the Army declined. The relationship between affiliated fund raising organizations and individual Army corps would continue to be a tug of war over many years.

An alternative to the tambourine, kettle and Chest allocations was the innovation of fund raising through a direct mail appeal to donors. In Washington, Lt. Colonel Wesley Bouterse explored the use of three mailings during the Christmas season to areas of the city where it was most likely to expect donations. The cost was relatively inexpensive, and, to the Army's joy, it was discovered that if someone took the time to send in a donation it was usually for a larger amount than could be collected in person by kettle or tambourine. The mail appeal would become essential to the Army's financial success in the emerging Information Age.

During Chesham's administration, the emphasis on Salvation Army camping programs was stressed. The Army had conducted camping programs in one form or another since the turn of the century. Now efforts were made to upgrade the camps themselves and to provide a more structured program for youth. Many of the camps had been little more than fields with few permanent buildings as campers roughed it in tents.

The desire to hold music camps and other specialized programs guaranteed this would have to change. The model camp up to this point had been Bena Lea, just outside of New Orleans. Few divisions even owned their own camp—many rented them from other organizations. But division after division, along with a few individual corps, initiated major efforts to develop their own camp facilities.

In Washington, the territory opened its first Harbor Light Corps at a dedication attended by Mrs. Harry (Bess) Truman and Supreme Court Justice William O. Douglas, and hailed by FBI directer J. Edgar Hoover. Aimed at alcoholics, the Harbor Light featured an "alcohol free tavern", beds for 48, and a chapel which seated 168. Men were allowed to stay as long as they didn't drink, but were required to attend nightly chapel services. Although the District technically had laws against public drunkenness, the Harbor Light met a great need and was an immediate success.

South of the border, the Army was in a boom time as corps after corps opened in the Republic of Mexico. Chesham held a conference of the South's divisional commanders in

Mexico City so they could see first hand the scope of the Army's program. Deeply impressed, the divisional commanders immediately pledged money to further the work there. Momentum was provided through the training college, which was turning out national officers whose zeal fired the Army's march.

The Gospel Crusade continued, with the Army responsible for the distribution of over four million Scripture portions. At one point the divisional commander, Lt. Colonel Gearing, persuaded a pilot to allow him to drop Gospel portions on remote villages inaccessible by conventional means. The success of the campaign was marred by the death of two Salvationists killed when their motor launch capsized at Vera Cruz.

In 1949 a devastating flood in Guatemala killed 4,000. The government accepted the Army's offer of help and Gearing quickly dispatched officers to the flood areas. Aided by Captain Sven Ruthstrom of the Men's Social Service in Houston, several tons of clothing were sent by airplane through New Orleans.

The service of the Army during this national disaster opened the door for the Army to return two years later to open the work there. A Mexican officer, Lieutenant Ildefonso Granados, was selected to spearhead this new opening. When Commissioner Chesham visited there in early 1952 he found a thriving corps and men's shelter assisted by a prospering advisory board. This promising opening was snuffed out when a change in the government forced the Army to leave the country.

In communities across the South, Salvationists were the heroes of the day. In Washington, a store detective chased a shoplifter into an open-air meeting where the band was playing "Silent Night." The suspect ran among the bandsmen trying to escape. In the scuffle that followed, the detective was knocked to the ground. "I came to the feet of a trumpet player," the detective reported, "That band hadn't missed a note." The suspect ran away in the confusion but was caught.

In Macon, Ga., an Army truck driver saw a combination coin laundry and dry cleaner on fire. A boiler had exploded, ripping the doors off, injuring the manager and setting the building on fire. Rushing in, the driver, Jim Miller, grabbed a pan and used it to throw water on the fire until someone brought him a garden hose which he used to bring the fire under control.

In Dallas, Lieutenant Sue Baker of the Dallas Compton Citadel saw a burning car by the road. She pulled the driver out, giving the man first aid, rushing him to the hospital. She was treated herself for burns. The Lions Club hailed her as "a woman of real valor."

In Gainesville, Ga., Lieutenant Howard Beane rescued a lady from drowning, reviving her through aritificial respiration. In Washington, an oil truck and a tractor trailer collided in a fiery wreck downtown. Brigadier Verner Vansyckle and Lieutenant Philip Collier were able to rescue one man from the flames.

A more sedate news item came from Miami where Sr. Captain Glenn Stovall reported that WTVJ Television Station broadcast the Sunday morning service, the first such broadcast in the Southern Territory. New ground was broken when Captain Leslie Hall successfully convinced the Army to produce its own radio program. "*Wonderful Words of Life*" began, a program now heard around the world.

In Dallas, an appreciative fire department decided to repay the Army for its services rendered to the department during major fires. Lt. Colonel John Morrison was called to the fire station for a cup of coffee. He found a giant cup containing a gift of $495.

The South was visited by General Albert Orsborn in 1952

to observe the twenty-fifth anniversary of the territory. He was again honored by a dinner in Washington, but the main event was a congress in Atlanta. Here he met with delegates from across the South which now represented citizens from not only the fifteen Southern states and the District of Columbia, but Mexico and Guatemala as well. During this visit he enrolled 99 new soldiers.

It was one of the last Southern functions overseen by Commissioner Chesham. Announcing his retirement for September, he commented, "You are on the driver's seat one day and off the tailgate the next."

Before leaving office, he authorized Lt. Colonel Wesley Bouterse to conduct the first Territorial Bible Conference. Bouterse had long believed officers and soldiers would be benefited by a week long series of meetings centered on the Bible in a recreational setting. Having lobbied for this for some time, his dream came true when the Bible Conference met for the first time in Clearwater, Fla., at Trinity College.

The speakers included Dr. F.J. Huegel, an internationally known author who also had been instrumental in the Army's founding in Mexico where he served as an advisory board member. Other speakers were Training College principal, Sr. Major Wesley Rich, and Bouterse himself. The Bible Conference changed locations several times but continues as a much-valued Southern tradition to the present.

Replacing Chesham was Lt. Commissioner William Dray. Even as he moved into his office difficulties were brewing in the far reaches of the territory.

Through the Years

Coffee is served by Adjutant Herman Lambrecht at the site of a train wreck in Texas, 1947.

The Texas Division participates in march of witness down Peachtree Street, Atlanta, during the 1951 Territorial Music Congress; Lt. Colonel John Morrison, divisional commander.

Candidates' farewell with Captain and Mrs. C. William Jaynes, Jacksonville, 1949.

Lt. Commissioner Albert E. Chesham, territorial commander, and Brigadier Richard Fitton, training principal, lead an open-air meeting on Auburn Avenue in Atlanta.

Mrs. Major Amos Varney with a typical troop of Girl Guards in the late 50s.

Happy children with Captain Houston Ellis at Christmas party, Parkersburg, early 50s.

Members of the first Men's Club in the South, Greenville, enjoy a game of checkers.

Bandmaster Alfred Ward (center) with Commissioner and Mrs. William Davidson, Commissioner and Mrs. Norman Marshall (Sr.), and members of his family: Mrs. Lt. Colonel Harry Ward, Lt. Colonel William Powell, Mrs. Brigadier Art Ward, Brigadier Ward, Lt. Colonel Harry Ward, Lt. Colonel Gordon Swyers, Mrs. Brigadier James P. Henry, Brigadier Henry, Mrs. Colonel Swyers, and Mrs. Colonel Powell.

Leadership at Candidates' Seminar in Dallas, 1965: seated, Mrs. Brigadier Gordon Swyers, Mrs. Lt. Colonel Harry Ward, Mrs. Captain Orville Salmon, and Major Virginia Kellner; standing, Brigadier Gordon Swyers, Lt. Colonel Harry Ward, and Captain Orville Salmon.

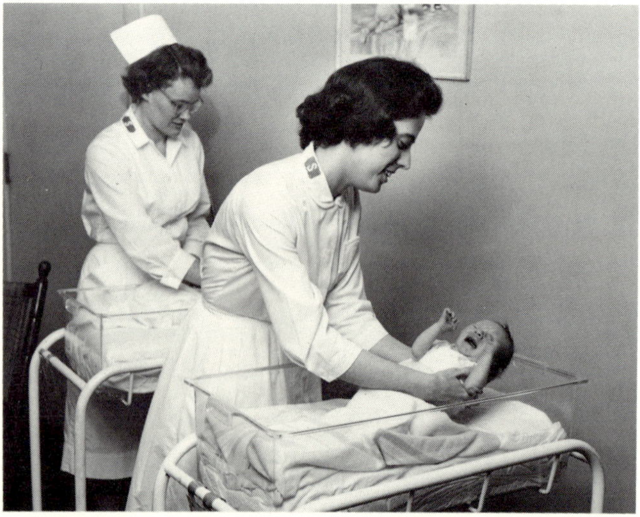

Mrs. Captain William Matthews and Lieutenant Billie Jean Vance, Birmingham. Home and Hospital, early 1960s, typify the dedicated service of Women's Social Service officers over the years in the territory.

Girl Guard Rally in the Carolinas in 1967: Captain Jack Waters; Lt. Colonel Gordon Swyers; Major Willard Evans; Captain Pat Wiley; Captain Jean Walser, DGD; Captain Sarah McClure, TGD; Mrs. Major Evans; Mrs. Colonel Swyers; and Mrs. Captain Waters. (Majo and Mrs. Evans, Southern trained officer and territorial youth secretary, later became territorial leaders in the U.S.A. West.)

Elizabeth (Buffie) Morrison says thank you for her Christmas doll with a big kiss for Mrs. Brigadier Gordon Swyers.

Lt. Colonel Paul Thronburg with Major George Woods as they greet Mrs. Winona Stimler, who taught Major Woods in Sunday School at Cumberland fifty years ago.

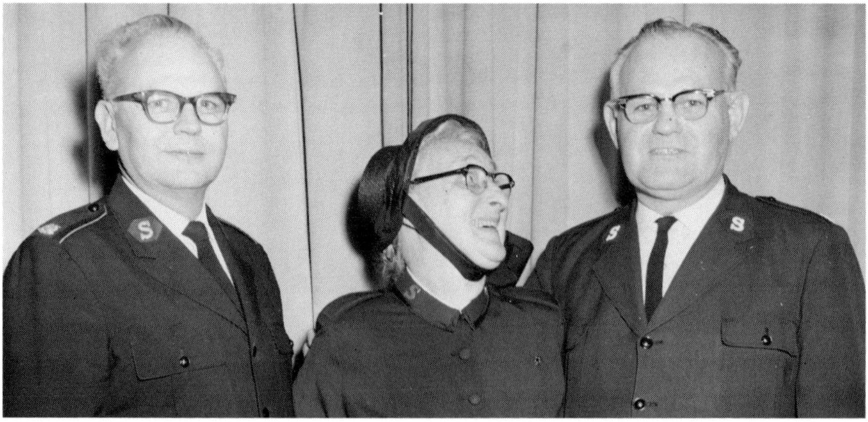

Youth band of Atlanta Temple Corps when S/Major Alfred Winkler was bandmaster and S/Captain Burl Wyatt, the corps officer.

Commissioner Ernest W. Holz presents a memento plaque to Major John Jordan, Property Secretary, who assumed responsibility for many of the details in connection with negotiations, renovations, and relocation to the Northeast Expressway Headquarters, 1976.

Brigadier Hubert Rawlin and Major Jack Waters prepare for the production of *Wonderful Words of Life* radio program with professionals at studio in Atlanta.

Mrs. Captain Allen Wiltshire and Captain Grace Cumberbatch lead singing company at Washington Ninth Street Corps.

Major Margaret Moore and General Eva Burrows relive moments of service in Zimbabwe (Rhodesia).

Some of the thousands of armed forces personnel who benefited from the dedicated service of Salvation Army workers in both USO and Red Shield Clubs across the South and around the world.

Captain Josué Saldivar takes Gospel portion to bracero in cotton field in Arkansas.

Operation Cotton Pickin' staff, who took the Gospel and other practical assistance to Mexican *braceros* working in the fields of Arkansas: Captain Raquel Gan, Brigadier Verna Davis, Lt. Colonel and Mrs. Harry Ward, with other members of the staff: Lieutenant Noel McBride and Captains Elias Yépez, E.H. Whaley, Isidoro Cerezo, Josué Saldivar.

Brigadier and Mrs. Ray Gearing, Southern officers, Mexico divisional commander; later, territorial commander, South America East.

The original Salvation Patrol at the beginning of work in Mexico.

Brigadier and Mrs. Reginald Clevett, who served in Texas and later as divisional leaders in Mexico.

Lt. Colonel Alfred Osborne oversees the operation of the concrete block machine used in the reconstruction of Tecpan.

Colonel Jacques Egger, territorial commander for Mexico and Central America, cuts ribbon to open Tecpan Corps Chapel. L. to r.: Major Jack Waters; Major Bernard Smith; Colonel Eggers; Commissioner Ernest Holz; Major Stanley Melton, divisional commander for Guatemala; Captain Daniel Guerra, commanding officer for Tecpan.

General Kjell Laguerud, president of Guatemala, with Commissioner Ernest Holz, cutting the ribbon at the dedication of construction of 527 houses, municipal building, and city market, following earthquake in Tecpan.

Major Harold Hinson, director of emergency reconstruction in Guatemala, looks on as Commissioner Ernest Holz, presents a plaque of appreciation to C.S.M. Hubert Phillips, who worked three months as volunteer construction consultant in Tecpan. Later Hubert Phillips was made a member of the order of Exceptional Service.

CHAPTER 16

MANEUVERING THROUGH MAYHEM

(1952–1957)

COMMISSIONER WILLIAM DRAY, born in Kent, England and raised in Canada, had spent most of his career in administrative positions. He had worked for 27 years in Canada with The Salvation Army Emigration Bureau, a service aimed at helping Europeans immigrate to Canada. In that position he had handled the cases of 200,000 people. His wife, Florence, had also been born in England and, like her husband, had moved to Canada as a child. Reflecting their heritage, they were somewhat reserved, especially when compared to Southerners noted for their open hospitality. If the Drays thought they would be able to slowly warm to their new land, they were shocked into reality soon after arriving.

Before 1946 when Mexico became a division, Alejandro Guzmán had led the Army in Mexico. Lt. Colonel and Mrs. Gearing came in that year to establish the new division. Though a fiery evangelist, Guzmán frustrated his leaders by his difficulty in complying with Army regulations and procedures. Dismissal was not the answer. As the guiding force in the Salvation Patrol and affiliation with the Army, dismissing him was not considered. It was decided to move him to supervise the northern section of Mexico as district officer. He eventually resigned from the Army, opening a farm for alcoholic men.

Mexican law forbade the Army to incorporate as a church. There was also a question of the legality of Army leadership being non-Mexican. Consultations with one of the attorneys on the advisory board resulted in the Army being incorporated as a mercantile corporation under the Companies Act, making it The Salvation Army Company. Later, other acts of incorporation would continue to solidify the Army's position.

Dray found encouragement with the territory's commitment to evangelism. In High Point, N.C., Captain Olvy Sheppard learned there were 140,000 children in rural areas of the state, 80% of them unchurched. With the young people of the corps, a postal Sunday school was devised. For fifty cents young people would receive eight weeks of lessons to be returned for a certificate.

Along similar lines, the Outer Circle Home League was initiated from territorial headquarters. Home League members in areas too distant from a corps were reached with a newsletter mailed to them. Aimed primarily at reaching women in rural settings, the Outer Circle reached as far as Greece when a Salvationist joined whose husband was stationed on a military base there.

In 1953, Captain Inez Newberry farewelled from Baltimore for an appointment in Ceylon, later renamed Sri Lanka. Serving most of her career in India, she rendered exemplary service on the mission field which was eventually recognized with her appointment as a territorial commander in her adopted country and promotion to the rank of commissioner—the first American woman to attain either position. In the same year, the South sent Sr. Captain Harlan Cleveland as the first corps officer delegate to the prestigious International College for Officers.

In the very first session of the International Staff College for Officers, later to become the International College for Officers, in January, 1947, from the South were Majors Carl Cone, W. Kenneth Howarth, and George Ribble.

Apprehension was in the air as 1954 unfolded. Senator Eugene McCarthy spread fear and suspicion with his spectacular hearings professing to expose Communists in government, show business and even in the clergy. In the ranks of the Army change was in the air as General Albert Orsborn announced his retirement and the convening of the High Council. It was while the High Council was in session to elect Wilfred Kitching as the next General that the United States Supreme Court rendered a monumental decision.

In *Brown v. Board of Education* the Court ruled that segregation was illegal, setting aside the previous 1896 ruling that established the "separate but equal" doctrine. Blacks were ecstatic after a long struggle seeking access to their constitutional rights. The undying hopes of a people could be seen in not only legal action but in art forms, as in this poem written by Langston Hughes:

> I, too, sing America.
>
> I am the darker brother.
> They send me to eat in the kitchen
> When company comes.
> But I laugh,
> And eat well,
> And grow strong.
>
> Tomorrow,
> I'll be at the table
> When company comes.

On the other end of the spectrum, the vast majority of Southern whites were concerned. South Carolina and Georgia vowed to close their public schools rather than to integrate. Twelve Southern political leaders gathered in Richmond, affirming their commitment to defy the order. In Georgia, two gubernatorial candidates called for the ouster of the Supreme Court to preserve segregation. White students marched in Baltimore and Washington to protest the ruling. In Jackson, Miss., voters disapproved integration by a margin of two to one.

The Army was quick to make its position clear. In November the United States Commissioner's Conference issued the following position statement:

> The Supreme Court's historic decision outlawing segregation in the nation's public facilities is heartily endorsed by The Salvation Army.
>
> A ruling so soundly based on Chistian principles cannot but receive understanding and cooperation from all Salvationists dedicated to the ideal that in Christ all men are one.
>
> We accept full Christian responsibility to work earnestly and sympathetically to the end that a practical implementation of the decision may be successfully effected.

Integration in the Army immediately began. In Washington, the Army was the first social service agency to integrate. Though the leadership of the Army was quick to embrace the decision, many individual Salvationists were as ambivalent as most other Southerners. These Salvationists probably did not question the need for the lot of blacks to be improved nor in the undeniable justice of integration, but they were as afraid as anyone else of their familiar lifestyle being changed.

Complicating the Army's position was the fact that the donor base of the Army was decidedly white. If the Army offended its white contributors, it would result in harm coming to all who benefited from Army programs, white and black. Like the rest of the churches in the South, it was a painful time. Everyone secretly hoped the blacks would be less confrontational and that the whites would be more restrained in their reactions.

When the Christian community attempted to speak out in favor of moderation, it was seen as betraying either the equality of all men on one hand or the sanctity of Southern life on the other. The Army would continue to accentuate the positive in race relations, attempting first to reach its own people with its ideals. Work started a few years earlier among blacks continued. In Little Rock, Perry A. Taylor became the first black advisory board member in the country.

The Army found itself in a difficult position, having long sympathized with the plight of blacks. As the epic civil rights struggle unfolded, the Army's unyielding refusal to involve itself in political issues left it unable to participate in the great demonstrations around the country.

Although frustrated on this issue, the Army knew some things were clearly right beyond any dispute. To these it now turned its energies.

Commissioner Dray continued to oversee advances with the work in Mexico. The editor of *The War Cry*, Brigadier Lillian Hansen, initiated publication of a Spanish language *War Cry*, *El Grito de Guerra*. Taking a night course in Spanish, she first had to pay a college professor $5 a month to edit the magazine. In other developments, Lt. Colonel and Mrs. Gearing were farewelled to take command of the South America West Territory. With this the Gearings became the first Southerners to be appointed as territorial leaders. The divisional secretary, Brigadier Reginald S. Clevett, became the new divisional commander.

It was also at this time that the Army began a major work in Mexico with the estalishment of children's homes. Beginning in Mexico City, children's homes sprang up across the division, in which Southern officer, Major Billie Jean DeArman, gave many years of valiant service. Many of these homes began when parents brought their children and simply left them with the Army officer, never to see them again. In one city, the officer had twenty children he had thus taken in living in his quarters. The Army was happy to receive help in this area from the Christian Children's Fund which eventually underwrote a large amount of the expense associated with the operations of the homes.

In a different outreach the Army in Mexico would serve in its first disaster there when the Los Remedios River broke through dikes, driving 60,000 from their homes. Salvationists took food by rowboat to people stranded on rooftops. The Men's Social Service began in the republic when officers from the United States met in Mexico City to help initiate that program. Meanwhile in Vera Cruz, a Home League was organized in the state prison.

General Kitching, came South in the fall of 1954. Besides holding a congress, he presented the venerable Brigadier Julius Mack Satterfield the Army's highest award, the Order of the Founder. Satterfield was called the "dean of corps officers." He especially left his mark in Winston-Salem, N.C., where he served for over twenty years. He was influential in the establishment of boys' clubs in the Carolinas, starting the one in Winston-Salem in a basement, with a budget of $8 a week.

Soon after this another Southern pioneer entered retirement. Major Cecil Brown, district officer of the Mountain Mission, was diagnosed with terminal cancer. The work of the Mountain Mission had changed considerably from the early days when she reached her people by foot or horseback. Her horse had been replaced in more recent days by a jeep.

The mountains changed as well. Following the war there was an exodus from the hills, as the young men took their families to seek opportunities elsewhere. Some of the communities where Brown had done her work ceased to exist altogether. Her ministry changed as the hills were made less remote by the advent of electricity, the telephone and other modern conveniences. New roads unlocked communities that had previously been almost inaccessible. Though still greatly loved, she wasn't needed as greatly anymore.

Added to this she began to feel the limitations of her age and then her illness. In her better days she could be difficult at times, but these changes brought her impetuous nature to the front. And to a woman who had learned to use the force of her will, the inescapable nature of her illness left her frustrated. She resigned herself to the inevitability of her retirement in 1956. In the quiet of the hills she loved, she died a little over a year later.

Another reminder of the past was seen in Dallas when the Veterans of Foreign Wars gathered in conference. Among the delegates was L.J. Smith of St. Petersburg, Fla., whose claim to fame was the possession of the only Salvation Army doughnut to survive World War I. Given the doughnut on the way to the front, it fell behind the seat of the truck he was driving. It survived there as Smith drove his truck through several battles. He found it again when he was cleaning the truck out months later and decided to keep it as a good luck piece. Displayed under glass at The Salvation Army booth, he said, "It's like The Salvation Army—something sturdy and not to be forgotten."

Advances in the South were discernible with the acquisition of a new territorial headquarters building in 1955. The revered Ellis Street building, showing signs of age, failed to provide the necessary room for the Army's growth. To replace it, Dray purchased the former Druid Hills Methodist Church. Also housed in the new facility was the Atlanta Temple Corps.

Further south, the first Senior Citizen's Club in the territory was opened in Jacksonville, Fla., as a joint project between the Army and the Pilot Club. Contrasting this was the activity of children in Salisbury, N.C., who went "trick or treating" on Halloween for The Salvation Army. One thousand children participated in the effort which collected food and clothing items.

In an unduplicated precedent, the Soul-Winners Session of officers commissioned in 1955 returned the next year without losing a single officer. This distinction was followed by another when Major Faye Gaugh opened the United States Senate in prayer, the first Salvationist to do so since William Booth prayed there in 1903.

Later, Commissioner Ernest Holz would open the Senate in prayer twice; also the House of Representatives. General Jarl Wahlström, as well as Commissioner Arthur Pitcher, was accorded this opportunity for spiritual ministry.

Texas and Louisiana were devastated when Hurricane Audrey smashed into the coastal areas, bringing with it a killer tidal wave. The damage was centered near Lake Charles, La., where a search was made in the bayous for some of the bodies of the 531 victims. The Army was quick to respond. In some areas the first vehicle to travel the cleared roads was the Army canteen, as it rushed drinking water and food to families stranded by the tidal wave. The first building erected in the town of Cameron was to house the Army relief efforts. Everyone associated with the rescue and relief work had to have typhoid shots as the stench of death hung over the devastated area.

The year of 1957 would be a year of change. America was shocked to learn the Russians had entered space by orbiting the satellite *Sputnik*. Spurred on by this challenge, America entered the space program in earnest. Key to this was the work done at Houston, the Red Stone Arsenal in Huntsville, Ala., and the test center at Cape Canaveral, Fla. The Army responded to the space age by pioneering its own work in the opening of corps in Huntsville and in Cocoa, Fla.

Commissioner William Dray ended his tenure in the

South when he was promoted to the Army's second highest position, the Chief of the Staff, in September 1957. Though his administration ended quieter than it began, it would not be a quiet time for his successor. He would find the challenge of streets in turmoil and the threat of nuclear war off the tip of Florida.

CHAPTER 17

A PAINFUL PASSAGE
(1957–1965)

IN THE next few years America would prove to be a collage of contradictions. While Americans were entering outer space, blacks were trying to enter restaurants. While Americans were being unloaded in Vietnam, boat loads of Cuban refugees were docking in Miami. While America was being charmed by the grace of the Kennedy White House, the president was in a deadly showdown with Khrushchev. In a time of unparalleled prosperity, the thump of rock and roll music voiced the rebellion of youth who were raised under the shadow of a mushroom cloud. How would an Army outfitted in Victorian uniform respond to this age?

As the Army rose to meet these challenges it was led by Lt. Commissioner and Mrs. William Davidson. Serving their early officership in their native Ireland where he commanded that country's largest corps, the Davidsons had come to the United States via Canada. Davidson had an advantage over any previous territorial commander, having served as Southern Chief Secretary for the last six months Dray was in command. The Davidsons took a tremendous interest in the family life of officers, quickly learning the names of all the officers' and many of the soldiers' children.

He was able to view with satisfaction the territory's commitment to evangelism. Within a year of taking command, the territory hit a record attendance in Sunday school. The recently begun radio program, produced by the Southern Territory, "*Wonderful Words of Life*", was already being broadcast on over 300 stations. The quality of the program was affirmed when the World Missionary Fellowship chose to add it to their programming from their "*Voice of the Andes*" station, whose transmission could be heard throughout the world. In addition, the Canadian-produced television program, "*The Living Word*", was carried by 75 stations.

There were individual stories that also heartened Commissioner Davidson. In Richmond, Lieutenant Omer McKinney was desperate following the loss of his pianist, the only musician in the corps. Having committed this problem to prayer, he was approached by a young man following the Sunday night meeting. The man had been a backslider but when confronted with the claims of the Gospel was not ready to yield. McKinney mentioned the need for music, inviting the young man to play in the meeting some day. He told McKinney that he had two friends, one a bootlegger and one a drunk, who played in a downtown bar. McKinney, over the expressed reservations of his wife, invited them to play in the meetings. All three were converted and the Sunday night meeting attendances picked up with the addition of the lively music.

The first visit to Mexico by the international head of The Salvation Army came with General Kitching's visit in 1959. He was greeted by another general upon his arrival, General Ruben Peralta, head of the Mexican army and chairman of the Mexico City Advisory Board.

An unusual honor came when General Kitching was received in the home by His Excellency, Adolfo Lopez Mateos, president of the republic. In their meeting, the General asked the President, "Is there anything we can do for you, sir?" The President quickly replied, "As a matter of fact, there is." He went on to explain his concern for Mexican migrant workers in the United States, known as *braceros*.

At the same time this conversation was taking place, Brigadier Harry Ward, divisional commander for the Louisiana-Arkansas Division, was driving across Arkansas with Major Verna Davis, his divisional finance secretary. Noticing the hundreds of Mexican migrants working in the fields, they began discussing ways they might reach them with the Gospel and help them with their many other needs. When they got back to New Orleans, Ward contacted territorial headquarters with his thoughts. By this time, Commissioner Davidson had been told of President Mateos' request. With that *"Operation Cotton Pickin'* " was born.

Plans were made to begin the work near Jonesboro, Ark. The Mexican division loaned two of its officers, Captain Jorge Gan and Captain Miguel Saldívar. Armed with Gospel portions, Davis and Ward joined the Mexican officers to form the first team.

Their first experience was less than successful. They had obtained permission from a farmer to go out to the fields to talk with the migrants. The workers panicked, thinking the four were police coming to arrest them and send them back to Mexico. This problem was solved by exchanging the customary blue uniforms for gray ones. In addition to going to the fields, the team went to the bunkhouses at night where they could spend more time talking. When they took slide projectors, they were gratified to find the workers attentive—most had never seen slides before.

The team went wherever they could find Mexican workers. One night they went to wrestling matches where they gave their testimonies between the bouts. Often they would go at night to have open-air meetings in sections of nearby towns where Mexicans gathered. The open-airs were especially thrilling for Mexican officers who were denied that privilege in their native land. In one city regular meetings were held in a movie theater.

They were also able to help in other ways. Often the migrants worked for farmers who could not speak Spanish, and few *braceros* could speak English. The team worked as translators in these circumstances. At other times, they were able to follow through with contacting relatives in Mexico, attending to medical needs, or supplying food to the braceros whose diet was meager at best.

"Operation Cotton Pickin' " continued for five years. In that time the number of Mexican officers increased to five each year, the number of migrants contacted reached over 30,000, while the number of conversions exceeded 4,000. The effort was finally discontinued after 1964 because the number of migrant workers dropped due to increased mechanization on the farm which made the handpicking of cotton, fruits and vegetables largely impractical.

Another outreach came through *"Operation West Virginia."* The *New York Post* had run a series of articles about the hardships faced by the unemployed in the mining areas of the state. With the use of donated trucks and assistance of the Men's Social Centers in the Eastern Territory, 20,000 pounds of clothing were brought to Welch for distribution. Efforts to alleviate the suffering in the coal mining areas continued beyond this effort as the divisional commander, Lt. Colonel Wesley Bouterse, supervised the collection and distribution of 21 tons of canned goods along with other gifts.

Not all the news from West Virginia related to poverty. In Fairmont, the South obtained an eventide home, the former Marion County Home, complete with its own coal mine, chicken farm and stocked fishing pond.

The most unusual project was in Bluefield where Captain Harold Hinson found himself the beneficiary of an anonymous gift of 3,000 new shoes, none of them having mates. Reported through the Associated Press, Hinson set up a free mail order service to amputees. If he was not able to fill an order, he referred them to one of his correspondents who needed the same size, but on the opposite leg.

At Arlington National Cemetery, the Army had been represented by the Chief Secretary, Colonel George Marshall, at a solemn ceremony at the Tomb of the Unknowns. At that time the remains of the Unknown Soldiers from World War II and the Korean War were laid to rest.

In visiting the shrine later, Brigadier Gordon Swyers noticed that conspicuously absent among the tributes to those who had died in the service of their country was one from the Army. Finally, in 1961, a plaque was presented in an impressive ceremony attended by 1,500 people that included participation by The Salvation Army National Capital Area Band and "The Old Guard—The President's Own."

On May 5, 1961, Alan Shepard Jr. became the first American in space with a flight which lasted a little over fifteen minutes. At about the same time, Lt. Colonel James Longino became the first Southern-born officer to be a Chief Secretary in the United States, an appointment which lasted a record eleven years. It took the South but thirty-five years for Longino's achievement.

Florida had been in a building boom since the opening of the space center at Cape Canaveral. The attraction to Florida was heightened by the advent of practical air conditioning for homes and automobiles, low taxes and real estate prices. This made the state more appealing, especially to retirees. But they were not the only ones who found Florida desirable. After the Cuban revolution that brought Castro to power, a steady stream of refugees began to flow from that island nation. By mid-1961 there were already 50,000 refugees, most of these settling in Miami. The situation there was compounded by the growing tensions between the United States and Cuba. On April 25, 1961, Cuban exiles made an attempt to invade Cuba with an amphibious landing at the Bay of Pigs. The attempt, flawed from the beginning, was quickly crushed by Castro's forces.

Strained relations worsened the next year when United States surveillance planes spotted missile bases under construction in Cuba. The bases, provided by the Soviet Union, would have allowed targets as far away as New York City to be struck by nuclear missiles. A confrontation between President Kennedy and Premier Nikita Khrushchev nearly plunged the world into World War III. Finally, the Soviet Union agreed to dismantle the bases if the United States would not invade Cuba.

Known as the Cuban Missile Crisis, this showdown affected and severed Cuban-American relations. More refugees fled the Communist government, most of these joining their fellow expatriates in south Florida. The Army began its outreach to the Cuban community when Captain James Osborne started holding in Miami simultaneous open-air meetings in English and in Spanish.

Soon after the missile crisis, Castro began broadcasting a program called *"Radio Free Dixie"*, aimed at blacks involved with the civil rights struggle and patterned after the Voice of America broadcasts. Contrasting this was a demonstration of both freedom of religion and freedom of speech, courtesy of The Salvation Army. Brigadier Ernest Holz in Washington reported that portions of an open-air meeting were recorded by Voice of America for use during the Easter season. The transmission went behind the Iron Curtain and to Asia.

The year of 1963 would be pivotal in American history. Unknown to the general public, the United States was escalating its involvement in Vietnam not only with additional troops, but also with orders that they could become directly involved in battles instead of acting only as advisors. Governor George Wallace would defy the federal government as he stood at the doors of the University of Alabama, vowing never to allow a black to enter there.

Two months later, Martin Luther King, Jr., would stand in Washington before a crowd of 200,000 and with unmatched eloquence intone one of the great speeches in American history, "I have a dream . . ." As if in answer to that, a bomb exploded during a Sunday school in Birmingham, killing four black girls. Then the final tragedy on November 22, 1963. The dream of Camelot came to an end when Lee Harvey Oswald aimed his rifle from the Dallas Book Depository and took the life of President John F. Kennedy.

America had been reeling from the events of the year, but the assassination of its young president shook the nation to the core. The new territorial commander, Commissioner Paul Carlson, called for memorial meetings in Atlanta. But in Washington, the Army had little time to mourn as it was called into the service of a grief-stricken nation. The body of President Kennedy lay in state at the Capitol Building. The order had been given to close the Capitol on Sunday night, November 24. But there were hundreds of thousands of mourners who wanted to bid farewell to their slain leader.

The DC Police Chief called Brigadier Ernest Holz with a request. Some of his men had been on duty for 24 hours without food. Could the Army do something to bring some hot food to his cold and hungry men? Responding immediately, Brigadier Wilbur Young came from the Men's Social Service Center with some men to serve coffee and donuts. Holz called Lt. Colonel C. T. McKenzie, the divisional commander in Philadelphia, requesting him to send three canteens, which were dispatched immediately.

Throughout the night, thirty officers served 4,500 police officers, guards and other personnel, staying until the president's body was moved. An additional service was provided to mourners, many of whom were overcome by the combination of their grief and the eight hour wait in line. Salvation Army personnel were stationed at the exit to console them as they departed. For its service the Army received a personal note of thanks from the president's brother, Attorney General Robert Kennedy, and a commendation was made a part of the Congressional Record.

The welcome of Commissioner and Mrs. Paul J. Carlson to the territory was understandably subdued, given the events soon after taking command. As territorial leaders in the South, the Carlsons would have the shortest appointment, lasting scarcely more than two years. Only the second American born officer to lead the territory, Carlson had been on headquarters his entire career. His wife, the former Ethel Glasco, had been involved in the Women's Social Service prior to their marriage in 1928. Though their tenure was short, it did not lack for excitement.

Following service in a major flood in Kentucky, the Army was heartened by the gift from their longtime friend, Colonel Harland Sanders of Kentucky Fried Chicken fame, beginning with a donation which entirely covered the cost of a new corps building in Louisville, appropriately designated Sanders Citadel. Traveling with either Lt. Colonel Ernest Pickering or Major Walter Swyers, Sanders visited advisory boards across Kentucky. As either Pickering or Swyers were talking to the boards about property needs, they would look over to catch Colonel Sanders' eye. If he nodded, they said, "Now, to start this campaign, Colonel Sanders has agreed to donate $25,000." Standing to confirm the gift, Sanders would say, "I made a lot of money. Here's the man that's spending it." In this way, Sanders made major gifts to ten corps buildings or officer's quarters.

Also in Kentucky was a massive response to a CBS television broadcast showing conditions in the mountains of eastern Kentucky. The network called the Army to handle the gifts it found overwhelming them. Food, clothing and toys were airlifted into the depressed areas where the Army took charge of distribution.

Carlson was challenged at once by the civil rights struggle. The year was full of tragedy, beginning with the deaths of three civil rights workers near Philadelphia, Miss. The Army had only recently come out with a stronger position statement on civil rights and non-discrimination. Especially, in light of this, was considerable embarrassment that Christmas. Civil rights activist Dick Gregory headed a campaign called *"Turkeys for Mississippi."* When he attempted to donate the food to the Army in Mississippi, the local advisory boards refused the gift. This action was quickly reversed by Carlson's announcement that the gift would be accepted and properly distributed, saying, "The Salvation Army anywhere in my command will accept gifts from anyone to alleviate suffering. We will meet the point of need without regard to race or creed."

Nor was this to be the last consequence of the civil rights movement. In February 1965, Martin Luther King, Jr., came to Selma, Ala., to dramatize the problems blacks were having when they attempted to register to vote. His arrival received massive media attention, especially when violence broke out between the police and blacks. Browns Chapel, the rallying point for the effort, was within one block of the Army building. While the demonstrations were going on this section of the city was blocked off, the Salvation Army soldiers having to cross through police barricades to reach the corps building. In addition, open-air meetings were prohibited for fear they might occasion further violence.

The Army had stated little about discrimination and civil rights in recent years, feeling that its traditional stand had proven itself through its actions over the years. But throughout 1965, the Army further clarified its position. *The War Cry* stated, "The Salvation Army is committed to furthering the cause of human dignity and equal justice for mankind . . . The Salvation Army opposes dicriminatory practices related to race or national origin at all levels of operation and administration . . . The Salvation Army knows that it must ever keep a compelling recognition of the need for involvement . . . The Salvation Army faces firmly and supports fully the imperatives of human and civil rights . . . The Salvationist shares, with every dedicated Christian, the conviction that the world's problems, especially this one, just won't go away . . . We are truly an international Army, a peaceful Army, yet united in battle against the forces of wrong, injustice and evil.

"With such a heritage, today's Salvationists can do no other than stand firm on the basic Salvation Army philosophy, Bible-given, that 'all men are created equal' for 'God hath made of one blood all nations of man for to dwell on the face of the earth.' Barriers, walls of prejudice, for reasons of race or color, are intolerable to the Salvationist who is committed to the brotherhood of all men."

The commitment to civil rights was proven the very next year when Maurice Smith became the first black to enter the School for Officers' Training in Atlanta. Entering from Washington, Smith was cautioned that he might not yet be welcome in all the South. He was reminded that he was breaking down a color barrier. For the most part, his time at the school was uneventful.

It was appropriate that these commitments were made in 1965 as the Army celebrated the centenary of the movement. And celebrate it did. A huge gathering in London was graced by the Queen of England. A less-ostentatious observance came in Baltimore when the Orioles hosted the New York Yankees baseball team. Proclaimed as "*Salvation Army Night*", led by Lt. Colonel Paul Thronburg, the Army flag entered the field to the sound of Meredith Willson's *"Banners and Bonnets,"* played by the Baltimore Area Band, Major W. R. H. Goodier, Bandmaster.

A more lasting honor came through efforts by both a Salvationist stamp collector, Brigadier Gordon Swyers, and by Brigadier Ernest Holz, divisional commander in Washington on 1965. Following negotiations with Postmaster General John A. Gronouski by Brigadier Holz in behalf of National Headquarters, came the announcement of a commemorative stamp recognizing the Army. The first day of issue took place in a public ceremony in New York City on July 2, the Army's hundredth birthday. And in Cocoa, Fla., a street was named in honor of the officers there, Major and Mrs. Vern Hall.

In an unusual set of circumstances, the South was unofficially involved in the opening of the work in another country. Leslie Lovestead, son of Major and Mrs. Lloyd Lovestead, intended to enlist in the US Navy. His elevator stopped at the wrong floor and he found himself with the Air Force recruiter. He was persuaded to enlist there and was subsequently sent to Taiwan. He was disappointed to learn that there was no Salvation Army in Taiwan.

He heard an inner voice say, "You will be there, and wherever you go, The Salvation Army goes with you." With this as his mandate, he began holding open-air meetings in Taichung. The city was one hundred miles from his base but he learned there were two former mainland Chinese Salvation Army officers there. With their help and that of another Salvationist serviceman, Robert McEaneny, he began the work.

When financing became a problem, young people in Florida belonging to the Corps Cadets sent nearly a thousand dollars. But Lovestead wanted to see the work permanent and knew that it was only a matter of time before he would be transferred. Accordingly, he wrote to General Frederick

Coutts and explained what was being done. Eventually Colonel and Mrs. George Lancashire came from Canada to officially open the work. When they arrived and met Lovestead they found a thriving corps of forty adults and one hundred young people.

Meanwhile, signs of the permanence of the work in Mexico came when Major and Mrs. Guillermo Pingarrón received their twenty-five year pin—the first officers to do so in Mexico. Later that year, Major and Mrs. Adolfo Guzmán, heroes of days gone by, became the first Mexican officers to retire.

An era passed when the Southern *War Cry* ceased publication in Atlanta with the September 25, 1965 issue. All publications were being consolidated in Chicago under the heading of National Publications. The Southern edition of *The War Cry* had recorded the largest circulation of all others in the world (except Great Britain), reaching in excess of 102,000 copies per week.

The year ended with a visit from General Coutts as the Army met in a Congress in Atlanta, the largest Salvation Army gathering to that date in the history of the territory. With his characteristic gentility, General Coutts visited the Fountainview Convalescent Home where he presented Bandmaster Alfred Ward a fifty year long service medal for his service as a local officer. Ward, originally from South end-on-Sea, England, had come South from Canada when Miami was little more than a fishing village and there labored faithfully as bandmaster. At the time of the presentation, five of his children were Salvation Army officers.

On December 18, 1965, came the announcement that Commissioner and Mrs. Carlson were ordered to proceed to Chicago to take command of the Central Territory. In the days ahead it would seem that the country was shaking itself apart.

CHAPTER 18

DISSENTS, DISASTERS AND DISTINCTION

(1966–1969)

ON AUGUST 1, 1966, Charles J. Whitman walked across the campus of the University of Texas at Austin. The architectural honor student, former altar boy and Eagle Scout, perched himself atop a 27 story tower, pulled out his rifle and began shooting. Before he was stopped by a bullet from an off duty policeman, he left thirteen dead, wounding thirty-three others. School officials were at a loss to explain what had happened. But this puzzling act of random violence was as much a reflection of the times as the later assassination of Martin Luther King Jr. and Robert Kennedy.

The nation would be even more desperate for answers as it watched its cities explode into riot, the massive proliferation of hallucinogenic drugs, the collapse of time-honored morals, the swelling numbers of war protesters, and the strategy of a war which seemed only to consume the ones who were sent to fight it. The old lines of authority were dismissed as hopelessly outdated, but nothing better suited was suggested. It seemed the flame of anarchy would spread from the smoldering college campuses, that America itself was on the verge of collapse.

Against the backdrop of protracted chaos, The Salvation Army busied itself with the casualties of revolution, pulling victims from the quicksand of their own folly, while still maintaining that purity had a place, that salvation was greater than the creative expressions of sin, that the great unchanging God could change any who would come. In a day when upheaval was in the air, the Army was confident in its roots.

To lead the Army at this critical time came Commissioner and Mrs. Glenn Ryan, whose most recent appointment had been territorial commanders of the Western Territory. Ryan, raised a Methodist in Illinois, had served in both corps and territorial appointments in the central and western states. He was married to the former Annie Blurton who came to the United States from her birthplace of Longton, England. When the Ryans assumed command they were the first territorial commanders who had been in charge of another territory before coming to the South. They found an Army trying to adapt its methods while remaining loyal to its message.

When 100,000 college students invaded Daytona Beach, Fla., during the annual spring break they found seventeen Salvationists ready to meet them. Conducting open-air meetings which featured folk music, followed by informal talk with the students afterwards, the team reached thousands of young people. Lieutenant and Mrs. Tom Jones, corps officers in Daytona Beach, also hosted a youth rally and band concert at the band shell on the beach.

Another venture to reach youth was found in Newport News, Va., where Captain and Mrs. Harold Hinson opened the first coffee house in the South. The coffee house ministry, an attempt to attract young people, used contemporary music, informal discussions called "rap sessions", and abundant refreshments. While coffee houses were considered to be an evangelistic outreach, they most often served as places where Christian young people could gather without the influence of a growing drug culture. Coffee houses sprang up across the South with varying degrees of success.

The Army found itself trying to serve youth going in two diverging directions. On the one hand, through its coffee houses and traditional ministries, it sought to reach out to young people of the "hippie" movement. Hippies were generally characterized by their long hair (both male and female), abuse of illicit drugs, advocacy of sexual freedom under the guise of "free love", use of loud music known as "acid rock" and general hostility toward authority which it labeled the "Establishment." This segment of the youth also embraced ecology, individuality and the brotherhood of man. As the movement grew the number of true hippies was always relatively small but their influence reached millions of young people who embraced their ideals to varying degrees. The one thing which seemed to fuel the hippie movement more than anything else was opposition to the Vietnam War.

As the war dragged on, protests against the war grew larger and more vocal in demanding that America withdraw. Whenever President Johnson filled speaking engagements, there were crowds of protesters, often taunting him, "LBJ, LBJ, how many kids did you kill today?" In Washington these protests grew from the first one in 1966 with 10,000 participants to 250,000 in 1969.

The Army was directly affected by the youth revolt as it watched its Sunday school attendances tumble by 25 percent from ten years before. The number of young people entering training for officership declined.

Contrasting this, there were those young people, mostly men, who followed their country's command to go to Vietnam. The Army had a few USOs in operation at the time when the United States became fully involved in the conflict, but no new services were added to accommodate the soldiers. Unlike the other times of war, the South was not affected by the growing numbers of enlisted men as they were routed to bases in the western United States instead. Still, the Army tried to supply something. Inductees were provided with a small box containing toiletry articles.

The first Salvation Army chaplain to go to Vietnam was Captain Kenneth Hodder, a son of officer parents in Great Britain, who completed his college work in Virginia and trained as a Salvation Army officer in the West. Hodder received his chaplain's training in Gulfport, Miss. From there he went overseas in March 1967, to serve, not only the military, but also the civilian population of Vietnam. As was the case with so many service personnel, he found it necessary to leave behind in Gulfport, his wife, a daughter of charter Southern officers, Lt. Colonel and Mrs. Richard B. Fitton, the Southern born Marjorie, and their three small children.

Not immune from the atmosphere around it, The Salvation Army would face an internal challenge. The Army had never claimed to be a democratic organization. Booth had started with a democratic organization during the Christian Mission days but, in his view, democracy was an inefficient form of rule for Christian warfare. The change of name to The Salvation Army sealed the form of government. It was to be an army, with a distinct chain of command. What was readily accepted in the nineteenth century was subject to challenge one hundred years later.

In 1966 a group of officers gathered informally in Charlotte, N.C. During a time of fellowship their conversation turned to affairs of the Army. "We are always rebuilding the Army when we get together," someone said, "Let's do something about it. We ought to put our feelings in writing." The result was the formation of the Concerned Officers Fellowship (COF).

The group began their activities by sending a bulletin to all officers in the South, expressing their concerns about certain issues. Among these was the feeling that the Army had become top heavy administratively, while demands upon corps officers increased. The COF was also distressed by the plight of officers entering retirement.

Active officers are provided a small allowance, supplemented by the provision of living quarters and an automobile. While this makes for a fairly comfortable situation during active officership, retiring officers had no equity built up in a home, owned no car and often no furniture. Retiring officers, who had commanded large centers with considerable numbers of people and managed Army resources, found themselves near poverty on their sixty-fifth birthday. It was not unusual to find one of these past leaders employed as a janitor or motel maid in order to earn enough money to live. These and other concerns made the COF feel officers needed an additional forum.

The COF was doomed by a couple of factors. First, some of those rumored to be involved with the organization seemed to have personal grudges which flavored their opinions. This made other officers suspicious of the motives of the COF. Those who were sympathetic were scared away by the administrative reaction to the unauthorized confederation.

Commissioner Ryan was understandably concerned. Considering the defiance of authority outside the Army's ranks, he did not want that within the Army. When word circulated about the strength of the administration's feeling against the activities of the COF, it was decided to dissolve the organization. The ultimate loyalty of the officers involved in the COF was evidenced by their refusal to respond to a network television reporter's inquiry to make their story known.

The administration considered that perhaps it was not completely in touch with some field officers. Following was the formation of the Territorial Officers' Advisory Committee (TOAC), which now meets regularly to discuss officers' concerns and needs. In addition, some of the concerns aired through the COF received further official attention, most notably the predicament faced by retiring officers.

A meeting of another small group produced an entirely different result. In Oklahoma City, a recently formed "Golden Agers" club became the nucleus of what would become the largest senior citizens' work carried on by The Salvation Army anywhere in the world. Eventually the program would include 23,000 retired people in multiplied centers, including one for Mexican-Americans and one for Native Americans. Providing hot meals, transportation, crafts, health services, educational classes, cultural activities, employment referrals and other services, the program continues to grow as America turns greyer.

More positive achievements were recorded by the territory. The South's contribution to missionary outreach, the Self-Denial/ World Service effort, saw a jump of almost 50 percent from $231,793 in 1966 to $316,919 in 1967.

The territory's missionary outreach found a new expression in the announcement in 1967 of the formation of the Mexico Youth Corps. Based upon the idea of the federal government's Peace Corps, college age youth were recruited across the territory to serve for a summer in Mexico. Under the supervision of the territorial youth secretary, Major Willard Evans, the first twelve journeyed south of the border during the summer of 1968. Scattered across the Mexican division, most would work in the growing children's home programs which now housed 1,300 young people. The Mexico Youth Corps was an annual feature until Mexico was separated from the Southern Territory.

The territory continued to blaze a trail with the Men's Fellowship Club. With a membership of over 3,000 the South had not lost its prominence as the world leader in this program, since its founding just after World War II. In 1969 the first ever Men's Congress convened in Atlanta. Under the supervision of Captain Harold Anderson, the congress boasted over 1,000 delegates from across the South and Mexico. The South had another reason to be proud when one of its officers, Major Phil Collier, became the first Southerner to head The Salvation Army National Publications as editor-in-chief.

The tragedies of the day continued to remind the Army of its ministry to the world. On April 4, 1968, civil rights leader Dr. Martin Luther King, Jr. was assassinated in Memphis. The funeral that followed the next week in Atlanta was attended by 75,000 mourners. Riots also followed in the wake of his death. In Baltimore and Washington, the streets became a battleground as enraged blacks vented their anger and frustration.

The Army found itself in a difficult position. During emergencies it traditionally served the rescue workers, National Guard and law enforcement officials. On a day to day basis it served the poor, many of them black. When riots broke out, the Army's service to the authorities seemed to some to be a betrayal of the poor. The Army continued, however, its service to the poor, many displaced when their homes were destroyed during the turmoil.

The Army felt it had to minister to the need, regardless of the interpretation some placed upon that service. Brigadier W. R. H. Goodier, divisional commander in Washington, supervised this dual role of the Army there. During the riot, a policeman was quoted as saying, "If it were not for them (The Salvation Army) we wouldn't be eating." At the same time, the Army set up collection points across the city for riot victims, mobilizing one hundred volunteers to assist those displaced by the riots in seven distribution centers.

Another outreach came in Atlanta at the hands of Colonel Dr. William Noble, who opened a medical clinic in the predominantly black section called Vine City. Using secondhand medical equipment and volunteer help of ten doctors from Emory University, Noble worked with the same dedication which had distinguished his labors in India.

The log for a typical day read: "Heavy schedule as medical consultant for Red Cross blood unit. At Red Cross Center at 7:30 AM and Lillian (his wife) picked me up at 6:30 PM. Quick hamburger at the Varsity (a well-known drive in restaurant); rushed to clinic to serve until 11 PM. Rewarding, when one knows the desperate need."

The Army was not always successful in sharing its vision with its own advisory board members. When some of the participants of the Poor People's March, led by Ralph Abernathy, came through Macon, Ga., on their way to join 50,000 others in Washington, the advisory board agreed with city officials in requesting the officer not feed the marchers, contrary to what had previously been announced. Fortunately, this kind of action became more and more rare.

When a Gallup poll was taken in 1968 it revealed that, for the first time, Americans considered crime to be the number one problem in the country. The Army stepped up its efforts to break the cycle of crime by providing services to both youthful offenders and ex-offenders. In Atlanta, a program called "Young Offenders" was started to work with juveniles. In addition, halfway houses for ex-offenders were opened in Atlanta, Orlando and Dallas. Halfway houses were opened a few years earlier under the auspices of the Men's Social Service in Houston and Dallas, but the thrust from this point on would be through the corps.

Within the walls of Atlanta Federal Penitentiary, the Army became active in the Yokefellows, a movement initiated by teacher and author Dr. Elton Trueblood. Two men from the School for Officers' Training, Cadet Lewis Hirzel and Cadet Ronald Liston, became the first Salvationists in the South to serve in this unique ministry. Called "Christian group therapy," the cadets met with Christian prisoners to discuss their problems of living in the prison, questions about the Bible and their hopes for the day when they would be released.

Speaking about the activities, Liston said, "We have no set plans. We open in prayer, and then just throw the meeting open so that the fellows can talk about whatever is on their minds. Usually one of the inmates opens in prayer, the main burden being, 'bless our families—make us assets to society when we are free again.' "

An innovative program for homeless men was begun in Roanoke, Va. Called the Voluntary Action Program, it was aimed at making transient men self-supporting citizens. Working with the Veterans Administration, Virginia Mental Health Department and local businesses, men were trained for employment and then assisted in establishing themselves independently. Despite the larger and more sophisticated programs involving the Army's resources, there was still the almost unseen personal involvement.

Captain Elbert Steadham, contacted about a homeless boy in Paducah, Ky., took him home, while checking out the young man's story. Feeling he could trust the Steadhams, he confessed that he was fifteen, that he had lied about his age in order to join the Job Corps, but had run away from the camp because of harassment from other boys. Steadham confirmed the boy's story and contacted his mother who was unable to send money to bring her son home. Steadham bought a small suitcase, stuffed it with clothing, purchased the boy a bus ticket and sent him on his way.

During these years, the Army continued to respond to disasters across the South. The federal government withheld recognition of the Army as an official disaster agency, but its efforts were appreciated by others.

The service unit director in Edinburg, Tex., received back an appeal envelope with a balloon, two pieces of chewing gum and a tin medal. Upon investigation he found a little girl, living with her family in a lean-to on the outskirts of town. Her family had been aided by the Army during Hurricane Beulah the previous year. Remembering this, she wanted only to share her gift to help other children.

The opportunity of sharing with other disaster victims would not be long in coming. On August 17, 1969, all previous Salvation Army disaster efforts were dwarfed by the fury of Hurricane Camille. Not since the hurricane that demolished Galveston in 1900 had the mainland of the United States been hit by a storm of this intensity. Even with advance warning of the approaching danger, over 300 people were killed as the storm flattened mobile homes, ripped apart houses and littered the landscape with uprooted trees and other debris along a path of destruction traceable from where it came ashore near Biloxi. The divisional commander for the Alabama, Louisiana and Misissippi Division, Major Leslie Hall, had anticipated the need for the Army's services and had canteens and personnel stationed at New Orleans, Mobile and Gulfport. Even with these advance preparations, the Army could not have been adequately prepared for the extensive damage in the wake of Camille.

As the magnitude of the storm's damage became known, Hall requested more help. Canteen units and personnel streamed in from across the country. Eventually, fifty canteens were employed in feeding victims, rescue workers and newsmen. The Army sheltered storm victims in seven schools and, at Pass Christian, in a circus tent.

At one point, the Army was unloading 150 trucks a day as supplies poured in from across the country. Estimates were that the food donated alone exceeded 100 million pounds. In their enthusiasm to help, some people misunderstood the needs. Among the donations coming in were surf boards, ice skates, and in one instance, a broken record player.

As disaster efforts continued, the Army was involved in locating over 100 missing persons, aiding 88,251 families, distributing in excess of two million pieces of clothing, serving 960,900 meals and distributing 16,000 Bibles and Scripture portions. In areas cut off from electrical power, the Army gave out 100,000 pounds of ice. "Baby kits" were assembled, complete with bottles, disposable diapers and milk. The Army's water purification unit was especially valuable as clean drinking water was at a premium.

As the storm's course took it northward, it entered Virginia where extensive flooding of the James River claimed another 100 lives. Canteen units in the stricken area served 10,000 meals a day, while trucks from the Men's Social Service helped in the evacuation and the return of people to their homes. Combined with the work in Louisiana and Mississippi, this made the efforts in response to Camille the largest relief effort of The Salvation Army since its founding. A gratifying, if not overdue, response by the federal government came when Congress designated the Army an official disaster agency.

At the end of 1969, Commissioner and Mrs. Glenn Ryan entered into the peace of honored (and much deserved) retirement. But for the territory the days of quiet were yet to be.

CHAPTER 19

REGROUPING WITHIN THE RAMPARTS

(1969–1974)

GENERAL ALBERT ORSBORN, in his autobiography, *The House of My Pilgrimage,* wrote, "The greatest disservice we could render to the past would be to adhere slavishly to our early methods."

If there was ever a territorial leader who took that to heart, it was Commissioner William E. Chamberlain. He came with the most diverse background of any person to occupy the office. He had not only served as a corps officer and in various levels of Army administration, he had also been a youth director. In addition, he was the only Southern territorial commander to have been a Men's Social Service officer or to have at one time resigned from officership.

His most recent appointment had been as territorial commander of the Caribbean and Central American Territory. His wife, the former Ethel Turner, before their marriage in 1931 had distinguished herself as a single corps officer and premiere bass player in the Training College band.

Confronting Chamberlain immediately was the mandate for a major reorganization of Army operations. A New York consulting firm, Booz, Allen & Hamilton, was asked to look at the American Army structure and make suggestions for needed changes which should be made. The national study, begun in 1968, was reveiwed by officers from all levels of the Army structure, with instructions to share their opinions of its findings.

The biggest impact was to be on territorial headquarters which, over the years, had evolved as changes were made in Army programming. The problem was that there existed overlapping responsibilities in a number of areas, while other matters were left unattended.

Headquarters looked in places like a house with an addition on an addition on an addition. The chain of command was equally confusing, with some departments reporting directly to the territorial commander, others the chief secretary, and still others working through another level of administration. After review by the Commissioners' Conference the plan was implemented.

At territorial headquarters the top two spots were retained by the territorial commander and chief secretary, respectively. Directly under them came a secretary for business administration, another for program and another for personnel. These top officers formed what became known as the territorial "cabinet."

Other recommendations were not put in place. Among these was a proposal that the four Schools for Officers' Training be eliminated in favor of a national school. The rationale for this change was based on eliminating the overhead of maintaining four separate schools which essentially duplicated each other's program. Although this received favorable recommendation from the committee made up of Southern officers, it was turned down by the Commissioners' Conference.

Their decision was based on more than sentimentality. They recognized that there were significant cultural differences existing within the country and the cadets needed to be able to respond to the settings where they would be serving as officers.

In addition, a national school would take the cadets away from three out of four of the territories, decreasing the visibility of the cadets and diminishing their territorial ministry. It was acknowledged that young people seeing the cadets themselves in action was a major recruiting tool for future officers.

Another suggestion left on the table was a reorganization of the divisional headquarters which would have resulted in there being a divisional commander with three divisional secretaries: one each for business administration, program and personnel, mirroring the structure of territorial headquarters. This idea was abandoned since it was felt it would have made the divisional headquarters administration top heavy.

Meanwhile, the Army agonized over the plight of the Women's Social Service Department. The network had shrunk over the years to seven maternity homes which had been begun in a time when to be an unwed mother meant being shunned by family and friends. The Army felt unlimited compassion for these young ladies, some as young as eleven years of age. The maternity homes had provided a haven for the girls as they awaited the arrival of their babies. With the kind guidance of the officers staffing the homes, the girls were helped to see what their options were for themselves and their children. A high percentage of them made professions of faith while in the homes.

But times had changed, and the changes eroded the work of the Women's Social. Hospital workers were receiving large increases in their salaries, increases the Army could not begin to match. Even if the home did not have a medical staff, the higher wages were reflected by the charges the hospitals were passing on to the Army when babies were delivered. The curse of legalized abortion, aided by financial assistance from health insurance companies, cut into clientele further.

Greater than these was the change in society's attitudes toward unwed mothers. As there was an increase in promiscuity, the inevitability of unplanned pregnancies was considered an acceptable price tag for those exercising their sexual freedom. Families and friends also encouraged girls to stay at home during the pregnancy and to keep their babies after they were born. This resulted in a drop in the maternity homes' populations which further resulted in decreased funding to support the program.

Still, the officers of the Women's Social clung desperately to the hope that the program would survive. The Women's Social Service Secretary, Brigadier Beatrice Combs, admonished her officers:

> Let's recognize that the situation could cause panic, which could manifest itself in several ways. It could immobilize us at the very time we need to be most keen and intelligently active. It could have us give up in despair and frustration. It could turn us inward on ourselves, cling to our past that is no longer there. Or have us running in circles wringing our hands in defeat, self-recrimination or blame and buck passing. Or we might just run. It could be a serious threat to our individual Christian faiths. All cop-outs.
>
> This could be the dawning of a new and even better age. I think we know that, but feel we are ill-equipped to do the necessary designing much less get around the roadblocks . . . it's in your laps and mine now.
>
> This could be the acid test of our faith. Either we believe God to this extent or we don't. If we can't believe it, we have based our faith on the wrong thing.
>
> Have we?

Valiant efforts were made to adapt the homes to other programs such as home care for pre-delinquent girls. The efforts had little success. The homes began to close one at a time, and the Women's Social Service Department was finally dissolved in 1977. Its record was astounding as typified by the home in Louisville where 8,000 girls had been served in sixty years.

The officers involved in this program mourned its passing, remembering the differences it had made in the lives of their girls. One girl, named Nedra, wrote a poem for the staff when she left the maternity home in Tampa:

> When you are in need of protection and care,
> For it's a child that you bear,
> Come to The Salvation Army Home
> And you'll never more need to roam.
>
> The Salvation Army Home
> Is made for girls like you and me,
> Who have made a mistake
> And wish to feel free.
>
> Girls like you and me have come
> With heavy hearts,
> And gone,
> To make a new start.

A different test came through the challenge of Captain Billie Jean McClure who had been commissioned in 1967 under special circumstances. McClure felt the financial pressure of raising a family on the limited allowance given an officer. Stating that men officers in similar circumstances were allowed more financial benefits and wider opportunities for service, McClure filed a complaint with the Equal Employment Opportunity Commission (EEOC).

She allied herself with the National Organization for Women (NOW), which group assisted and encouraged her efforts in this direction, including picketing of an Army Congress in June, interestingly called "The Wonderful World of Women."

The Army had recommended McClure's termination as an officer on the basis of previous unsatisfactory service and considered disloyalty prior to this action. At the Board of Inquiry she pleaded guilty to one charge and was found guilty on all others. She chose not to appeal this decision within the time limit proffered to any officer under such circumstances.

Meanwhile, McClure's case was wending its way through the courts, although the Army had maintained the courts had no jurisdiction over this ecclesiastical matter. It further stated that the Army, in any case, had not violated McClure's civil rights. The EEOC, as a "friend of the court", filed a brief on McClure's behalf. The District Court dismissed the suit, agreeing with the Army that it lacked jurisdiction in this matter.

McClure appealed to the United States Court of Appeals for the Fifth District. The Court of Appeals agreed with the lower court ruling and refused to hear the case. She appealed this decision to the Supreme Court which denied a hearing since she failed to file in a timely matter. With that the matter was officially closed.

This was not the only trial for the Army. In Mexico, the Army received substantial funding for its children's homes from the Christian Children's Fund (CCF). When funding was cut off, the Army inquired as to the reason. The problem was that corps buildings were frequently housed in the same facilities as the children's homes, making it impossible to completely separate either the function or expense. In a country where the per capita income at that time was $276, the loss was a severe one. Territorial headquarters advanced the needed funds, calling on Salvationists to help in the crisis. Eventually, an understanding was reached with the Christian Children's Fund and funding was restored and improved.

A wider ranging struggle was waged with the United Way. Formerly known as the United Fund, the organization changed more than its name. It became more centrally coordinated and saw itself not as a federation of agencies, but as a representative of donors. The change in emphasis justified its feeling that it could set priorities in funding agencies, enter into the purchase of services that an agency might offer, while refusing to fund those which it did not like, and, if it felt it was warranted, drop an agency altogether. The change made the United Way see itself as a controlling entity on the donor's behalf.

The Army felt the impact of this change in philosophy when in some communities it left the United Way. In others, the United Way demanded that the Army surrender outside fund raising efforts, including the traditional Christmas appeal. Because it had a tighter network, if the Army gave ground in one community, news of this was quickly communicated to another.

The Army faced the challenge by standardizing its practices, recruiting more strong leaders for its advisory boards and by insisting upon sovereignty in clearly defined areas as part of its partnership agreement. In a report to International Headquarters, it was noted that "relationships (with the United Way) are hardening and there are increased tensions because of (this) reorganization."

Despite the difficulties of the day, there were those refreshing reminders of the Army's purpose and mission. When Captain Judy Moore traveled through the city of Atlanta, she passed through the area of town known as Peachtree Strip, dominated by the "hippie" culture. Noticing how young some of the girls were, she could not get them off her mind, feeling something had to be done to save them from ruining their lives.

Approaching the Army leadership, she brought a plan to open a girl's lodge for young ladies under sixteen years of age. The girls were allowed to stay there up to three days.

While there, they were referred for medical attention if needed, and encouraged to call home. In the first year, the lodge housed 387 girls, forty percent of whom returned home. A similar program was opened in Birmingham under the auspices of Brigadier Luther Smith, directed by Beth Fountain.

Both programs received notable recognition. Word of the ministry in Birmingham reached the White House prompting President Nixon to write, "Your outstanding efforts deserve the praise and commendation of all our fellow citizens, and I want you to know of my admiration for your fine humanitarian concern." During a crusade in Atlanta, Captain Moore was surprised by a visit from Billy Graham associate Cliff Barrows. Moved by what he saw, he asked Moore to be a part of the meetings the following week. Before 50,000 in the stadium and a television audience of millions more, Captain Moore shared her personal witness, prompting Graham to comment, "After hearing this marvelous testimony we hardly need a sermon tonight." (He preached anyway.)

Other social service advances were seen across the territory. In Danville, Va., Captain Sam Crowder initiated a program of delivering hot lunches to elderly and handicapped individuals. In McAlester, Okla., Captain Fred Musgrave received a national award for The Salvation Army coffee house. In Miami, a ministry to Cubans was headed by Lt. Colonel Moises Suárez. Suárez, a native of Cuba, had been a divisional commander there, but was forced to flee when Castro outlawed The Salvation Army.

On January 24, 1972, the Supreme Court ruled that residency requirements for welfare aid were unconstitutional. This had a dramatic effect on government administered assistance programs. The Army had always helped regardless of the length of time a person was in the community, but the consequence to the Army was the mobility which this ruling gave to the poor. With the residency requirements waived, the poor could travel to any part of the country where conditions looked promising.

This resulted in a mass migration, especially to the South where jobs were available in places like Disney World and Cape Kennedy. The Army was inundated with clients who, though eligible to receive governmental services, still had to wait for public welfare certification and/or appointments to determine their eligibility.

The Army continued to render disaster services in hurricanes on the East Coast, mine disasters in West Virginia and an earthquake in Mexico. It was aided not only by the federal government's recognition of the Army as an official emergency agency, but by a similar law in Texas passed in 1971—making Texas the first state in the Union to recognize the Army in this way.

The Men's Social Service Department was able to report the success of its program when it showed that over one-third of those who entered the program were able to soon return to independent living. A new venture proved fruitful at Florida's Camp Keystone when the first Men's Social camp was held for the men of the centers.

A spontaneous spiritual revival began at the School for Officer's Training. Cadet Vernon Jewett had been reading *One Divine Moment,* the story of a recent revival at Asbury College in Wilmore, Ky. On a Saturday following lunch Jewett stood before the other cadets, confessing hs own need and asking the other cadets to pray for him. When he went to the chapel he was followed by other cadets. As the Holy Spirit moved among those gathered in prayer, there was a time of confession, rejoicing and petition.

The meeting continued as different cadets maintained a prayer vigil through the night. The next day the cadets went to surrounding corps and told of God's blessing which resulted in outpourings of the Holy Spirit's blessings in these corps as well. That night the prayer vigil was resumed.

When attempts were made the next day to begin classes again, only the Bible classes met, and these became times of sharing what God was bringing about in lives. Then, as cadets called and wrote home, the revival spread to the Atlanta Lakewood Corps and to corps in Kinston, Durham and Gastonia, N.C. A result of the revival was seen the following fall when six mobile housing units were purchased to accommodate the influx of cadets.

Along a similar vein, what should have been a great spiritual breakthrough simply died out. The Army joined enthusiastically with representatives from thirty-four Protestant denominations, seven independent evangelistic organizations and three evangelistic associations for an effort called Key 73. With the theme, *"Calling our Continent to Christ,"* the plan was to present the Gospel to every person in North America. In a kickoff television broadcast, two Salvationists, Rick and Jim Mikles, were featured with a musical they had written entitled *"The Encounter"* based on Saul's conversion.

There was little question of the Army's commitment, as corps, institution and headquarters officers joined soldiers in total involvement. Members of most of the other participating organizations did not enter in with the same dedication. With the Army representatives almost singlehandedly carrying the torch, the flame flickered out.

In fairness to those involved, the news events of the year were so shattering as to eclipse almost everything else. Israel inflicted a stunning defeat on the Arab nations in what was known as the Yom Kippur War. In retaliation for their defeat, the Arab nations placed an embargo on any nation friendly with Israel. Almost immediately gas prices in the United States skyrocketed as long lines queued up at gas stations in a quest for the once bountiful commodity. Also, in that year, the last troops were withdrawn from Vietnam.

The Vice President, implicated in tax evasion, resigned and Senator Gerald Ford was named as his replacement. The media began carrying stories about a senseless break in at Democratic Headquarters located in the Watergate Apartments in Washington. What seemed at first an insignificant event would drive President Nixon from office the next year and make Americans cynically suspicious of leadership for the next generation. And, in a confirmation of the South's maturity, Atlanta elected Maynard Jackson as the first black mayor of a major Southern city.

This last event was proof of what Southerners already sensed was happening—the South was "coming into its own." *Business Week* magazine reported, "By all accounts the southward migration of people and business will continue into the 1980s. It is fast earning . . . the title, the new rich South." The magazine's glowing statements were not misplaced. The South was where things were happening.

All of America was enjoying a hit television series based on a Southern family. *The Waltons* was as refreshing to Southerners as it was to people in the rest of the country in its portrayal of the warmth of family and its break from the media tendency to portray Southerners as backward.

In the world of sports, the Army could feel gratification as advisory board member Hank Aaron of the Atlanta Braves on April 4, 1974, entered the record books as the man who broke Babe Ruth's career home run record.

For the Army this bright promise of the future could be no more clearly seen than in Texas. Major Neal Keeton was looking for property to expand the operations in San Antonio. Peacock Military Academy was closing its doors and an approach was made to see if part of the property could be purchased. The Peacock family made it known was not interested in having the property, which had seen honorable service for three generations, divided piecemeal.

When the Peacocks countered with an offer to give the Army the property, there was a question as to how funds could be obtained to operate the twenty-acre, twenty-building site. In a step of faith, it was finally decided to accept the property as a whole and to rename it The Salvation Army Peacock Community Service Center. The property now houses the Citadel Corps, a senior citizens' apartment complex, a girls' home and a community center.

The changes were not over. Commissioner Chamberlain received his orders to become National Commander, the first Southern territorial commander to proceed directly to that position. The surging South was now to be commanded for the first time by one of her very own.

CHAPTER 20

THE RISING SOUTH

(1974–1979)

THE SOUTHERN TERRITORY had been commanded by officers from Canada, England, Ireland, Germany, and individuals from other sections of the United States. After almost fifty years of existence, the territory was to have one of its own at the helm, Commissioner Ernest Holz. It was almost too good to be true—instead of having a leader who would have to adapt to Southern ways, the Army was to have one who not only understood the South but helped build the Army there.

Born in Pittston, Pa., Holz had a great heritage as the grandson of early Salvation Army greatheart, Commissioner Richard Holz, and son of Southern pioneer, Brigadier Ernest R. Holz. Married to Mina Krunsburg in 1938, Holz served as corps officer in Sapulpa, Okla., and then in administrative appointments. In 1970 he was appointed Chief Secretary of the Western Territory, followed by an appointment as National Chief Secretary. From this position, he was selected to command the South. Holz possessed a keen mind with a tremendous capacity to not only comprehend complicated facts, but to recall them at will in amazing detail.

More history was being made. Holz's brother, Commissioner Richard Holz, was territorial commander of the Western Territory, making it the first time in history that two brothers were territorial commanders at the same time in this country. When Commissioner Richard Holz came to Atlanta for the installation ceremonies, it was also the first time a U.S. territorial commander had been installed by his brother.

When he assumed office, Holz would find advances being made across the territory. In Florida, the state legislature passed The Salvation Army Act, making the Army eligible to operate a rehabilitative program for misdemeanor offenders. A similar program was developing in Tennessee.

At the same time, both the federal and state governments began using Army facilities for pre-release placement of prisoners nearing the end of their sentences. Aimed at breaking the cycle of crime, both programs showed remarkable success as they continued to spread across the South. In Oklahoma, a joint project between the Army and the El Reno Federal Correctional Institution resulted in a "Children's Toy Shop" where inmates crafted wooden toys for nurseries and day care centers.

A totally different service was being offered at opposite ends of the territory. Ft. Chaffee, Ark., near Little Rock, had become a resettlement center for 100,000 Vietnamese refugees. Both the State Department and the Department of Health, Education and Welfare called on Major Klon Kitchen to help feed and clothe the internees. Within six weeks, 2 million pieces of clothing were given out, while three canteens helped serve the thousands in the camp. Later in Miami, the Department of Immigration and Naturalization would call on the Army to provide residential care for non-documented aliens as an alternative to incarceration while they awaited deportation.

Advances were seen in areas other than social services. The South boasted the largest membership in Nurses (later Medical) Fellowship, a nondenominational organization which provided Christian fellowship to the medical community. The North and South Carolina Division led the way under the leadership of Mrs. Major James Rickard, herself a nurse. Of the 600 members in the division, Mrs. Gerry Jordan of Rocky Mount, N.C., had recruited 323.

The Men's Club forged ahead, this time by naming the first annual Territorial Man of the Year in 1975. The recipient was Clyde Workman of Raleigh, N.C. As manager of Sears Automotive, he administered an operation that grossed $10 million per year. On his staff were seven Salvationists, most of whom he had personally won to the Lord. Of these, two would later become officers.

America was celebrating its bicentennial in 1976, but the Army ended up being almost too busy to notice. On February 4, 1976, a devastating earthquake in Guatemala, registering 7.5 on the Richter scale, left over 24,000 dead and 77,000 seriously injured. Of the country's total population of less than six million, 1.2 million people became homeless. One-third of all Guatemalan families suffered a death in the immediate family, including more than 5,000 children who were orphaned. In Guatemala City, only two of the seven hospitals were left operating. The Country's eastern port, Puerto Barrios, was neutralized by one hundred landslides.

Responding quickly, Brigadier Newton McClements, Disaster Relief Coordinator for the Caribbean and Central American Territory, arrived with Major Shirley Cox to assess what the Army's role of relief would be. Contacting the United States for help, it was decided relief efforts would be handled through the Southern Territory. Commissioner Holz immediately dispatched Captain Stanley Melton and Major Aida Garcia, both Spanish speaking, to Guatemala; also Captains Frias and Martinez from Mexico. In addition, he named Major Harold Hinson as the coordinator of relief efforts for the United States.

With destruction so widespread, it was easy to see that everything imaginable was needed without delay. In little over a month, the South would send supplies in excess of 3,500,000 pounds, valued at $4,000,000. Miami was one of the staging areas, where the City Commander, Major Emery Frierson, estimated that 250 tons of supplies had passed through there alone. At one point, Major David Mulbarger, Miami Men's Social Service Officer, had one of his warehouses jammed with 300,000 pounds of supplies. Even that was not enough.

Eventually the work was turned over entirely to the Southern Territory when the government of Guatemala asked the Army to accept the responsibility of rebuilding the city of Tecpán, located in an area of the severest damage. The city of 23,000 had suffered destruction of all 998 homes. When the Guatemalan army arrived, it was decided to bulldoze the entire area where houses once stood.

The Army started by distributing clothing, blankets and food, and then opened a medical clinic. The nights could be bitterly cold, so the need to build houses was urgent. Lt. Colonel and Mrs. Alfred Osborne (R) arrived in early April to begin the operation of a cement block plant provided by gifts from the United States, Canada, Great Britain and the Netherlands. The problem was the machinery wasn't there and wouldn't be for another five weeks.

In the meantime, Osborne began looking for a location, realizing when he finally found one that it was the only place within 69 miles that had proper electrical wiring. The block plant finally arrived and was put into immediate use. When the Army was finished, it would have constructed 500 homes and sold building materials for another 500 to those able to pay or work for them.

When the first 31 homes and the large community center

were finished, Commissioner and Mrs. Holz came to dedicate and turn them over to the city of Tecpán. It was a night of rejoicing for the community, as it celebrated with a fiesta which included fireworks, a marimba band and the raising of the Guatemalan and Salvation Army flags.

At the same time, ground was broken for the new corps as the government gave its consent for the Army to again open its work in the country. Captain and Mrs. Stanley Melton were placed in charge of the work and proceeded to Guatemala City to open a second corps there. Left in charge of the new opening in Tecpán were Captain and Mrs. Daniel Guerra, Mexican officers who had joined the rescue efforts.

The opening of the corps underscored the Army's witness to the devastated city. One Saturday following the earthquake there were a series of severe aftershocks. The head of a company of Mexican engineers approached an Army officer and asked, "My men are frightened to death. Will you come over and speak to them?" The captain spoke to the men and when he ended in prayer, all the men stood shivering around a lantern, repeating every word.

A year after the earthquake Commissioner and Mrs. Holz returned to Tecpán to join Guatemalan President Kjell Shell Laugerud in a dedication ceremony for the corps building and 524 cement-block, steel-reinforced homes. The president's brother said, "The Salvation Army was one of the most dedicated of all the agencies who came to help rebuild our little country. They worked diligently finishing and rebuilding Tecpán as they had promised."

Corps Sergeant-Major Hubert Phillips from Anniston, Ala. would be later recognized for his service following this and other disasters by The Salvation Army's Order of Exceptional Service.

A study of the Army's effort was done four years later by

JoAnn E. Glittenburg, an anthropologist who had made studies of similar efforts in other countries. In her paper she made the following statements:

> The Tecpán project is superior to most others based on these observations:
>
> 1) Completion of what was promised.
> 2) Just and equal distribution of materials and work.
> 3) Democratic decision making process.
> 4) Close technical supervision of the work.
> 5) Culturally acceptable housing, size, etc., after consultation with the people.
> 6) Urbanization completed as part of the total reconstruction process. Did not see housing as separate from the other needs of the community, such as drains, electricity, etc.
> 7) Women were granted legal rights as heads of households (this is not true in all communities).
> 8) A close cooperation between The Salvation Army personnel and the official government representatives.
> 9) A clear cooperative effort between Salvation Army personnel (Captains Melton and Guerra) as well as other voluntary organizations . . .
> 10) Leadership style of Captain and Mrs. Guerra in Tecpán make them well accepted in the community.
> 11) A sense of pride in Colony Iximche, a family approach to living, a sense of child-orientation with the nursery school and playground.

The spiritual value of this work could be seen when ten years later an anniversary celebration in Guatemala revealed a growth to ten corps, a men's residence and feeding center, an Alcoholic Rehabilitation Center, three outposts, eight day care centers and 8,000 children being taken care of through sponsorship programs.

The earthquake was not the only story from Latin America that year.

Prior to farewelling from Atlanta on October 31, 1974, the

former Territorial Commander, Commissioner William Chamberlain, had recommended to the General that Mexico be separated from the Southern Territory to be a part of a new Spanish speaking command comprising all of Central America. No staff discussions or planning had been initiated in Atlanta and the matter had not been brought to the attention of the Divisional Commander in Mexico. Commissioner Chamberlain in a confidential letter to his successor covering officer personnel, attached to his farewell brief, wrote: "*MEXICO—Brigadier Howard Whitehead*—This is not an easy assignment and I feel the Brigadier should not be asked to fulfill this responsibility for more than another year or so. ——-I have great respect for his service in Mexico. However, I do feel further dramatic changes are going to take place and eventually this should be part of a Spanish speaking territory and not be attached to the South. We are attempting to "Americanize" Mexico and this should not be."

Commissioner Holz, long familiar with Mexico and the Army's growth and development under the sacrificial leadership of devoted Southern officers, was somewhat surprised to receive a letter from the International Secretary in London within a week after taking command of the South that advised the General was prepared to act on establishing the new territory, within three months if feasible.

While not opposed to Mexico being separated from the South, Commissioner Holz was alarmed that no formal discussions or even plans had been made concerning the financing, personnel requirements, legal status of the five Mexico S.A. corporations and the role and commitment the Southern Territory would play, now and in the future, as the new territory was established. Writing to the General he pleaded, "It is my opinion that we have not sufficiently reviewed or researched the implications of this change and I urge that we make no announcement nor enter into formal decision until further input is received from the USA Southern Territory".

General Wiseman, who was scheduled for special meetings in the territory early in the new year, indicated he would review the matter at the time of his visit. The result of that consultation was satisfactory to Commissioner Holz as the General and he agreed that the announcement of the new Territory would be delayed a year, with the change over to take place October 1, 1976.

This provided for an orderly transfer of all legal, personnel, financial, property and insurance records covering forty years of territorial development and administration of The Salvation Army in Mexico and Guatemala. Further, it enabled Commissioner Holz to present the matter to his Territorial Executive Council whose support was needed for the continued financial support of the new territory.

From the inception of the work in Mexico in 1937 Southern Salvationists had not only met annual Self Denial/World Services financial goals but also had raised substantial funds each year for the support of the work south of the border. Mexico was the South's "baby". In 1975 $275,000.00 was required to keep this thriving infant growing and expanding. More than $50,000.00 of this amount was raised annually by the Home Leagues of the South whose special projects included the Mexico children's homes and day care center in fifteen cities.

International Headquarters acknowledged that the new territory could not survive without this continuing financial help. The Territorial Executive Council wholeheartedly endorsed the financial commitment of over $200,000.00 annually and this commitment was continued by each succeeding territorial administration.

On August 20, 1976, the announcement was made that the new territory would consist of Mexico, Guatemala, Costa

Rica, Panama, the Panama Canal Zone, Honduras, Colombia, Venezuela, El Salvador and Nicaragua with territorial headquarters in Mexico City.

November 20, 1976, was a momentous day for Salvationists in Mexico City. The time had come for The Salvation Army in Mexico to "spread its wings", leave the sheltering nest of the Southern Territory USA. Throngs of Salvationists and friends of the Army from other churches and the advisory board made their way to the "Principe de Paz" (Prince of Peace) church located in the heart of the city. The strains of martial music filled the air as the Texas divisional band led by Bandmaster Jack Morrison could be heard from afar.

As standard bearers entered with the national flags represented in the new territory, hearts were moved by the colorful pageant and jubilant voices joining in singing "Adelante, pues, Ejercito de Salvacion!" (The Salvation Army is marching along). Anticipation welled up in the hearts of the pioneer Mexican Salvationists who vividly recalled the early days of The Salvation Army in their country and thanked God for sparing them to see this historic day. Major Leon Ferraez, acting Divisional Commander and a Southern officer who served faithfully many years with Mrs. Ferraez in Mexico, ably piloted the jubilant celebration. In contrast was the solemn moment when Commissioner Holz officially announced the "cambio de guardia" (change of command) transferring into the new territory 30 corps, 34 institutions, 99 officers and cadets, 2,571 junior and senior soldiers and all properties and equipment.

Commissioner Chamberlain, now National Commander, was present to represent the General and conducted the installation of Colonel and Mrs. Jacques Egger as the territorial leaders of the new command. The colonel and his wife, experienced missionary officers, publicly pledged themselves to their new field of labor. The band struck up the closing cry as the great crowd raised their voices in a song of dedication:

> So we'll lift up the banner on high,
> The salvation banner of love;
> We'll fight beneath its colors till we die
> Then go to our home above.

The Mexico and Central America territory had taken its place in the Salvation Army world.

Little time was allowed to mourn the loss of this cherished part of the Southern Territory. The Army expanded its services to older Americans by dedicating its first senior citizens' residence in Fort Worth, Tex., called "Friendship House." It included furnished apartments, a library, laundry facilities and nine acres for gardening.

The opening in Ft. Worth was quickly followed by similar projects in Charlotte, Cumberland, Md., and Orlando. The need to provide for America's older citizens has remained critical. By 1984, seven states had more than a million people 65 or older—double the number ten years earlier.

On October 19, 1976, forty corporate and professional leaders from every part of the USA, recruited by territorial and divisional commanders, gathered in New York City for the organizational meeting of the first National Advisory Board. Chaired by Dr. Jerome Holland, former ambassador to Sweden and US delegate to the United Nations, the South was represented by 13 influential and knowledgeable members. One of them, Mr. Robert Sellers, president and chief executive officer for the Cities Service Oil Corporation of Tulsa, Okla. was elected chairman. Two years later he was succeeded by another Southerner, Mr. Prime Osborn, chairman of the board of the C.S.X. Corporation of Jacksonville, Fla. Mr. Osborn headed the national advisory board from 1978 to 1983.

In 1989, another Southerner, Mr. B. Franklin Skinner, chief executive officer of Southern Bell Telephone Co., serves as national advisory board chairman.

Among its many accomplishments has been bringing together bi-annually over a thousand delegates to a national advisory organizations conference; also guiding the Army on issues, concerns, and opportunities of national importance. In November 1989, the conference will be held in London, England, so members can take part in special functions at the birthplace of the international Salvation Army.

The Southern Territory indulged itself in a joyous celebration of the fiftieth anniversary of its opening. The year of 1977 was proclaimed the Year of Jubilee. The observance was begun the previous year when a new territorial headquarters building was dedicated. Ideally located next to Interstate 85 in Atlanta, the building had 55,000 square feet on five acres of choice land.

The real celebration came in October when Salvationists convened in Atlanta for the Jubilee Congress featuring newly elected General Arnold Brown. The over 4,000 delegates were treated to a weekend of near-flawless meetings. Included in the congress was Heritage Hall, an exhibit area which honored the Army's Southern heritage with eighty booths. The old and the new Salvation warriors were honored as fifty new soldiers were enrolled by the General under their own corps flag and fifty-four veterans received long service badges for fifty years of soldiership. The congress was a fitting testimonial to Commissioner Holz's characterization of the South's fifty years of service as "one unbroken note of praise and love to God."

The modern spirit of Salvationism could be seen in smaller ways besides the congress. In Melbourne, Fla., Bandmaster Nicholas McCloud celebrated his 102nd birthday, one hundred years of that spent in The Salvation Army. That same year the corps officer and soldiers took their stand at an open-air meeting outside a theater where a traveling company presented the nude musical "Oh, Calcutta!"

Milestones continued to be erected. With the proliferation of government grants and foundations, territorial headquarters appointed veteran officer Brigadier Leslie Hall to head up a new Social Services Department. At the School for Officers' Training there was excitement as a major building program was initiated with a groundbreaking. The first new building, designed to house married cadets and their children, would be named after Colonel Dr. William Noble, Southern hero of the faith, who had recently been promoted to Glory.

The cadets themselves brought an innovation with their outreach. Cadet Will Cundiff suggested that the cadets go out late at night to witness on Peachtree Strip, an area notorious for drugs and prostitution. The outreach, dubbed *"Night Watch,"* saw cadets volunteer to go and testify through individual contact and midnight open-air meetings. Another victory came in the 1978 Self Denial/World Service effort, when the South brought in over one million dollars for the first time in its history.

In Lafayette, La., Major Sam Crowder laid plans to begin the first battered women's shelter in the South. The problem of battered women had always existed but the women's liberation movement focused attention on this national disgrace. As time went on, the Army's commitment to the needs of the victims of domestic violence would result in a proliferation of shelters across the South, including Charleston, W.Va., and other locations.

After local unhappy problems, it was decided to send Auxiliary Captain and Mrs. John Jones to command Harrisonburg, Va. The picture of practical godliness, the Joneses gently worked among the shocked corps people and community. Even if people didn't like the Army, they had to love this couple. Although their stay was relatively short, the effectiveness of their ministry was proven when the community erected a new corps building for the Army within ten years.

The skills of Commissioner and Mrs. Holz in guiding the South through its trials and its triumphs came on February 16, 1979, when they made history again as the first Southerners to be appointed as National Commander and National President of Women's Organizations. Holz would lead the nation in a centennial celebration of the Army's one hundredth year in the United States. It would be a time of soul-searching and prayerful self-study as the Army looked to the best way to express its sense of mission to reach the challenge of its second century in the United States.

CHAPTER 21

A SENSE OF MISSION

(1979–1982)

AFTER A GENERATION of constant change outside and continued progress inside, The Salvation Army approached with excitement and eagerness this new era.

The South had reversed the 10 year downward trend in Sunday School attendance in 1978 when a 6,000 increase was recorded. Corps Cadet enrollment also increased that year. The Home Leagues and Men's Clubs reported increases each year from 1971 to 1979. Self Denial/World Service giving increased each year during the 1970's, surpassing one million dollars for the first time in 1977. 91 new centers for service had been erected during the five years from 1975 to 1979, continuing the surge to build for practical expression of Salvationism. Larger sessions of cadets for training for Salvation Army officership came during this time. 13,000 first time converts had been won in 1977 alone; with Cartridge giving (members' tithes) increasing each year during the 70's.

To this time came Commissioner and Mrs. Arthur Pitcher as territorial leaders. Raised in the fishing town of St. John's, Newfoundland, the Pitchers not only shared the same home corps but a rich Army heritage. Their appointments had taken them to The Salvation Army schools of Newfoundland, corps work and then to administrative appointments in Canada.

Pitcher came to the Southern Territory following service as chief secretary in South Africa and an appointment as territorial commander of the Caribbean Territory.

Coming to the United States was not easy for Pitcher. The "American" system now installed at territorial headquarters was completely foreign to him, as were the series of annual inspections at the divisional centers across the territory. The Army's vast network of social services and sophisticated means of fund raising and public relations represented challenges not felt as keenly by other territorial leaders as by Pitcher. He listened to his colleagues and kept the momentum going. However, his greatest contribution to the South would not be in these areas.

Possessed of a poetic eloquence, Commissioner Pitcher crisscrossed the South preaching messages that were welcomed as rain in a parched land. He appreciated the heritage of a people living in the "Bible belt", understood instinctively the needs of the Army at this point in its history and, with evident devotion, faithfully proclaimed the Word of the Lord. His gifts, under the guidance of the Holy Spirit, created a quickening of the spiritual tempo in the territory. The text of the message of his welcome service was significant. He spoke on Joshua 15:19, "Give me a blessing; for thou hast given me a south land; give me also springs of water."

Throughout his service in the South, Pitcher was aided by his wife, Betty, who carried on her own ministry though handicapped by a visual impairment which left her nearly blind. The effectiveness of their spiritual influence was reflected in the jump in the number of decisions for Christ from 2,301 in 1979 to 3,437 in 1982.

The Pitchers soon became aware, through a series of disasters, of the extent of Army social services. Tornadoes ripped through northern Texas, causing widespread destruction. Sections of the city of Wichita Falls were decimated. In Jackson, Miss., the Pearl River inundated the city. No sooner had the final reports of the Army's service been penned in these disasters than Hurricane David blew into Florida.

The last winds of David had hardly stilled when Hurricane Frederic smashed into the Gulf Coast of Florida, Alabama and Mississippi. Serving in these disasters, the Army put together over a million meals, dispensed clothing, furniture, food and other emergency needs to tens of thousands of homes, and counseled multiplied hundreds who were shocked by the onslaught of nature.

The Army's emergency service would not be limited to natural disasters. On the foggy night of May 9, 1980, a ship plowed into a piling of the Skyway Bridge in Tampa Bay, knocking out a span. In a matter of seconds, a bus and four cars plummeted from the heights of the bridge into the water below.

As skin divers began their gruesome task of searching for bodies and attempting to get a count of the dead, the Army canteen served the only food and beverages available to the workers. Ten days later, race riots broke out in Miami. Again the Army served in its dual role, helping both the law enforcement officers and those victimized by the disturbance.

Later, the city of Atlanta was terrorized by an unknown killer who preyed primarily upon young black boys. When it became apparent that this was the work of a serial killer, massive searches in the area turned up more bodies of missing children. Army personnel participated in the searches and served the workers. During the crisis, a black corps, Atlanta West End, instituted a "missing-in-action" program. The officer called the names of the children missing from Sunday school, asking the soldiers to contact all of them before the next Sunday. This was not only to serve the Sunday school but to insure that none of the Army's children were among the killer's victims.

At the height of rush hour on a frigid winter day in Washington, an Air Florida jet crashed into a bridge, then into the icy waters of the Potomac. Within thirty minutes Salvation Army emergency teams made their way through the snarled traffic to serve hot food and beverages to the chilled rescue workers. The Army set up a large tent as a refuge from the stinging cold. Major James Hipps coordinated the efforts, using three canteens, fifty officers and staff. At nearby hotels officers were on hand to offer spiritual counsel and comfort to families and friends of the victims.

In April 1980, President Carter announced he would welcome refugees who were now allowed to leave Cuba with Castro's permission. Within two months, over 100,000 had fled to the United States in a massive exodus, dubbed the Mariel Sea Lift. This influx of people completely overwhelmed the resources available in South Florida where the refugees entered. The Army was called on to help.

In Key West, Auxiliary Captain Lawrence Holmes distributed cold drinks and Spanish language Gospel portions, giving out more than 200,000 pieces of literature to the Cubans who landed daily. In Miami, Captain Warren Fulton took charge of a temporary housing facility at the North Miami Armory providing food, clothing and other emergency needs to the displaced people as they awaited travel arrangements.

At Ft. Lauderdale, Major Fred Smith was called on to feed and clothe the arriving refugees. In Ft. Walton Beach, the Army received an urgent request for clothing for 20,000 men housed at Eglin Air Force Base. Long after the initial crisis passed, the Army was involved in serving this new wave of immigrants to America.

Meanwhile, the Army continued its work with Vietnamese refugees. When Ewing Diep was given a choice of places for his family and him to settle, he chose Ft. Walton Beach,

Fla., although he had never heard of it before. Having had considerable wealth while in Vietnam, he now chose this location, recounting, "I was told this was at the ocean—that if I did not have money to buy food I could fish to feed my family." Arriving there, he went to the Army seeking warm clothing for his family.

Diep was already a Christian and had heard that the Army was an evangelistic organization, but was unaware that it was a church. After becoming actively involved in the corps with his family, he soon convinced Captain Ron Smith that a work could be done among the Vietnamese in the area. Together they began holding services for Vietnamese, Smith preaching and Diep, a translator for the military seventeen years, interpreting the message to his people. The fervor of his evangelism was further demonstrated by his distribution of tracts he had written in Vietnamese through Oriental food stores. When he and his family became American citizens in May 1981, he said, "I have a wonderful feeling of belonging."

The ideals of the Men's Social Service ministry were personified in Frank Dyer, a convert at the Adult Rehabilitation Center in Miami. Sentenced by a judge to the Army center, the judge told him, "You have been the most arrested and convicted alcoholic in the city of Miami and no other facility nor treatment center of ours has had any effect on you." Receiving Christ as Savior, Dyer celebrated his tenth anniversary of a new life as a Christian and of victory over alcohol, not as a beneficiary, but as a counselor for other men who shared his affliction.

One hundred years after George Scott Railton and his "magnificent seven" stepped out on the dock at Battery Park in New York, the Army was celebrating its centennial in grand style. The South began the year under the national theme, "Celebration Proclamation", with the Texas Divisional Band marching in the famous Cotton Bowl Parade in Dallas. However, the main focus of this milestone would not be within the bounds of the South but in Kansas City where the first national congress in fifty years was held.

Even after one hundred years of history, the congress would be able to boast a first. It was the first time there had been a national commissioning of cadets, thirty-nine of them from the South. It was also the largest gathering of Salvationists on the North American continent. Of the over 12,000 delegates, 2,500 were from the South. Participation was divided evenly among the four United States territories. The South was represented musically by the National Capital Area Band under the baton of Bandmaster Campbell Robinson.

The excitement of this unprecedented gathering was captured in the thrilling opening pageant under the expert direction of Major and Mrs. Raymond Cooper. But the congress was a celebration that rose above any regional pride. It was a weekend when both the diversity and unity of Army expression found a place.

Among the presentations of the congress was a Council of War where the results of a study by the International Marketing Group of McLean, Va., were revealed. Under the title of "*Second Century Advance*", information was shared with the delegates about both the current perceptions of the Army's strengths and weaknesses, and the challenge of what was to be done with the future. The research included queries to donors, human service recipients, officers, soldiers, advisory board members and the general public.

The research confirmed what most Salvationists already knew—hardly anybody understood what the Army was. Only 11 percent of the public perceived the Army was a religious organization, while at the same time the Army led the way among social service agencies, with 98 percent of the population knowing of its existence. The Army was encouraged to go back to its roots, to firmly and consistently witness to its own religious convictions, and to take advantage of its strengths to let the country know what it was about.

An encouraging showcase of the growing Army was Florida. In 1981 the Florida Division had a congress of its own with over 2,000 delegates. The growth in the state was evidenced when three new corps in Naples, Orange Park and Port Richey were presented their flags. Before another year had rolled around, additional corps would be opened in Plant City and Venice. A further evidence came when General Arnold Brown conducted the enrollment of 108 junior and senior soldiers. The next year would see the Men's Club of Orlando win the first Territorial Men's Club of the Year Award.

Florida Governor Bob Graham gave his recognition to the Army in one of his famed work days. In Orlando, he began his day by serving breakfast to 130 transients, changing bed sheets, and conducting other housekeeping duties. At a meeting of volunteers, he asked to lead them in prayer. Throughout the day, Graham took applications from needy clients and then returned to the transient lodge that night to check in homeless men and feed them supper.

During this time, there were the beginnings of several notable trends. One was signified by a change in name. The Men's Social Service Centers were renamed Adult Rehabilitation Centers to signify a broadening of their ministry to the growing number of alcoholic women. In the South, the number of women participants and the practicality of service to them was extremely limited. The change in name was more to conform to a national move than to signify any significant shift in that direction.

Related to service to alcoholic and homeless men was the rise of the Corps Salvage and Rehabilitation Centers (CSRC). While existing in more or less informal ways prior to this designation, the CSRCs existed in communities too small to

THE SALVATION ARMY

SOUTHERN TERRITORY

Lt. Commissioner and Mrs. William McIntyre, first Southern territorial leaders, 1927–1930, with Lt. Commissioner and Mrs. Albert Cheshar territorial leaders from 1946–1952.

Lt. Commissioner and Mrs. Alexander Damon, territorial leaders, 1930–1935.

Lt. Commissioner and Mrs. Ernest I. Pugmire, territorial leaders, 1935–1939; later, National Commander.

Commissioner and Mrs. William C. Arnold, territorial leaders, 1939–1946.

Lt. Commissioner William Dray, territorial leader, with Mrs. Dray, 1952–1956; later, Chief of the Staff.

Lt. Commissioner William Davidson, territorial leader, with Mrs. Davidson, 1956–1962.

Lt. Commissioner and Mrs. Paul J. Carlson, territorial leaders from 1962 to 1966; later, National Commander.

Commissioner and Mrs. Glenn Ryan,
territorial leaders, 1966–1969.

Commissioner and Mrs. William C. Chamberlain, territorial leaders, 1969–1974; later, National Commander.

Commissioner and Mrs. Ernest W. Holz, Southern trained officers, territorial leaders, 1978–1982; later, National Commandeer.

Commissioner and Mrs. Arthur R. Pitcher, territorial leaders, 1978–1982.

Commissioner and Mrs. Andrew S. Miller, territorial leaders, 1982–1986; National Commander, 1986–1989.

Commissioner and Mrs. James Osborne, Southern trained officers, territorial leader; National Commander, November 1989.

Colonel and Mrs. Kenneth C. Hodder, Chief Secretary and Territorial Home League Secretary, 1989, and territorial leader, November 1989.

support Adult Rehabilitation Centers, but large enough to support more than just a thrift store selling items "as is." With a client load of 10 to 15 men, the CSRCs were the size of the original Industrial Homes. These programs were placed under the same guidelines as the Adult Rehabilitation Centers in required services to the men involved with their programs, as well as other operating standards.

It is possible for CSRC programs to develop a large enough program to become full fledged Adult Rehabilitation Centers, as did the one in Norfolk in 1984. For the present, they are seen as an alternative for medium size communities.

The services to homeless saw a shift of populations from the typical single man to more family units. This distressing development meant that the traditional idea of the homeless had to be redefined. Both women and children are in far more danger if adequate shelter and food cannot be provided. The Army's adapting to these changes included modifying the design of its buildings. Usually laid out in dormitory fashion to serve single men, adequate family facilities are even now often at times severely limited in many communities.

Further demands came on the Army's services not only by changes in the faces of those seeking assistance but in changes in the federal government. With the election of Ronald Reagan as president, there was a mandate to cut the federal budget. Slow-downs in federal social programs resulted in an immediate increase of demands among private agencies, including the Army. At the same time, higher professional standards in programming and fiscal accountability raised the cost of operation.

Changes in Army finance were also clearly in evidence. In the short time between 1978 and 1986 the portion of Army funding from the United Way fell from 30.4 to 19.1 percent. On the other hand, the Army's own fund raising efforts provided an increase for the same period from 20.3 to 29.6 percent. The losses of United Way income were more than compensated by the success of fund raising done in the Army's own name.

By 1981 the computer had entered the American mainstream. No longer the behemoths which occupied entire rooms, the development of the microchip allowed a user to have incredible capacity in a unit hardly larger than a typewriter. As prices plummeted, the computer became feasible for everyday Army operations. Following the headquarters centers, the Adult Rehabilitation Centers were the first field operations to go on computer. Despite misgivings by some personnel, the computer continues to figure more prominently in Army operations.

Multiplied both in number and intricacy, Army programs were run less and less by officers and more by employees. A gradual trend began in the sixties, increasing the ratio of employees to officers. In 1967 there were 2.69 employees for every officer. Twenty years later, the number had skyrocketed to seven employees for each officer. The most dramatic increase started during the administration of Commissioner Pitcher.

While to some it might seem a negative trend, the Army's ministry would be severely hamstrung if not for the employment of competent employees, both professional and otherwise. On the down side, officers have become more removed sometimes from daily contact with many of those in need, as they have had to sharpen their management skills. Whether good or bad, the trend is likely to continue. At the current rate, the ratio of employees to officers will possibly nearly double by the year 2,000, with employees probably outnumbering commissioned officers 13 to 1.

A disturbing trend resulted as a side effect of the collapse of sexual morals in the general public. Teen pregnancy skyrocketed. Venereal disease became epidemic as new strains of old diseases resisted traditional means of treatment. Genital herpes alone, an incurable venereal disease, infected 20 million victims, adding more victims at the rate of 500,000 a year. A frightening new venereal disease, Acquired Immunity Deficiency Syndrome, known as AIDS, made its appearance. First spread through the homosexual community and then into the population as a whole, AIDS has yet no known cure and is fatal. Spread primarily through illicit sexual relations and drug use, the wisdom of God's laws becomes all the more apparent in the face of these developments. The depth of the tragedy is seen as the innocent are swept away as surely as the guilty.

The fear of AIDS has highlighted another trend directly affecting the work of the Army. In the 1960s and 70s, the concept of zoning became popular in the United States. An effort to preserve neighborhoods and control growth, the laws often serve to restrict work among those in need. With the worn cry of "Not In My Back Yard", residents have successfully frustrated efforts to help those in need, including AIDS victims, the homeless, battered women and children, and others. When communities drafted zoning laws, they failed to take into account the needs of the afflicted in their midst, and continue to raise a formidable barrier to any who compassionately reach out to shelter the suffering.

The Army has won some zoning battles, while losing far more. The Army joins other human service providers in its frustrations that so many neighborhoods still fail to make provision of any kind for treatment centers which work best in a community setting. This results in a new form of legalized discrimination by communities which seek to deny both the existence of problems in their area and their obligation to help those in need.

Through these changes, Commissioner Pitcher led his troops, mindful of the trials, but certain of the outcome. In

September 1982, the Pitchers returned to Canada to command the Army forces there. The next leader was a man who never entered a room quietly.

CHAPTER 22

CHARGE!

(1982–1986)

NOT SINCE Commissioner William McIntyre did the South have a territorial leader as colorful as Commissioner Andrew S. Miller. Enthusiastic and outgoing, it was not unusual to see Miller mixing with people in the audience when it was time for a meeting to start. His spontaneity delighted the rank and file, while sending his staff officers scurrying to adjust to the latest unanticipated move. A revealing portrait of his personality comes from an incident that occurred while he was still serving in New York.

One afternoon Miller started home in his car. From the back seat where he had concealed himself, a man put a gun to Miller's head. He told Miller to keep driving, that he intended to steal the car. Miller began talking. "Do you realize how much trouble you can get into if you steal this car? You're a young man. You don't want to ruin your life. Besides, this isn't much of a car anyway. I was just about to take it into the shop because of all the problems I'm having with it. You really don't want this car." After listening for awhile, the thief replied, "Shut up. I'm going to steal this car. Get ready to pull over."

Miller answered, "Well, if you are intent on stealing this car, then I need to have a word of prayer with you." It was enough. Telling Miller to stop at the next corner, the thief got out of the car saying, "Leave it to me to pick one of these nuts."

At his side was his wife, the former Joan Hackworth, every bit the equal of her mobile mate. Her warmth and caring did not hide her own high level of competence and skill. Like many officer wives, she learned, as the occasion demanded, to command the platform or sit in quiet support.

Heading off in full gallop, Miller was quickly challenged by programs initiated by his predecessor, Commissioner Pitcher. The first was the opening of the Office of Media Ministries (OMM). The Army had long wished for the opportunity to share in outreach provided by television, but the costs were prohibitive. That changed with the advent of inexpensive videocassette player/recorders and access to satellite transmission of broadcasts.

The goal of OMM was twofold: to supply the internal needs for teaching resources and permanent video records of Army events; also to provide for external outreach through production of public service announcements and television programming. Lt. Colonel John Mikles, divisional commander for Texas, had both the vision to see what could happen and the grasp of technological developments which made this new venture practical.

On January 29, 1983, Commissioner Miller traveled to Dallas for a dedication service of the first Salvation Army television production center under the direction of Mr. Ian Adnams. Soon after the dedication, each Salvation Army corps and institution was provided its own commercial grade video player.

The provision of these machines proved a mixed blessing. Most everyne was delighted with a means to use new materials provided by OMM. The problem was that the machines played tapes at a different speed than generally in use, making it impossible to use any tapes other than the ones the Army produced. Meanwhile, Christian video tapes were proliferating at a faster rate than OMM could either produce in the new format or secure copyright permission to do so.

At first, the planned monopoly of OMM was protected by not allowing Army units to purchase any other type video players. When it was realized that OMM would still be the major provider of thousands of tapes, that they had distribution of Army tapes, and that Army units were being hurt by their inability to use other materials, the ban was lifted.

The first major accomplishment of OMM came with the release of a Christmas television special entitled *"Blood and Fire."* Documenting the early history and present ministries of the Army, the one hour program was shown on 151 television stations, while being broadcast 206 times. Anticipated results came when viewers called to inquire about the Army's ministries. Another benefit came from increased donations to the Christmas effort. Later, the special was also produced in a thirty minute format.

Miller tackled the execution of another project, whose groundwork had been begun by Commissioner Pitcher, with the launching of the largest financial campaign in the history of The Salvation Army. With a goal of $27.3 million dollars, the campaign sought to strengthen the officers' retirement fund, medical plan, cadets' scholarship fund, and expansion of the School for Officers' Training. Never before had a financial campaign focused on the needs of Army personnel. Assessments received from Army units had paid the costs involved in these programs, but the dramatic increase in health and education costs was placing a heavier burden on already strained budgets.

Convinced the public would respond to the needs of Army officers who were noted for their sacrificial service with nominal remuneration, Miller inaugurated the campaign.

Under the direction of the Community Relations Department led by Major Jack Waters, the effort was aided by veteran capital campaign director, Mr. Jack McDowell. To chair the drive, the Army enlisted the help of Mr. Alex Schoenbaum, chairman of the board of Shoney's Incorporated, an enterprise which included numerous restaurant chains and hotels.

The thrust of the campaign was made through local advisory boards. Each community was asked to commit an amount to the effort, reminding each board that the success of the campaign would not just improve the quality of life for officers, but would ease the burden placed on each community through the assessments which had been the sole source of financing for these programs.

While initially reporting that the campaign had exceeded its goal by almost $3 million dollars, the final amount fell just short of the goal, when one of the key contributors failed to follow through on a verbal commitment. Nonetheless, the campaign allowed the Army to strengthen areas which had become dangerously weak and paid for the much needed expansion of facilities at the School for Officers' Training.

In 1983 a congress was scheduled. Never a small undertaking, the congress under Miller's direction would have some unusual twists, not the least of which was the "*Salvation Fair.*" The fair, held in the exhibition hall of the Atlanta Civic Center, was in part a huge flea market which included an automobile auction to raise money for missionary efforts. Miller's vision was that the fair would attract outsiders who could then be evangelized. Musicians provided evangelistic entertainment, while individuals moved through the vast crowd to do personal witnessing. At the same time, a marathon Bible reading ran throughout the weekend.

For the first time, the Adult Rehabilitation Centers were musically represented in the meetings by a 175 voice "*Chorus of Redeemed Men,*" all recovering alcoholics, smartly outfitted in maroon jackets. They provided inspiration not only by their music but by their testimony. The department would have another first the following year when its first woman administrator, Major Mrs. Lynette McConniel, was placed in charge of an Adult Rehabilitation Center following the sudden death of her husband.

During the meetings, General Jarl Wahlstrom presented Mrs. Ruby Ferraez Laudun with the Order of the Founder, the first soldier in the South to receive this high honor. Her exemplary service in the New Orleans Citadel corps and, as Salvation Army social worker in that community, earned her the title "Mother of the Needy."

Also honored were the heroes of Harrisonburg, Auxiliary Captain and Mrs. John Jones. The General presented them with the Certificate in Recognition of Exceptional Service. These humble servants of the Lord had served valiantly in many cities, despite Mrs. Jones' severe handicap. She had been the victim of a hit-and-run accident involving a drunk driver in 1978. The resulting injury had permanently fused her neck and left her with artificial knees, wrist and hand, confining her to a wheelchair. She and her husband faithfully worked without complaint though the years continued to take away her mobility, as the injuries left her in more debilitating pain.

Brigadier Elmer Capp would also later be recognized as a member of the Order of Exceptional Service because of his evangelistic service among adults and children; especially for his nearly a lifetime of preparing printed material for children's meetings.

At the time of the congress, a new territorial newspaper was introduced entitled, *The Southern Spirit.* Under the expert hand of Mr. Ralph Miller, the newspaper compensated for changes made in *The War Cry* which eliminated regular coverage of much territorial news.

Other strides could be seen in places like Lynchburg, Va., where soldiers visited all the area coin laundries to invite patrons to corps meetings. A more involved outreach was in Ft. Lauderdale, under the command of Captain and Mrs. William Crabson. Following up on programs begun by his predecessor, Major Fred Smith, Crabson used the talents of a dedicated core of young adults. Beginning with a Christian rock group named *Last Adam,* the group operated under the banner of "Front Line Ministries."

They were particularly touched with the plight of prostitutes and endeavored to reach out to them. When the police cracked down on prostitution by sending offenders to a special jail, aptly dubbed "Hooker Hilton," the group followed them there, leading to a ministry in the jails. The group also took a booth at a flea market, selling Christian books and witnessing to those who stopped by to peruse their materials. The efforts of Front Line Ministries culminated in the opening of *"The Home Front,"* an emergency shelter for runaway teenage girls.

Other advances in Florida came through the burgeoning correctional service program. In existence for less than ten years, it had become the largest private probation system in the United States, with 86,500 probationers assigned to it at the end of 1982. The state legislature had passed tougher drunk driving laws in 1981, and the case load swelled to a degree that exceeded the wildest imagination. Mr. Jordan Rothbart, director of the program, had spearheaded the initiation of this Salvation Army service with the guidance of Lt. Colonel Harlan Cleveland, Divisional Commander, and Major Robert Tritton.

The growth of the correctional service program was accompanied by parallel activity in other social service areas. The change in the federal government's funding of social services was continuing to leave more people without the provision of the most basic needs. Long abandoned soup kitchens began to reappear at Army centers across the South as the number of homeless in the United States mushroomed to an estimated 350,000. People across the country turned to the Army to help combat this baffling problem that existed amidst incredible wealth.

It wasn't just the homeless who were suffering. The number of poor people in America had reached astronomical proportions by 1983 when 35,300,000 were living in poverty. To meet this crushing problem the Army added a variety of programs such as the mobile soup kitchen in Nashville. Caring for 75-80 people a night, the canteen served a hot meal, the only food of the day for some of those who awaited the nightly rounds. The Army was aided in its efforts by a growing number of companies which wanted to become involved in helping the needy. Beginning in Mississippi with *Project Concern*, utility companies not only made corporate donations to the Army's work, but allowed customers to participate by including an extra amount when paying their utility bills. In 1985 alone, $2.3 million dollars was given through this means for the Army's relief efforts.

A unique individual effort was initiated by Bob Carver of Vicksburg, Miss. Taking vacation from his job as a research hydraulic engineer, Carver began the "*Santa Express.*" Hauling loads with a semitrailer, he covered 7,800 miles through 25 states in twelve days. He donated $1,672 to the Army for its Christmas program—the entire proceeds of his trip.

Aiding the victims of disaster continued to involve Army resources. Whether tornadoes in the Carolinas, a plane crash in Dallas, or the ravages of Hurricane Juan which wreaked havoc in Virginia and West Virginia, the Army mobilized with incredible efficiency and effectiveness. The biggest challenge at this time came outside the country.

One survivor related, "I heard a tremendous noise. I grabbed my daughter and jumped out the window. I had no chance to help my wife, who was killed when she was buried in the rubble." The killer quake in Mexico City had registered 7.8 on the Richter scale, with an aftershock registering 7.3. It was estimated that 10,000 were killed or trapped. Major David Mikles, from the Community Relations Department at territorial headquarters, was appointed to coordinate Army relief efforts from the United States, which included truckloads of material and mountains of medical supplies.

Headway continued in the Army's spiritual endeavors, beginning with the creation of the Adult Ministries Department under the leadership of Major and Mrs. Paul Kellner. The department further enhanced the evangelistic work of the territorial evangelist and the Army's radio program, *"Wonderful Words of Life,"* now broadcast weekly on over a hundred stations, including several overseas, literally taking the program around the world. But the department's main thrust was to be the growth of existing Army corps and the planting of new ones. As evangelistic as the Army was, it had never had any department specifically assigned to the organization's growth.

Proof of this burgeoning growth could be seen at the commissioning service in 1984, when five new corps openings were presented Salvation Army flags. Two of the corps had a common connection. The Port Richey, Fla., Corps, opened for three years, by 1984 had sent two couples into officership, who in turn opened new corps in Jacksonville, N.C., and Brooksville, Fla. A different twist came in the remaking of an older corps in Miami where the Citadel Corps changed from the traditional white metropolitan corps to a Spanish-speaking corps.

The music forces of the South received a boost from three different corners of the territory. In Dallas, a piano school was operating. In the Georgia Division, a seven week music conservatory gave concentrated instruction to 23 teenage musicians. In the affluent community of Fairfax, Va., the Leidzen Institute for the Performing Arts opened to provide professional and small group instruction to both adults and children.

Old ideas were shattered by what was happening in Norfolk, Va. Generally, Salvationists had resigned themselves to the thought that Army meeting attendances would be small. Noting that the public often failed to perceive the Army corps as a place of worship, and that Army officers were stationed in appointments for seemingly unacceptably brief periods of time, there was a general notion that Army meetings would be poorly attended.

Coming to Norfolk, which already had one of the largest Sunday schools in the South, Captain and Mrs. Dan Delaney were convinced it could be bigger. The attendances continued to climb, surprising the cynical. On October 18, 1985, the corps had its first "Super Sunday." The all-out effort resulted in a record attendance at a Southern Salvation Army Sunday school of 1,218. Succeeding years would result in numbers which passed 2,000 in the annual event. The large number was not just a fluke. The Sunday school on any given Sunday would have in excess of 700 people. The idea that Army attendances in the United States had to be small was thus nullified.

In an impressive ceremony later conducted by the next territorial commander, Commissioner James Osborne, during the Commissioning weekend in June, 1989, YPSM Clara Paige, of the Norfolk, Va. Corps, was honored posthumously with the prestigious Order of the Founder recognizing her compassionate ministry in helping to develop the Sunday School to such a phenomenal point. However, this represented only one aspect of this superb Salvationist's activities.

Even at the time of her critical illness just a few days earlier, Clara's spirit had been radiant and vigorous. She had said, "God has been good to me. I am still in the fight for God and right. It is my determination to continue in this fight as long as God gives me breath . . . fighting as a soldier in The Salvation Army."

In the summer of 1986 the High Council convened to elect the replacement of General Wahlstrom. The mantle of leadership fell on Eva Burrows, who would serve as the Army's second woman international leader.

Soon afterwards, General Burrows would announce the appointment of Commissioner Miller as the next National Commander of The Salvation Army in the United States, following Commissioner Norman Marshall. Marshall had spent teen-age years in Atlanta where his father had been Territorial Youth Secretary and Training Principal.

Commissioner Marshall had become National Commander after the untimely death in office of Commissioner John D. Needham. Needham, raised in the South by officer-parents, was also trained at the Southern School for Officers Training, serving successively in various corps, territorial department, and divisional commander appointments. Outside the South, Commissioner Needham, with his wife Florence at his side, had been territorial commander in the Caribbean Territory, the Central USA Territory, and British Commissioner.

Just before he assumed his new responsibilities, Commissioner Miller traveled to Dallas once again, this time to dedicate the largest Salvation Army social service complex in the world. The Carr P. Collins Social Service Center was financed by a capital campaign that raised $15,645,717—the largest amount ever raised for a Salvation Army building. The 475 bed facility had 134,000 square feet, which included lodging for homeless men, women and families, a domestic violence shelter, a detoxification unit, a halfway house for ex-offenders, and a 20,000 volume library. Separating the men's and women's wings was a chapel, the spiritual and architectural center of the complex.

When the Millers left, the territory was moving at full throttle. The new leader would take a look and then echo the Founder's words, "This and better will do."

CHAPTER 23

VISION TO VICTORY
(1986–1989)

TO READ any contemporary book on leadership would be to gain insight into the personality of Commissioner James Osborne. The second Southerner to command the territory, he brought with him a towering intellect, an ability to discern the significant in people and events, and a total commitment to the Army and its principles. Direct in correspondence, conversation and on the platform, Osborne has known little of wasted words or movement. At his side is his wife, the former Ruth Campbell, daughter of revered Southern officers, Major and Mrs. John Campbell, whose contagious enthusiasm is coupled with a commanding platform presence which will not tolerate lethargy. Building on the momentum of the Millers, the Osbornes clearly envisioned the potential of the Army's place in what they affectionately call the "scintillating South."

The Osbornes found the Army program in the South to be on the upswing. Sunday school attendance, which had been falling steadily from the fifties to the seventies, had turned around and was creeping back up. "*Wonderful Words of Life*" radio program had seen an astounding increase in the number of stations carrying it, from just over 100 two years before to 155 in 1987. The listener response to the program was gratifying, continuing to increase with 37 percent of its correspondence coming from foreign countries.

In new departures, the territory had recently appointed Major John Merritt to become the first archivist. His appointment paved the way for the South to move ahead with a long hoped for museum to be located on the campus of the School for Officers' Training.

A Stewardship Bureau was begun with the appointment of Major Richard Ulyat. Financial support from soldiers and others attending Army services had been embarrassingly low throughout the Army's service in the South. While aiming at turning around this situation, the Stewardship Bureau has designed a program that "is to encompass the broad spectrum of stewardship—time, talent and treasure."

An addition to the territorial headquarters building in 1988 provided a much-needed conference center and enlarged facilities for the Supplies Department which, among other achievements, had become recognized as a leading publisher of Salvation Army books, including holiness classics by Samuel Logan Brengle and others.

The memorial chapel in the conference center was dedicated in full salute to a great leader, Commissioner William A. McIntyre, pioneer Territorial Commander of the Southern Territory from 1927 to 1930.

Soon after Osborne took office the nation was shaken by scandals involving television evangelists. All of these scandals brought division among the saints, scorn from unbelievers, and a shadow on Christian ministries as a whole. The Army faced to some degree the same questions which all ministries confronted. The public wanted to know how it could be sure its money was used properly, that the Army's leaders were as they said they were, that the Army could still be trusted. Fortunately, the Army had both a proven track record and visible display of its charitable activities. Though there was a slight initial loss of income, this was soon overcome as public trust of the Army continued more than ever.

The Army made further adjustments due to changes in the financial climate. Continued decline in oil prices, a boon to the consumer, wreaked havoc with the economy in Texas, Oklahoma and Louisiana. As more people were hurt by the recession, the Army was squeezed by those seeking its help on the one hand and its traditional supporters unable to contribute on the other.

While these and other distractions were going on the Army found its resources strained by increasing needs of the homeless. The nation as a whole became conscious of what the Army had always known—the solution to homelessness was more than a bed and a meal. The problem before had been that, though the Army knew this, it could never fully convince the public of the need. Consequently, it could not get the funding needed to run more effective services for the homeless.

As awareness increased, funds became available through federal, state and private sources. With these, the Army expanded its services to the homeless to include referrals for job placement, medical and mental health assistance and new programs of public assistance.

Army officers were considered resident experts and were appointed to boards trying to address the problem. The Southern Territory already had more homeless shelters than any other region of the country, but now found even more demand for its bed space.

Other needs became more apparent to the public and offered a place for ministry. This was no more clearly seen than in the services to battered women. By the end of 1987, there were eighteen Salvation Army-operated battered women's shelters in the South and another twelve women's shelters which served battered women, as well as a variety of other needs. This network of shelters not only exceeded the number of battered women's shelters offered in the other three United States territories combined, but made the Army the leader in this field in the South. No other organization comes close to having an equal number of battered women's and women's shelters.

Interestingly, the trend to provide these services came without any persuasion from headquarters. Field officers simply responded to the needs of their community by providing services to these sad victims of domestic violence.

The value of the battered women's shelters to the individual communities cannot be overestimated. The Army literally saves the lives of women and children. (Half the beds of any shelter are occupied by the children of the women who come. Many of these also have been abused.) The communities as well have responded with compassion by providing funding, buildings and other support.

The battered women's shelter in Roanoke, Va., had been turned down on two separate occasions when seeking a zoning variance. When a third attempt was made, a crowd of 300 thronged the city council chambers to support the Army's successful bid to obtain the necessary exception. While not filling the void left by the Women's Social Service Centers, this new Army program is unquestionably a valuable service to women in this generation.

Another significant change has been in the Army's outreach to minorities. While, in some circumstances, minorities were targeted, most of the change has come without design. After the Army's many noble, but notably unsuccessful, attempts to reach blacks, it now has its most successful ministry ever among them.

Over one third of the corps in the South have a significant number of blacks attending religious activities. While a few of these are all black corps, the vast majority are corps which have been all white until recently. Nor is this inclusion limited to blacks. Over one tenth of the corps have a significant number of Hispanics, while a handful more have embraced Orientals.

Evidence of the advance of women's rights came in May 1987 with the Supreme Court ruling that Rotary Clubs could not exclude women from their membership. In the wake of this landmark decision, other service clubs joined Rotary in opening their doors to women. Following soon after, Lieutenant Janice Schnell of Petersburg, Va., became the first woman Salvation Army officer to join Kiwanis International.

Like the rest of the country, the Army had to adjust to a culture permeated with drugs. The Adult Rehabilitation Centers found themselves serving an increasing number of men who had not only an alcohol dependency but a drug dependency as well.

Insurance prices soared as crime increased, a direct result of drug users' quest to find money to support their habits. The drug epidemic was graphically illustrated in a Conrail train accident which killed 13 and injured 175 near Baltimore. It was disclosed that two of the train conductors had traces of marijuana in their bodies.

Another manmade tragedy came on November 23, 1987, as Cuban detainees seized control of the Atlanta Federal Penitentiary. Holding 89 hostages for 11 days as they burned down the institution around them, the Cubans were protesting the lack of action related to their status and imminent plans to deport them back to Cuba. The tense standoff continued while distraught family members, law enforcement and media representatives crowded around, waiting for a break in the crisis.

The Army immediately set up its canteens and started to work. Its biggest contribution was the unplanned assignment of Mrs. Captain Martha Mothershed to the relief efforts.

Mothershed, herself a Cuban native, became the center of attention for the families of the detainees. *The War Cry* reported:

> Finding someone from their own homeland who spoke their language, the distraught wives of the Cuban prisoners made her the center of their questions and complaints, everyone talking at once, some screaming obscenities, many weeping, all angry and confused.
>
> Mrs. Captain Mothershed kept her cool, spoke loudly enough to make herself heard over the tumult, firmly enough to get their attention and calmly enough to quiet the clamor. When things were reasonably under control, she began to pray.
>
> Mrs. Captain Mothershed was the rock to which those anxious women clung. She was messenger, interpreter, adviser, disciplinarian, mother, a tower of strength in a storm of doubt and fear.

In late September, 1989 Southern Salvationists responded with speed to the needs of victims of Hurricane Hugo; then supported Western Salvationists serving those affected by the major earthquake in the San Francisco area October 17th.

No one could have been more appreciative than Commissioner Osborne, who insisted that the Army make sure it could live with both the anticipated movements and the unexpected challenges of the present. In addition, Osborne has demonstrated both an appreciation for the past and impatience for the future. Demonstration of this was the launching of a campaign he has called *"From Vision to Victory."*

Not since McIntyre's first five year plan for the territory had the South been challenged to such diverse and definitive goals. Noting that the territory had grown from its original 220 corps to 305, Osborne quickly put it into perspective, stating: ". . . the fact that this numerical increase represents an approximate annual growth rate of 1 percent also compels us to confess that such a level of development is not consistent with the divine, growth-centered intention of the life-giving Head of the Church. Nor does it match the vision of the brave pioneer officers and soldiers who made the Southern Territory possible. And neither does it satisfy the longing for victory for which Southern Salvationists have fought more than 60 years."

Osborne further expounded his conviction that the time was ripe for a major effort, reasoning, "We have the best Salvation Army we have ever had. We are reaching more people with more ministries than at any time in our history."

Although the campaign covers a wide variety of areas for expected growth in the period of 1988–1992, the most dramatic is the challenge to open fifty new corps during that span of time. Focusing the effort primarily in the cities, it was noted that, while half the population of the South lives in the cities, only one-fifth of the corps are there. Dubbed the *"Battle for the Cities,"* the success of this effort would result in making the South the largest territory in the country, fourth largest in the world, behind Great Britain, India Northern and Canada.

The key to this success was outlined by Commissioner Osborne in an address he made at Congress 88, a gathering of evangelicals from around the country:

> An organization succeeds not because it is big or long established, but because there are people in it who live it, sleep it, dream it and build future plans for it.
>
> What will keep us from doing it?
>
> 1. The time lost getting started.
> 2. Being too easily diverted from our major objectives.
> 3. Establishment of goals that are too low, that do not make a difference.
> 4. The continuance of our inferiority complex.
> 5. Being too easily satisfied.
> 6. Getting weary in well doing.

In late summer of 1989 word reached Salvationists across the South that General Eva Burrows has appointed, effective

November 1st., Commissioner and Mrs. Osborne to be the National Commander and the National President, Women's Organizations, respectively.

In related news, it was announced that Commissioner and Mrs. Andrew S. Miller, former Southern territorial leaders and now national leaders, will be entering retirement and moving back to the South at that time.

The new territorial leaders of the Southland will be Colonel and Mrs. Kenneth L. Hodder, present Chief Secretary and Territorial Home League Secretary, promoted to the rank of commissioner also as of November 1st.

With the close working relationship of the Hodders and the Osbornes, it is expected that the goal-setting and goal-reaching comprehensive campaign that has brought the Army growth will continue at an ever-quickening tempo; as well as *"The Battle for the Big Cities"* in updating Army facilities and strengthening the Army's balanced ministry in the South's major inner-city areas; also the vital *"Impact On The Future"* campaign to expand the School For Officers' Training and to establish an endowment fund for the training of S.A. officers.

At the time of this writing, the Southern Territory is in the second year of the "Vision to Victory" campaign. Whether the territory accomplishes all goals outlined will be the subject for another historian. The question is whether this vision can be shared by those who live far from the board rooms and offices where Army policies are made.

Can it be translated to the single mother existing on food stamps or the elderly man who can barely maintain his independence? Can it find a way into the heart of the officer who knows he will not command the gleaming citadels in other cities or to the one who knows she must teach and reteach again the most basic lessons? Can a vision of this magnitude touch the heart of a teen and beckon him or her from the gloss of a magazine's definition of success? Can the Army make its voice heard above the din, or will it be a whisper amid the uproar?

When the battle began in London, to be then carried to America and the dusty streets of an indifferent South, the warriors of the past sometimes fell in defeat. But they tasted victory often enough to sense that the fight for God and man was worth the sacrifice.

Today, as then, in each loyal Salvationist's life again and again there comes the time when leaving the Army would make little sense but staying at the post does, when being accepted is much less important than being distinctive, when there is more to give than to be taken away.

We are reminded once again of Commissioner Osborne's vision for The Salvation Army both in the South, in the country, and around the world:

> I want a Salvation Army that stands commandingly tall in the world, not because of the excellent edifices it constructs or the significant sums of money it receives, but because it follows the servanthood example of our Lord, our founder and our forebears.
>
> I want a Salvation Army whose light will so perpetually shine that it will illumine the pathway of millions who seek to rise from being sinners to become sinners saved by grace.
>
> I want a Salvation Army that remains constant to its ideals and purposes, resolute in honoring its commitments, and true to its responsibility to provide daring evangelical leadership.
>
> I want a Salvation Army whose officers and soldiers clearly understand the true meaning of our majestic balanced ministry to the whole person.
>
> I want a Salvation Army of today and tomorrow that recognizes and appreciates its rich heritage, that values its unique opportunities, and fears no foe.
>
> I want a Salvation Army whose people are more concerned about service than security, better at accepting responsibility than rewards, and more involved in the ministry than the mechanics.

> I want a Salvation Army that is constantly loyal to its principles, faithful to God, and is courageously aggressive in making a good Salvation Army a better Salvation Army tomorrow.
>
> I want a Salvation Army that becomes a spiritual juggernaut and massive evangelistic force. I want that not just to be our aim but our magnificent obsession and, I pray, our brilliant achievement.

It is an absolute certainty that this mission will never get any easier nor will conquest from the initial vision to glorious victory come without cost. The Army's future will be triumphantly answered by each succeeding generation of Salvationists in the scintillating South, in quiet moments before the God who has raised up this peculiar and rare movement called The Salvation Army.

So we close this brief and far from all-encompassing history of Salvationists in the Southern Territory USA with the song of George Scott Railton again in our hearts and upon our lips:

> We are sweeping through the land,
> With the sword of God in hand,
> We are watching and we're praying while we fight;
> On wings of love we'll fly
> To the souls about to die,
> And we'll lead them to behold the precious light.

APPENDIX A

TERRITORIAL COMMANDERS OF THE SOUTHERN TERRITORY

1927	**Lt. Commissioner William McIntyre**
1930	**Lt. Commissioner Alexander Damon**
1935	**Lt. Commissioner Ernest I. Pugmire**
1939	**Lt. Commissioner William Arnold**
1946	**Lt. Commissioner Alfred E. Chesham**
1952	**Lt. Commissioner William Dray**
1956	**Lt. Commissioner William Davidson**
1962	**Lt. Commissioner Paul Carlson**
1966	**Lt. Commissioner Glenn Ryan**
1969	**Lt. Commissioner William Chamberlain**
1974	**Commissioner Ernest W. Holz**
1978	**Commissioner Arthur R. Pitcher**
1982	**Commissioner Andrew S. Miller**
1986	**Commissioner James Osborne** (National Commander designate—Nov. 1989)
	Colonel Kenneth L. Hodder (Territorial Commander designate—Nov. 1989, with rank of Commissioner)

CHIEF SECRETARY

1927 Colonel Alfred Chandler
1930 Lt.-Colonel A. E. Marpurg
1931 Colonel Arthur E. Smeeton
1935 Colonel Albert E. Norris
1936 Colonel Richard F. Stretton
1942 Colonel Edmund Hoffman
1948 Colonel P. L. DeBevoise
1952 Colonel Alfred G. Gilliard
1954 Colonel A. E. Ramsdale
1957 Colonel William Davidson
1957 Colonel George H. Marshall
1961 Colonel James Longino
1972 Colonel W. R. H. Goodier
1974 Colonel Orval A. Taylor
1978 Colonel John W. Paton
1982 Colonel Stanley E. Ditmer
1985 Colonel Bramwell H. Tillsley
1989 Colonel Kenneth L. Hodder
1989 Lt.-Colonel Harold D. Hinson (designate—Nov. 1, with rank of Colonel)

ASSISTANT CHIEF SECRETARY

1989 Lt.-Colonel John Mikles

ASSISTANT TO THE CHIEF SECRETARY

1983-86 Lt.-Colonel John Jordan

FIELD SECRETARY

1927 Colonel W. George Peacock
1928 Colonel Henry D. Bale
1930 Colonel A. E. Marpurg (C.S. and Field)
1930 Major J. Arthur Fynn
1933 Adjutant Sidney E. Cox Responsibility for Field under Chief Secretary
1941 Lt.-Colonel George H. Marshall
1947 Colonel P. L. DeBevoise
1948 Lt.-Colonel Charles Dodd
1950 Lt.-Colonel Robert Rose
1955 Lt.-Colonel G. A. Stephan
1961 Lt.-Colonel Ernest Pickering
1968 Colonel Carl Cone
1970 Colonel Paul Thronburg

SECRETARY FOR PERSONNEL

1973 Lt.-Colonel C. William Jaynes

FIELD SECRETARY FOR PERSONNEL

1974 Colonel Charles Talmadge
1976 Lt.-Colonel George Marshall
1981 Lt.-Colonel Harlan Cleveland
1983 Lt.-Colonel Rodolph Lanier

DIRECTOR OF OFFICER DEVELOPMENT

1989 Lt.-Colonel W. Edward Laity

STAFF SECRETARY

1960 Brigadier Carl Cone
1968 Brigadier Ernest Holz
1970 Brigadier W. R. H. Goodier
1971-73 Colonel Gordon Swyers

SECRETARY FOR BUSINESS

1973 Colonel Gordon Swyers
1974 Lt.-Colonel Floyd Hooper
1979 Lt.-Colonel Edward J. Johnson
1989 Lt.-Colonel Wesley Faulkner

FIELD SECRETARY FOR PROGRAM

1973 Colonel Paul Thronburg
1974 Lt.-Colonel C. William Jaynes

PROGRAM SECRETARY

1976 Brigadier Rodolph Lanier
1983 Lt.-Colonel Harold D. Hinson
1986 Lt.-Colonel Orville Salmon

MEN'S SOCIAL SERVICE SECRETARY

1927 Lt.-Colonel A. Baillie
1929 Ensign A. Baldwin
1935 Major W. H. Range
1938 Adjutant A. Baldwin
1946 Major Gilbert S. Decker
1953 Lt.-Colonel L. Turrel
1960 Brigadier William DeVoto
1967 Lt.-Colonel Warren Johnson
1979 Major David Mulbarger

WOMEN'S SOCIAL SERVICE SECRETARY

1927 Lt.-Colonel Martha Hamon
1929 Colonel Mary Stillwell Cox
1930 Brigadier Emma Dale Webb
1933 Brigadier Florence Wykes
1944 Brigadier May Wilmer
1955 Brigadier Margaret Wilkins
1963 Major Beatrice Combs (Closed as a separate dept.—1977)

ALABAMA, LOUISIANA, MISSISSIPPI

Gulf
1926 Staff-Captain J. Arthur Fynn
1930 Staff-Captain W. Herbert Bartlett (G.S.)
1930 Brigadier Harry H. Bayes

Combined with Alabama—1934
Louisiana and Southern Arkansas—1937
1935 Major W. Herbert Bartlett
(added Mississippi)—1939

Gulf—1939
1941 Major Willard S. Evans
1947 Brigadier Herbert W. Young
1950 Major William T. Powell
1953 Brigadier W. Kenneth Howarth
1955 S/Major Paul Thronburg

Arkansas and Louisiana
1957 Brigadier Harry Ward

Combined with A.L.M. or Ok.-Ark.—1966

Dixie
1926 Major Thomas Seaver

Alabama and Mississippi—1928
1928 Major C. J. Hickey
1928 Staff-Captain Geo. Rose
1935 Brigadier A. Baynton

Alabama, Mississippi and West Georgia—1935
1938 Brigadier James Asher

Dixie—1938
1941 Major Ray Gearing
1944 Major Gustav A. Stephan
1946 Lt.-Colonel George Rose
1947 Lt.-Colonel John Morrison

Dixie (without Atlanta)—1948
1948 Lt.-Colonel Verner J. Huffman
1950 Brigadier Willard S. Evans

Alabama and Mississippi—1957
1961 Brigadier Frank Longino
1968 Brigadier Leslie Hall

Alabama, Louisiana, Mississippi—1969
1976 Lt.-Colonel Harlan M. Cleveland
1978 Major John Mikles
1981 Lt.-Colonel Orville Salmon
1986 Lt.-Colonel W. Edward Laity

1989 Lt.-Colonel Jack Waters
1989 Lt.-Colonel David Holz

FLORIDA

Florida
1925 Major Donald McMillan

Florida and Georgia—1928
•1931 Brigadier Alfred Tyler
1935 Major Ernest Higgins

Florida and South Atlantic—1936
1936 Lt.-Colonel Harry Bayes

South Atlantic—1937
1940 Brigadier C. J. Hickey
1944 Major Ernest Pickering
1950 Lt.-Colonel H. W. Young

Florida—1950
1958 Lt.-Colonel Harold Stout
1966 Brigadier Ernest Holz
1968 Lt.-Colonel William T. Pyke
1973 Lt.-Colonel Harlan Cleveland
1976 Lt.-Colonel C. William Jaynes
1978 Lt.-Colonel James Osborne
1980 Lt.-Colonel Maro Smith
1985 Lt.-Colonel Harold D. Hinson
Lt.-Colonel John Busby (Divisional Commander designate—Nov. 1989)

GEORGIA

Georgia and South Carolina
1925 Major Bertram Rodda
1927 Adjutant J. Rivers Lebby

Georgia—1928
Georgia combined with Florida—1929—also see Dixie, Training College Command

Georgia—1957
1957 S/Major Paul Thronburg
1960 Major John D. Needham
1966 Major George Marshall
1970 Lt.-Colonel Guy Hepler
1973 Major Ralph I. Miller
1976 Major Harold D. Hinson
1983 Major Jack T. Waters
1989 Major Warren Fulton

Training College Command
1930 Brigadier Norman Marshall
1935 Brigadier Ernest R. Holz
1938 Major Sidney E. Cox

Atlanta
1948 Major Kenneth Howarth
1953 S/Major William T. Powell

KENTUCKY AND TENNESSEE

Kentucky and Tennessee
1927 Major Alfred Tyler
1931 Major David Boyd

Kentucky, Tennessee, and Arkansas—1933
1933 Brigadier Harry H. Bayes
1937 Major Wesley W. Bouterse
1942 Major Herbert W. Young
1947 Brigadier Willard S. Evans
1950 Brigadier Ernest Pickering
1955 Lt.-Colonel Edward Laity

Kentucky and Tennessee—1957
1960 Major Walter Swyers
1966 Lt.-Colonel Harold Stout
1971 Lt.-Colonel C. Wm. Jaynes
1972 Brigadier Rodolph Lanier
1973 Major John Mikles
1978 Major David Holz
1981 Major J. B. Matthews
1988 Major David Mikles

MARYLAND AND WEST VIRGINIA

Chesapeake
1923 Brigadier Fred Seiler
1929 Major George Rose

1933 Major George H. Marshall

Maryland and Northern West Virginia—1933

1941 Major Charles H. Dodd
1946 Lt.-Colonel Robert Rose
1950 Lt.-Colonel Verner J. Huffman
1958 Brigadier Carl Cone
1960 Brigadier Paul Thronburg
1966 Brigadier Walter Swyers
1971 Brigadier James Osborne
1973 Lt.-Colonel Wm. T. Pyke
1973 Major Wallace C. Conrath
1978 Major Edward J. Johnson
1979 Major W. Edward Laity

Maryland and West Virginia Division—1983

1985 Major Raymond Cooper
1989 Major Philip Swyers

West Virginia

1923 Brigadier David Main
1927 Lt. Colonel A. E. Kimball (Ret.) (Pro Tem)
1929 Staff-Captain David Boyd
1931 Major Joel M. Chamberlain
1933 Major Robert Rose

Combined with Virginia or Maryland—1934

NATIONAL CAPITAL AND VIRGINIA

Potomac Division

1926 Staff Captain Ernest R. Holz
1929 Staff Captain James Asher
1938 Major Charles Dodd

Virginia Division

1931 Lt.-Colonel F. W. Seiler

Virginia and Southern West Virginia—1933

1938 Lt.-Colonel Albert E. Baynton
1941 Major Robert Rose
1944 Brigadier Richard B. Fitton
1952 Lt.-Colonel Charles H. Dodd
1955 Lt.-Colonel Ernest Pickering
1958 Lt.-Colonel Wesley Bouterse
1962 Brigadier Guy Hepler
1966 Brigadier John D. Needham

National Capital Division—1939

1941 Brigadier James Longino
1946 Lt.-Colonel Wesley Bouterse
1951 Lt.-Colonel William Range
1959 S/Major B. Gordon Swyers
1961 Brigadier Ernest Holz
1966 Brigadier W. R. H. Goodier
1968 Lt.-Colonel William T. Powell

National Capital and Virginia—1971

1971 Lt.-Colonel John D. Needham
1973 Brigadier James Osborne
1978 Lt.-Colonel Maro Smith
1980 Lt.-Colonel Fred Ruth
1986 Lt.-Colonel Gordon Swyers
1989 Lt.-Colonel Jack Waters

NORTH AND SOUTH CAROLINA

North Carolina

1925 Brigadier Arthur Hopkins (continued as N.C—Div. Comm. 1927)

(at start of territory all of South Carolina with Georgia)

D.C., South Carolina:

1927 Staff-Captain W. E. Hickman

North and South Carolina—1929

1929 Lt.-Colonel Fred Seiler
1929 Staff-Captain William Gilks

The Carolinas—1935
1935 Lt.-Colonel Alfred Tyler
1942 Brigadier Wesley Bouterse
1946 Brigadier G. A. Stephan

Carolinas (All N.C.; part S.C.—1947)
1955 Lt.-Colonel Robert Rose

North and South Carolina—1957
1959 Lt.-Colonel William Range
1966 Lt.-Colonel B. Gordon Swyers
1971 Lt.-Colonel W. R. H. Goodier
1972 Lt.-Colonel C. William Jaynes
1973 Lt.-Colonel George Marshall
1976 Lt.-Colonel Orville Salmon
1981 Major David Holz
1989 Lt.-Colonel Raymond Cooper

OKLAHOMA AND ARKANSAS

Oklahoma
1921 Staff-Captain W. B. Sowers
1923 Major L. C. Bennett
1929 Staff-Captain Ernest Holz
1935 Brigadier Albert Baynton
1935 Brigadier C. J. Hickey
1940 Brigadier George Rose
1946 Brigadier Edward Laity
1953 Lt.-Colonel Wesley Bouterse
1958 S/Major Guy Hepler
1962 Major George H. Marshall

Oklahoma and Arkansas
1966 Lt.-Colonel C. William Jaynes
1971 Lt.-Colonel Harlan M. Cleveland
1974 Major Orville Salmon
1976 Brigadier Howard Whitehead
1976 Major John Jordan
1983 Major B. Gordon Swyers
1986 Lt.-Colonel John Busby
Major Harold Anderson (Divisional Commander designate—Nov. 1989)

TEXAS

Southwestern
1924 Lt.-Colonel Edwy White

Texas—1928
1928 Lt.-Colonel David Main
1935 Lt.-Colonel William Gilks
1944 Brigadier Ray Gearing
1946 Brigadier Charles H. Dodd
1948 Lt.-Colonel John A. Morrison
1958 Lt.-Colonel Ernest Pickering
1961 Brigadier B. Gordon Swyers
1966 Lt.-Colonel Paul Thronburg
1970 Lt.-Colonel Gordon Foubister
1973 Lt.-Colonel Guy Hepler
1978 Lt.-Colonel Harlan M. Cleveland
1981 Major John Mikles
1989 Lt.-Colonel B. Gordon Swyers

MEXICO

1946 Brigadier Ray Gearing
1954 S/Major Reginald E. Clevett
1966 Brigadier Harlan M. Cleveland
1971 Brigadier Howard Whitehead

Mexico became Mexico and Central American Territory—1976

APPENDIX B

SESSIONS OF OFFICER TRAINING AND TRAINING PRINCIPALS

Name of Session	**Date**	**No. Commissioned**
Lt.-Colonel Harry Bayes	1927	
Invincible Crusaders	1927	43
Torchbearers	1928	56
Centennial	1929	46
Trailblazers	1930	55
Brigadier Norman Marshall	1930	
Climbers	1931	52
Fight It Through	1932	42
(No session due to the economic depression)	1933	
Do and Dare	1934	40
Brigadier Ernest R. Holz	1935	
Challenge	1935	35
The World for God	1936	51
Guardians of the Covenant	1937	52
Brigadier Sidney E. Cox	1938	
Enthusiasts	1938	60
Dauntless Evangelists	1939	49
Hold Fast	1940	67
Crusaders	1941	54
Steadfast	1942	75

Name of Session	Date	No. Commissioned
Lt.-Colonel Alfred Tyler	1942	
Valiant	1943	62
Liberty	1944	59
Fearless	1945	47
Challengers	1946	39
Brigadier Richard B. Fitton	1946	
Warriors	1947	65
King's Messengers	1948	43
S./Major Wesley Rich	1949	
Peacemakers	1949	58
Standard Bearers	1950	42
Ambassadors	1951	51
Intercessors	1952	53
Heralds	1953	46
S./Major William T. Powell	1953	
Shepherds	1954	45
Soul Winners	1955	37
Sword Bearers	1956	37
Faithful	1957	48
Courageous	1958	42
Pioneers	1959	40
Great Hearts	1960	40
(First Two Year Session)		
Soldiers of Christ	1962	45
Servants of Christ	1963	53
Heroes of the Faith	1964	47
Lt.-Colonel Charles Talmadge	1964	
Proclaimers of the Faith	1965	47
Defenders of the Faith	1966	40
Witnesses to the Faith	1967	69
Messengers of the Faith	1968	68
The Evangelists	1969	57
Undaunted	1970	39
Brigadier George Marshall	1970	
Victorious	1971	35
Lightbringers	1972	49
Blood and Fire	1973	50
Major W. Edward Laity	1973	
Followers of Christ	1974	39
Soldiers of the Cross	1975	43
Overcomers	1976	38

Name of Session	Date	No. Commissioned
Major Fred L. Ruth	1976	
Companions of Christ	1977	32
Disciples of Jesus	1978	37
Joyful Evangelists	1979	31
Proclaimers of Salvation	1980	39
Major Raymond Cooper	1980	
God's Soldiers	1981	41
God's Messengers	1982	41
Heralds of Hope	1983	54
Servants of God	1984	54
Guardians of the Truth	1985	44
Major Philip D. Needham	1985	
Proclaimers of the Gospel	1986	31
Messengers of Peace	1987	43
Messengers of Joy	1988	45
Ambassadors for Christ	1989	36
Witnesses for Jesus*	1990	52
Servants of Jesus*	1991	40

*PRESENTLY ENROLLED

Number commissioned, in some instances, includes spouses reaccepted. In addition, officers were commissioned following training in the Mexico Division.

The author expresses appreciation to Captain Jeanne Miller of the Officers' Record Section of the Field Department, Lt. Colonel Houston Ellis (R), and Brigadier Mrs. Eileen Purdum (R) for assistance with the appendices.

APPENDIX C

SOUTHERN RECIPIENTS OF SALVATION ARMY HONORS

THE ORDER OF DISTINGUISHED AUXILIARY SERVICE

(Non-Salvationists who have rendered distinguished service to The Salvation Army; the recommendations having been considered and approved by the Chapter of the Order, consisting of the Chief of the Staff, the Senior Commissioner at International Headquarters, and the International Secretaries, who have made their proposals to the General, with whom alone rests the authority to admit an individual to the Order.)

Mr. Preston S. Arkwright	Atlanta, Ga.	1944
Judge Richard A. Billups	Oklahoma City, Okla.	1944
Colonel Frank B. Shutts	Miami, Fla.	1944
General Charles P. Summerall	Charleston, S.C.	1944
Governor Thomas L. Bailey	Jackson, Miss.	1945
Mr. Wm. E. Mitchell	Atlanta, Ga.	1954
Judge C. Compton	Dallas, Texas	1959
Mr. Harry Wright	Mexico City, Mexico	1959
Mr. Oliver R. Rowe	Charlotte, N.C.	1959
Mr. & Mrs. Carl I. Wilson	Miami, Fla.	1964
Mrs. Harold H. Burton	Washington, D.C.	1965
Dr. F. J. Huegel	Mexico City, Mexico	1966

Dr. C. E. Gaines	Birmingham, Ala.	1967
Colonel Harland Sanders	Louisville, Ky.	1977
Mr. Graham Miller	Miami, Fla.	1978
Mr. Jack McDowell	Jacksonville, Fla.	1981
Mr. Donald Peacock	San Antonio, Texas	1982
Mrs. Ruth Sharp	Dallas, Texas	1986
Mr. Tommy Thomas	Panama City, Fla.	1987
Mr. Richard Rathgeber	Austin, Texas	1987
Mr. Charles Towers, Jr.	Jacksonville, Fla.	1988

THE ORDER OF EXCEPTIONAL SERVICE

Brigadier Elmer Capp
A./Captain John Jones
Mrs. A./Captain John (Miriam Hoggard) Jones
Hubert Phillips

THE ORDER OF THE FOUNDER

Major Cecil Brown
Brigadier Julius Satterfield
Colonel (Dr.) William Noble
Mrs. Ruby Ferraez Laudun
Mrs. Brigadier Keitha Holz
Y.P.S.M. Clara Paige

APPENDIX D

SALVATION ARMY OPERATIONS IN THE SOUTH

The following information on corps and social institution openings and closings has been compiled primarily through information supplied in the *Disposition of Forces*. At times this information is incomplete or lacks a precise date. Where this source has not been helpful, *War Cry* reports are used or help supplied through The Salvation Army National Archives and Research Center. Some of the towns listed below have ceased to exist or have been incorporated into larger areas.

The longest continually opened corps in the South is Petersburg, Va., which opened in October, 1887. The first corps opened in the South was Baltimore (South), Md., later closed for a time. Baltimore claims the first Adult Rehabilitation Center, opened originally in 1900 as an Industrial Home, and is also the longest continually opened social service institution in the South. The Maternity Home in Birmingham, opened in 1905 was the first institution of its kind opened in the South.

The initials MSA mean that there was a corps in that city operated by the Moore Salvation Army. The initials HSA mean that there was a corps operated by the Holz American Salvation Army prior to the reunification of his forces with The Salvation Army.

Early Army leaders considered record keeping to be important, with meticulous detail. Yet corps were opened and closed in some places with official records having been lost over the years. Some of the earlier dates are approximate based on reports in *The War Cry* or other sources. Closing dates are particularly difficult to ascertain.

Abilene, Tex. 2/08–4/17; 9/17
Acapulco, Mexico 9/53–Transferred to Mexico-Central American Territory in 1976
Ada, Okla. 7/03–12/04; 2/38
Aiken, S.C. 1/27
Albany, Ga. 2/19
Alexandria, La. 4/07–5/07; 10/21
Alexandria, Va. 1885–closed same year; 7/88–9/88; 1/89–5/89; 2/98–12/00; 7/02–11/02; 6/15
Alexandria, Va. #2 (Colored) 1885–closed same year
Alexandria, Va. (Korean) 3/1986
Altus, Okla. 2/29
Alva, Okla. 10/01–10/05
Alvarado, Mexico 3/50 Transferred to Mexico-Central American Territory in 1976
Amarillo, Tex. 12/03–11/09; 1/20–5/25; 3/27
Americus, Ga. 7/6/19–12/23
Anadarko, Okla. 7/29–10/30
Anderson, S.C. 2/10
Annapolis, Md. 1885–7/92; 1/93–1/96; 8/21–4/22; 8/24–10/24; 5/25
Annapolis, Md. #2 (Colored) 1885–closed same year
Anniston, Ala. (MSA 5/88) 6/02
Appalachia, Va. 7/29–10/30
Appalachicola, Fla. 3/14–10/15
Ardmore, Okla. 1/05–4/09; 2/20
Arlington, Tex. 6/85
Arlington, Va. 6/53
Asheboro, N.C. 9/71
Asheville, N.C. 11/1890–3/93; 10/05
Ashland, Ky. (MSA 2/1886) 4/09
Athens, Ga. (MSA 5/1887) 3/16
Atlanta, Ga. #1 (Temple) (MSA) 2/1887–1/91) 11/90
Atlanta, Ga. #2 4/1895–1/96; 3/30–3/31
Atlanta, Ga. #3 (Fulton) 11/27
Atlanta, Ga. #4 (Bellwood) 3/28–11/72; reopened 1987
Atlanta, Ga. (Clark-Howell) 9/54
Atlanta, Ga. (Lakewood) 6/35
Atlanta, Ga. (Peachcrest) 6/1983
Atlanta, Ga. (West End) 9/70
Atlanta Evangeline Residence 10/49–11/51
Atlanta, Ga. Industrial Home 1/09; now ARC
Augusta, Ga. (MSA 3/1887) 5/91–7/92; 9/00–5/01; 3/07
Austin, Tex. 2/1889
Bainbridge, Ga. 11/53–11/58
Baltimore #1 (South), Md. (MSA 10/1884–9/89) 5/1881–8/1896; 2/98

There were two corps in Baltimore at the time of the Moore split. Nothing is known about the second corps, but it is believed it might have been a colored corps. Both corps became attached to Moore's Salvation Army of America. Only 5 persons, all soldiers, remained with the international Army. A Sister Yaegge and 4 other soldiers secured a church building in West Baltimore and continued SA work. Captain Wray, the divisional officer, came from Philadelphia to help them get organized. Mrs. Yaegge was made an acting captain and was in charge of the corps for two months until officers could be sent to take command.

There is no record of the second corps which finally closed during the Moore split.

Baltimore #2, Md. 5/89–5/1892; 1/93–1/99; re-opened 7/1902 as colored corps, closed same year.
Baltimore #3 (East), Md. 1/1891–1/94; 4/03–11/06; 4/09–1945 when it merged with #5 (Highlandtown) and became the Patterson Park Corps, keeping its number and history.
Baltimore #4 (Temple), Md. 4/1892–9/93; 2/94–1901; 3/21
Baltimore #5 (Highlandtown), Md. 5/1892–10/93; 1921-1945 (Merged with #3 (East Baltimore) and became Patterson Park.
Baltimore #6 (Hampden), Md. 9/1892–1/99; 1903 re-opened as #2 Corps.
Baltimore #6 (Colored), Md. 10/21–10/22; re-opened then closed 1930
Baltimore #6 (Washington Blvd.), Md. 11/27–3/31
Baltimore Slum Post, Md. 3/01–6/19
Baltimore Salvage, Md. 7/00 Became Industrial Home 11/01–04. Now ARC
Baltimore Popular Hotel and Beacon Light Hotel, Md. 1902–04. Industrial Home, and 2 hotels destroyed in Baltimore fire
Baltimore Slum Nursery, Md. 1/08 Now Day Nursery
Baltimore Home for Destitute Women, Md. 1910–?
Baltimore Emergency Home for Women, Md. 12/30
Baltimore Men's Lodge, Md. 1931–
Baltimore Red Shield Boys' Club, Md. 1936
Bartlesville, Okla. 4/07–2/17; 5/21
Barton, Md. 1888–2/1890; 5/91–6/92
Baton Rouge, La. 5/05–4/10; 10/19
Beattyville, Ky. 12/04–1/06
Beaufort, S.C. 8/1890–3/93; 6/73
Beaumont, Tex. 2/01
Beaumont, Tex. Citadel Hotel 10/02–5/09
Beckley, W. Va. 1/69
Bessemer, Ala. 7/03–8/22; 3/29
Big Spring, Tex. 3/30–33; 11/36
Biloxi, Miss. 2/1971
Birmingham, Ala. #1 (Citadel) (MSA 9/1889–10/90) 12/1899
Birmingham, Ala. #2 (Ensley) 7/24
Birmingham, Ala. Industrial Home 4/08; now ARC
Birmingham, Ala. Rescue Home 11/04; now Maternity Home
Blackwell, Okla. 10/24–10/24; 6/26–3/31
Bladensburg, Md. (Prince Georges) originally Washington D.C. # 5 Moved to Colmar Manor, Md.
Bladensburg 11/63 then Hyattsville, Md. 11/68
Bluefield, W. Va. 1/11–4/20; 8/21
Bogalusa, La. 4/47–11/63
Borderland, W. Va. 7/20–8/21
Borger, Tex. 6/54
Bowling Green, Ky. 1/01–1/04; 3/21–2/29; 9/39
Bradenton, Fla. 6/23
Breckenridge, Tex. 4/01–5/32
Brenham, Tex. 2/1890–1/91
Bristol, Tenn. (MSA 3/1888–9/89) 4/97
Bristow, Okla. 8/23–11/58
Brooksville, Fla. 11/1984
Brownwood, Tex. 5/00–1/11; 10/21–10/23

Brunswick, Ga. 5/00–11/00; 12/10–1/24–; 3/27
Burkburnett, Tex. 3/21–8/24; 3/27–4/33
Burlington, N.C. 6/27
Bush Run, W. Va. MSA 1/1886–12/86
Catlettsburg, Ky. MSA 3/1886–7/86
Cambridge, Md. 4/13
Camden, Ark. 8/23–3/28
Canadian, Tex. 12/21–8/24
Carlos A. Carillo, Mexico 11/50–11/54
Charleston, S.C. #1 (MSA 9/1887–1/88) 1/06
Charleston, S.C. #2 (Colored) 6/13–1/23
North Charleston, S.C. (Ferndale Outpost) 5/75–11/81
Charleston, S.C. Industrial Home 8/22–11/33; turned over to corps 11/33; closed 1/37
Charleston, W.Va. #1 (Citadel) (MSA 3/1886–6/87) 12/04
Charleston, W. Va. #2 (Oakland) 2/22
Charlotte, N.C. (Temple) (3/1887–9/88) 2/04
Charlotte, N.C. (Belmont) 10/37 Service Center 9/81
Charlotte, N.C. (City Command) 1/49, changed to Area Command 10/86
Charlotte, N.C. (North) 6/40–5/48
Charlotte, Men's Social (ARC) 3/50
Charlottesville, Va. 2/12–8/19; 10/20
Chattanooga, Tenn. #1 (Citadel) (12/1886–6/89) 4/93
Chattanooga, Tenn. #2 11/27–2/29
Chattanooga, Tenn. #2 (Alton Park) 7/48 later changed to East Lake
Chattanooga, Tenn. Industrial Home 4/09–9/18
Chickasha, Okla. 7/29
Chihuahua, Mexico 7/57 transferred to Mexico-Central America Territory in 1976
Childress, Tex. 8/23–5/25; 3/27–3/31
Ciudad Juarez, Mexico 7/57 transferred to Mexico-Central America Territory in 1976
Clarksburg, W. Va. (MSA 9/1887–12/88) 8/03
Clarksville, Tenn. 4/09–2/11; 12/21–8/25; 7/89
Clayton Co., Ga. 1/1985–6/86
Clearwater, Fla. 3/26
Cleburne, Tex. 1/1896–7/98; 3/09–2/17
Cleveland, Tenn. 12/1988
Clifton Forge, Va. 12/12–12/14; 8/21–4/22; 11/31–1/37
Clinton, Okla. 11/31–4/69
Coalgate, Okla. 12/1902–1/04
Coatzacoalcos, Mexico 2/59 transferred to Mexico-Central America Territory, in 1976
Cocoa, Fla. 8/58
Colmar Manor, Md. See Bladensburg
Columbia, S.C. (MSA 3/1887–12/87) 1/06
Columbus, Ga. (MSA 5/1887–3/88) 2/96–1/04; 12/08
Columbus (Beallwood), Ga. 8/52–10/66
Columbus, Miss. 3/14
Concord, N.C. 5/30
Conroe, Tex. 7/87 (was outpost)
Conway, S.C. 9/49
Corbin, Ky. 10/30–5/32

Corinth, Miss. MSA 12/1887–4/88
Corpus Christi, Tex. 2/09–2/18; 11/25
Corsicana, Tex. 1/1897
Covington, Va. 11/26
Crittendons, Va. HSA 1889–closed same year
Cuernavaca, Mexico 3/57 transferred to Mexico-Central America Territory in 1976
Culiacan, Mexico 8/67 transferred to Mexico-Central America Territory in 1976
Cumberland, Md. (Citadel) 12/1899
Cumberland, Md. (South) 1/52–11/62
Cushing, Okla. 8/23
Dallas, Tex. #1 (Citadel) (MSA 6/1889–1/90) 3/92
Dallas, Tex. (Compton) 11/24
Dallas, Tex. #2 (Southside) 2/25 later renamed Cedar Street
Dallas, Tex. #3 (Oak Cliff) 1/65
Dallas, Tex. (Pleasant Grove) 9/65
Dallas Industrial Home 4/07 now ARC
Dallas, Tex. (Social Services) 7/86
Dalton, Ga. 11/49
Danville, Ky. 1/10–10/14; 12/47
Danville, Va. 3/07
Daytona Beach, Fla. 6/23–5/28; 7/39
Decatur, Ala. 3/04–3/27; 3/40
Denison, Tex. 2/1898–11/01; 1/07–12/07; 11/16–2/29; 2/77–6/81
Dothan, Ala. 12/12
Dover, Okla. 1/1894–3/96
Drumright, Okla. 2/17–11/51
Dumfries, Va. (Prince William) opened as Woodbridge, Va. 6/74
Duncan, Okla. 11/26–10/46
Durham, N.C. 1887–1/88; 5/10
Durham, N.C. Home and Hospital 5/32–11/74
East Knoxville, Tenn. 11/26–3/27
East Nashville, Tenn. (Nashville)
Eastland, Tex. 4/20–8/20; 1/21–3/21
Easton, Md. 11/27–2/29
Eden, N.C. 1/1980
El Dorado, Ark. 12/22
El Reno, Okla. 11/26–11/33
Elberton, Ga. 6/60; later Service Unit
Elizabeth City, N.C. (MSA 7/1888–3/89) 6/16–4/19; 9/37
Elizabeth City, N.C. #2 6/16–5/19
Elizabethton, Tenn. 7/29; closed
Elkins, W. Va. 8/24–11/27
Elkton, Md. 11/88–2/89; 1892–10/97
Ellicott City, Md., 1888–1/89
Elm Springs, Tex. 9/1890–12/90
Enid, Okla. 11/1893–1/97; 4/09
Ensley, Ala. 12/02–7/03; 7/24 (See Birmingham, Al. #2)
Erwin, Tenn. 7/29–10/30
Eureka Springs, Ark. 4/1895–12/99
Fairfax, Va. 11/58
Fairmont, W. Va. 5/1898–1/04; 10/12
Fairview, Md. 6/30/1888–closed same year
Falls Church, Va. (Fairfax) 10/56–11/68
Fayetteville, Ark. 4/1895–12/99; 9/68
Fayetteville, N.C. 2/24
Fitzgerald, Ga. 9/1897–11/04; 11/27–2/29
Florence, Ala. 7/05–4/08; 2/14–10/21; 3/27
Florence, S.C. 9/24

Fort Lauderdale, Fla. 2/26
Fort Lauderdale, Fla. Men's Social 1/64, now ARC
Fort Myers, Fla. 10/51
Fort Pierce, Fla. 8/64
Fort Scott, Tex. 11/1898–1/99
Fort Smith, Ark. 1/1896
Fort Walton Beach, Fla. 6/68
Fort Worth, Tex. (MSA 4/1889–12/90) 1/91–5/92; 6/93–1/96; 1/00; now Northside.
Fort Worth, Tex. #2 2/26–2/29; 2/32–11/33
Fort Worth, Tex. Industrial Home 7/07; now ARC
Frankfort, Ky. 9/1897; transferred to South 6/1989
Franklin, Va. HSA 6/1889–10/1889
Frederick, Md. #1 1886–1/1899; 4/16
Frederick, Md. #2 (Colored) 1886–1/91
Fredericksburg, Va. 1886–7/1888; 8/19
Freeport, Tex. 1/66
Front Royal, Va. 3/57
Frostburg, Md. 1887–1/90; 5/91–5/92; 12/99–11/02; 4/20–11/33
Fulton, Va. 1/24–7/29
Gadsden, Ala. 3/15–9/18; 7/20–11/25; 3/29
Gaffney, S.C. 6/20
Gainesville, Fla. 3/21–5/25; 10/62
Gainesville, Ga. 2/29–11/31; 12/48
Gainesville, Tex. 1/1896–6/04; 11/31–11/33
Gaithersburg, Md. (Montgomery Co.) 6/1985
Galena, Tex. 11/1898–1/00; 2/01–3/01
Galveston, Tex. #1 1/1892
Galveston, Tex. #2 11/1892–5/95
Garland, Tex. 2/1980
Garfield, Md. MSA 10/1886–9/1887
Gastonia, N.C. 7/21
Glasgow, Ky. 5/32–1/35
Glen Burnie, Md. 1968/72 Outpost; 12/72; Service Center 6/87
Goldsboro, N.C. 1/1888–1/33; 10/33
Grafton, W. Va. 1/24
Graham, Tex. 7/30–1/35
Greensboro, N.C. 11/04
Greensboro, N.C. (Haywood) 9/70–8/74
Greenville, Miss. 6/05–7/07; 4/10–4/14; 7/42
Greenville, N.C. 1887–5/88; 6/27
Greenville S.C. 1/1888; 10/04
Greenville, S.C. Children's Home (Bruner Home) 6/17–11/49
Greenville, S.C. Maternity Home 7/08–11/33
Greenville, Tex. (MSA 9/1889–12/1890) 12/01–6/04; 2/26–3/28; 2/61
Greenwood, Miss. 3/42
Greenwood, S.C. 7/21
Griffin, Ga. (MSA 9/1886–12/1888) 11/12–10/16; 10/24
Guadalajara, Mexico 3/50–transferred to Mexico-Central American Territory in 1976
Guatemala City, Guatemala 2/50–11/53; 4/76–turned over to Mexico-Central American Territory in 1976
Gulfport, Miss. 1/07
Guthrie, Okla. 1/1892–7/98; 1/00–2/17; 12/21–3/27
Hagerstown, Md. (MSA 9/1885–10/1888) 12/01
Hagerstown, Md. #2 10/21–8/22
Hamburg, Md. 11/1890–3/91

Hampton, Va. (MSA 9/1888–10/89) 2/98–7/99; 3/21–5/25; 9/55
Hanover, Md. 1/20–10/20
Harlan, Ky. 1/37–11/58
Harlingen, Tex. 3/28
Harrison, Ark. 8/1897–8/98
Harrisonburg, Va. 8/25
Hattiesburg, Miss. 3/07
Havana, Cuba 1/12–8/13
Havre de Grace, Md. 1886–10/97; 1/99–11/02; 8/24
Haynesville, La. 8/22–8/23
Hazard, Ky. 10/39–11/58
Helena, Ark. 5/02–4/04
Henderson, Ky. 1/39
Henderson, N.C. 9/21
Hendersonville, N.C. 5/25–11/33; (Outpost of Asheville 5/55) Corps 1/64
Hennesey, Okla. 1/1893–3/96
Henryetta, Okla. 4/20–1/35
Hialeah, Fla. 1/1975
Hickory, N.C. 1/25
High Point, N.C. 4/13
Hillsboro, Tex. (MSA 5/1889–12/89) 3/95–1/97
Hinton, W. Va. 2/14–11/17
Hobart, Okla. 7/03–12/04; 5/07–1/11; Service Center 5/1989
Hopewell, Va. 8/24–7/45
Hopkinsville, Ky. 8/16–8/23; 3/27
Hot Springs, Ark. 2/1897
Hot Springs, N.C. 1/1986
Houma, La. 6/1984
Houston, Tex. 6/1889–1/90; 4/93
Houston, Tex. Harbor Light 1/50
Houston, Tex. Industrial Home 2/25; now ARC
Houston, Tex, Workingman's Hotel 8/89–2/01
Houston, Tex. Wood Camp 8/98–11/03
Humble, Tex. 7/05–1/07
Huntington, W. Va. #1 (Citadel) (MSA 2/1886–3/88) 6/02
Huntington, W.Va. #2 (West Side) 2/22–11/51
Huntsville, Ala. 12/02–3/04; 1/56
Hyattsville, Md. (Prince Georges) originally (Washington #5 (Northeast) then moved to Colmar Manor, Md., then Bladensburg, Md. 11/68
Irvine, Ky. 3/31–1/35
Irving, Tex. 11/87
Jackson, Ky. 5/15–11/31
Jackson, Miss. 4/00–1/01; 2/06
Jackson, Tenn. 1/01–10/01; 4/08–12/09; 4/51
Jacksonville, Ark. 3/1983
Jacksonville, Fla. #1 (Citadel) 1/1891
Jacksonville, Fla. #2 4/19–1/20
Jacksonville, Fla. #2 (Fairfield) 1/34–11/53
Jacksonville, Fla. Industrial Home 6/11; ARC 1/27
Jacksonville, N.C. 12/1984
Jacksonville Beach, Fla. 5/1983–8/87
Jonesboro, Ark. 3/01–2/18; 5/25
Johnson City, Tenn. (6/1888–3/89) 3/10–2/17; 5/21
Kenner, La. 1/1987
Kerrville, Tex. 1/86
Keyser, W. Va. 1887–6/88; 5/25–11/33
Key West, Fla. 7/07–1/37; 2/54
Kingfisher, Okla. 5/1891–3/96
Kingsport, Tenn. 4/17
Kinston, N.C. 2/1888
Knoxville, Tenn. (MSA 5/1887–9/89) 1/99
Lafayette, La. 6/48
La Grange, Ga. 4/17–7/44
Lakeland, Fla. 10/21

Lake Charles, La. 1/04
Lake Worth, Fla. 11/53; Outpost 1925
Laredo, Tex. 12/21
Laurel, Miss. 10/20–11/33; 6/39
Lawrence, Md. 6/1888—closed same year
Lawrenceville, Ga. 2/1985
Lawton, Okla. 3/04–4/09; 12/22
Lehigh, Okla. 5/02–12/02
Lexington, N.C. (Outpost of High Point 2/52) 1/61
Limestone, W. Va. 11/26–3/28
Lindsberg, Va. HSA 6/1889–10/1889
Little Rock, Ark. (Citadel) 9/1896–10/70
Little Rock, Ark. (Geyer Springs) 9/82; became (South) 9/86
Little Rock, Ark. Industrial Home 5/25–11/33; 1/48; now ARC
Littlefield, Tex. 1/37–10/46; 12/48–2/71
Logan, W. Va. 10/24
Lonaconing, Md. 1886–2/90; 5/91–6/92; 6/98–5/04
Longview, Tex. 12/1882
Loudon, Tenn. MSA 8/1888–3/1889
Louisville, Ky. #1 1883–1884; 1/95
Louisville, Ky. #2 6/1897–8/98; 8/21–8/23
Louisville, Ky. (Brook St.) 4/1989
Louisville, Ky. (Portland) 7/29
Louisville, Ky. #3 (Point) 11/1897–8/98; 6/38—renamed Sanders Citadel in 1964
Louisville, Ky. #4 8/1898–1/04; 1/07–2/10
Louisville, Ky. (South) 11/44–10/46
Louisville, Ky Industrial Home 2/05; now ARC
Louisville, Ky Maternity Home 8/1919–11/74
Lubbock, Tex. 12/22
Lufkin, Tex. (Outpost 9/41); Corps 2/43
Luray, Va. Outpost closed 10/86
Lynchburg, Va. #1 5/05
Lynchburg, Va. #2 3/21–4/22; 1/24–1/25
Macon, Ga. (MSA 4/1887–9/1889) 12/99
Madisonville, Ky 6/77
Makota, Va. HSA 1889–10/89
Manchester, Va. 8/95–1/96
Mangum, Okla. 5/02–12/04
Mannington, W. Va. 11/26–3/27
Marietta, Ga. 2/68
Marshall, Tex. 2/1898–1/99; 8/26–11/27
Martinsburg, W. Va. 4/03–5/04; 6/12–1/13; 1/20
Martinsville, Va. 10/30–9/43; 10/71
Matamoros, Mexico 9/53 transferred to Mexico-Central American Territory in 1976
Mazatlan, Mexico 11/50 transferred to Mexico-Central American Territory in 1976
McAlester, Okla. 2/01–1/04; 4/07–5/17; 12/21
McAllen, Tex. 11/31–5/32; 4/42
McComb, Miss. 4/72 (outpost) 2/89
McKinney, Tex. 12/01–6/04
Mechanicsburg, Md. 1/1886—closed same year
Melbourne, Fla. 6/71
Memphis, Tenn. #1 (Citadel) 8/1890–11/93; 11/00—name changed to Temple then Ben Lear 11/55
Memphis, Tenn. #2

(Ft. Pickering) 8/24–11/61
Memphis, Tenn. (North) 9/43–12/48
Memphis, Tenn. (Southside) 1/49
Memphis, Tenn. Industrial Home 10/23–11/33; turned over to corps 11/33; reopened 10/37; now ARC
Memphis, Tex. 8/22–8/23
Mena, Ark. 7/03–11/03
Merida, Mexico 9/67—transferred to Mexico-Central American Territory in 1976
Meridian, Miss. (MSA 9/1887–6/1888) 5/02
Messic, Va. HSA 4/1889–10/1889
Mexia, Tex. 4/22–11/33
Mexicali, Mexico 10/58—transferred to Mexico-Central American Territory in 1976
Mexico City, Mexico (Temple) 11/39—transferred to Mexico-Central American Territory in 1976
Mexico City, Mexico (Romero Rubio) 3/52—transferred to Mexico-Central American Territory in 1976
Mexico City, Mexico (Rio Blanco) 10/56—transferred to Mexico-Central American Territory in 1976
Mexico City, Mexico (Col. Revolucion) 4/62—transferred to Mexico-Central American Territory in 1976
Mexico City, Mexico (Col. Argentina) 10/68—transferred to Mexico-Central American Territory in 1976
Mexico City, Mexico Men's Social 3/52–10/66
Miami, Fla. (Citadel) 4/13
Miami, Fla (Edison Court) 7/40
Miami, Fla. Men's Social 1/48; now ARC
Miami, Okla. 3/31–11/33
Middlesboro, Ky. 3/08
Middlesburg, Md. 7/1886—closed same year
Midland, Tex. 6/56
Mineral Wells, Tex. 5/07–2/09
Mobile, Ala. 1886—closed same year; 9/99
Mobile, Ala. Industrial Home 2/09–9/18
Mobile, Ala. (Northside) 6/89; also see Prichard, Ala.
Monroe, La. 3/27
Monterrey, Mexico 2/44—transferred to Mexico-Central American Territory in 1976
Montgomery, Ala. (MSA 8/1887–9/1889) 12/99
Montgomery, Ala. (West End) 11/57–11/59
Montgomery, Ala. Industrial Home 1/11–10/15
Morgantown, W. Va. 6/1898–3/11; 2/18
Morristown, Tenn. MSA 8/1888–2/1889
Moundsville, W. Va. (MSA 5/1886–7/1888) 2/17–2/20; 8/59
Mount Airy, N.C. 8/22–3/27; 2/29–11/33; 6/40
Mount Pleasant, Md. MSA 9/1886–3/1887
Mount Sterling, Ky. MSA 5/1886–12/1886
Muskogee, Okla. 5/00
Naples, Fla. 2/1981
Nashville, Tenn. #1 (Magness Citadel) (MSA 1/1887–1/1890) 7/90–4/91; 2/92
Nashville, Tenn. #2 (North) 10/1890–4/91; 3/93–1/94; 4/97–7/98; 9/43; (Citadel)

Nashville, Tenn. Industrial Home 1/09–3/11; 8/23–11/33; turned over to corps 11/33; reopened 1/37–3/46; 11/50; now ARC
Natchez, Miss. 12/04
New Bern, N.C. 2/87–10/1893; 12/10
Newberry, S.C. 10/30–11/33
Newkirk, Okla. 4/1894–8/95
New Orleans, La. 1886—closed same year; 1/97
New Orleans, La. #2 12/1898–7/99; 1/00–10/00; 7/28–11/33; 10/37–7/44
New Orleans Industrial Home 8/11–1/37; corps operated 1/37–7/39; reopened 11/39; now ARC
Newport News, Va. #1 1/1899–8/01; 4/04–1/82
Newport News, Va. #2 (Colored) 2/20–7/20
Norfolk, Va. (Only corps to come over from Moore Army in South.) Opened 2/1888; 11/89–7/92; 4/05
Norfolk, Va. #2 (Colored) 8/20–10/23
Norfolk, Va. #3 (Berkley) 3/21–11/33
Norfolk, Va. Industrial Home 11/13–7/19; 4/22–11/31; now Tidewater ARC 6/84
Norman, Okla. 3/92–8/1893; 8/73
North East, Md. 6/1889–10/93; 1/95–10/97
Northern Virginia Adult Rehabilitation Center–Alexandria, Va. 6/1984
North Little Rock, Ark. 3/41
Norton, Va. 11/26–3/28
Nuevo Laredo, Mexico 6/48—transferred to Mexico-Central American Territory in 1976
Oak Grove, Okla. 12/1891–3/96
Oak Ridge, Tenn. (Service Center) 6/1889
Oakland, Md. 7/1888–8/88
Oakview, Md. 7/1894–12/94
Oakview, Okla. 7/1894–8/95
Ocala, Fla. 2/1893–8/95; 11/27
Odessa, Tex. 1/52
Oklahoma City, Okla. 10/1891–7/98; 11/00
Oklahoma City Industrial Home 3/24; now ARC
Oklahoma City, Okla. Maternity Home 12/05–2/08
Okmulgee, Okla 2/20
Orange, Tex. 3/03
Orange Park, Fla. 2/1981
Orangeburg, S.C. 4/27
Orlando, Fla. 4/20
Orlando, Fla. Men's Social 1/69; now ARC
Owensboro, Ky. 2/06–11/08; 11/27
Paducah, Ky. (MSA 9/1889–1/1890) 5/00–11/02; 11/06–1/12; 3/31
Palestine, Tex. 5/00–6/04; 6/26–11/27
Pampa, Tex. 12/29–11/33; 9/37
Panama City, Fla. 10/36
Panhandle, Tex. 3/27–7/29
Paragould, Ark. 8/11–4/20
Paris, Tex. 4/1896–1/00; 3/09–1/11; 1/25–7/29; 1/35
Parkersburg, W. Va. (MSA 2/1885–1/1888) 4/02
Pasadena, Tex. 1/51
Pascagoula, Miss. 3/66
Pawhuska, Okla. 8/22–1/35
Pekin, Md. 1887–2/90
Pensacola, Fla 6/01
Perry, Okla. 11/1893–7/98; 1/00–10/01
Perryton, Tex. 2/22–5/25; 3/27–11/27
Petersburg, Va. 10/1887

Petersburg, Va. Industrial Home 1/24–5/25
Phenix City, Ala. 2/66–6/77
Piedras Negras, Mexico 7/64—transferred to Mexico-Central American Territory in 1976
Pine Bluff, Ark. 3/02–10/05; 8/20–10/30; 11/62
Pinellas Park, Fla. 1/60—originally St. Petersburg (Clearview)
Pitcher, Okla. 10/22–7/29
Pittsburg, Tex. 1/1899–1/00
Plainview, Tex. 2/29–9/32; 1/36
Plant City, Fla. 1/1984
Ponca City, Okla. 10/22
Port Arthur, Tex. 7/06–1/15; 2/16–5/21; 10/24
Port Charlotte, Fla. 7/1987
Port Deposit, Md. 1887–4/92
Port Richey, Fla. 10/1981—later West Pasco Corps
Portsmouth, Va. (MSA 3/1888–3/1889; HSA 3/1889–10/1889) 4/10
Prichard, Ala. 9/56; now Mobile Northside
Princeton, W. Va. 12/36
Puebla, Mexico 10/47—transferred to Mexico-Central American Territory in 1976
Pulaski, Va. 2/20
Radford, Va. 8/21–10/23
Raleigh, N.C. 1887–4/88; 2/12
Raleigh, W. Va. 12/17–3/30
Ranger, Tex. 7/20–10/30
Rasco Neck, Va. HSA 3/1889–10/1889
Reidsville, N.C. 5/30
Reynosa, Mexico 11/53—transferred to Mexico-Central American Territory in 1976
Richmond, Ky. (Service Center) 8/1989
Richmond #1, Va. (Temple) 4/1886–4/92; 1/96–8/96; 1/05–5/53
Richmond #2, Va. 4/1888–6/89; 6/15–8/25
Richmond, Va. (Manchester) 2/22; renamed Dunstan Citadel 12/51; later Richmond (Citadel) 9/80
Richmond #3, Va. (Church Hill) 4/20–3/46
Richmond #4, Va. (Oregon Hill) 6/53–5/56
Richmond, Va. Industrial Home 4/05–5/07; 1/20; now ARC
Richmond Maternity Home 4/23–11/74
Roanoke, Va. (12/1888–3/1889) 1886—Closed same year; 4/92–1/93; 5/07
Roanoake #2, Va. 3/21–9/21
Roanoke #3, Va. 3/21–4/22
Roanoake #4, Va. (Norwich) 3/21–4/23; 3/27–6/30
Roanoke Rescue Home 10/20–7/45
Rock Hill, S.C. 3/30
Rocky Mount, N.C. 9/14–4/18; 2/25
Rogers, Ark. 2/1897–6/99; 1/85
Rome, Ga. Outpost Industrial Home 5/17–3/19
Rome, Ga. (MSA 9/1887–12/1889) 5/97–1/03; 12/08
Russellville, Ark, 11/88
Salem, Va. 1/1892–1/93; 3/21–4/23
Salisbury, Va. 12/13
Salisbury, N.C. 10/12
Saltillo, Mexico 4/64—transferred to Mexico-Central American Territory in 1976
San Angelo, Tex. 10/01
San Antonio, Tex. 2/1889–12/89; 2/98
San Antonio, Tex. (Southside) 4/1984
San Antonio, Tex. Industrial

Home 11/29–1/35; operated by corps 1/35–1/37; reopened 1/37; now ARC
San Antonio Palms Hotel 10/37–3/46
San Antonio, Tex. Rescue Home (Home and Hospital) 3/11–11/75
San Luis Potosi, Mexico 4/59—transferred to Mexico-Central American Territory in 1976
Sand Springs, Okla. 7/29
Sanford, Fla. 2/29
Sapulpa, Okla. 11/07
Sarasota, Fla. 3/27
Savannah, Ga. (MSA 4/1887–1/1890) 3/00–6/02; 1/10
Savannah, Ga. Industrial Home 10/10–11/33; turned over to corps 11/33
Sayre, Okla. 8/23–2/26
Sebring, Fla. 5/15
Selma, Ala. (MSA 8/1887–8/1888) 1/03–1/18; 5/21
Seminole, Okla. 3/31–11/68
Shawnee, Okla. 3/01–4/09; 2/18–5/18; 1/21
Sheffield, Ala. 10/21–11/33
Shelby, N.C. 6/36–11/39; 1/65
Shelton Laurel, N.C. (Mountain Mission 1935) 6/84
Sherman, Tex. 1/97–12/07; 11/21–6/29; 4/42
Shreveport, La. 4/1897–8/02; 2/04
Siloam Springs, Ark. 4/1898–12/99
Sistersville, W. Va. 5/1898–11/02
Sleepy Valley, N.C. 11/50 (Mountain Mission 1935)
Smithfield, N.C. (Outpost of Goldsboro-Wilson) Corps 5/55
Smithton, W. Va. MSA 9/1887–12/1887
Smoke Town, Md. 12/1886–3/1887
South Pittsburg, Tenn. 8/1890–4/91
Spartansburg, S.C. 8/08
Springdale, Ark, 2/72
Springville, Ala. MSA 8/1889–1/1890
St. Augustine, Fla. 1/92–10/93; 1/17–3/17; 6/84–12/86
St. Petersburg, Fla. 10/12
St. Petersburg (Clearview) Fla. 8/1960 changed to Pinellas Park in 1983
St. Petersburg, Fla. Men's Social 8/1956; now ARC
Statesville, N.C. 2/1906–2/07; 1/27–12/44; Outpost 6/47; Corps 5/81
Staunton, Va. (MSA 8/1889–12/1889) 4/10–12/10; 2/12
Sterling, Ky. MSA 1887–1888
Stillwater, Okla. 4/1894–8/95; 3/04–10/05
Suffolk, Va. (HSA 6/1889–10/1889) 3/13–2/16; 8/24
Sumter, S.C. 7/28
Tallahassee, Fla. 7/51
Tampa, Fla. 4/94
Tampa, Fla. #2 2/22–11/31
Tampa, Fla. Home and Hospital 2/32–6/76
Tampa, Fla. Industrial Home 2/26–11/33; turned over to corps 11/33; closed 1/37; ARC 11/50
Tampico, Mexico 10/47—transferred to Mexico-Central American Territory in 1976
Taylor City, Tex. 11/1889–8/91
Tecpan, Guatemala 4/76—transferred to Mexico-Central American Territory in 1976
Temple, Tex. 11/1893–7/98; 3/00–3/01; 8/25–1/37
Terrell, Tex. 10/01–6/04
Texarkana, Tex. 4/1896
Texas City, Tex. 7/1981
Thomaston, Ga. 11/27–7/28

Thomasville, Ga. 3/28–7/29; 10/66
Thomasville, N.C. (Outpost of High Point 11/49) 1/64
Tidewater Adult Rehabilitation Center—Virginia Beach, Va. 6/1984
Tijuana, Mexico 4/59—transferred to Mexico-Central American Territory in 1976
Titusville, Fla. 5/69
Toccoa, Ga. 11/50
Tonkawa, Okla. 8/25–10/30
Torreon, Mexico 11/48—transferred to Mexico-Central American Territory in 1976
Tulsa, Okla. 11/06
Tulsa. Okla. #2 11/27—11/33
Tulsa, Okla. Home and Hospital 2/29
Tulsa, Okla. Men's Social 6/40; now ARC
Tupelo, Miss. 7/29–10/30; 1/72
Tuscaloosa, Ala. 10/10
Tyler, Tex. 5/57–6/04; 10/24–6/27; 8/31
Union, S.C. 6/19
Union Bridge, Md. MSA 12/1885–9/1886
Valdosta, Ga. 8/24
Van Buren, Ark. 7/38–11/39
Venice, Fla. 9/1983
Veracruz, Mexico 11/53—transferred to Mexico-Central American Territory in 1976
Vicksburg, Miss. (MSA 9/1887–3/1889) 3/02
Victoria, Tex. 1/58
Vidalia, Ga. 10/88
Waco Tex. (MSA 5/1889–3/1890) 5/91–12/00; 3/03–12/04; 7/05
Walkersville, Md. 1887–8/88; 1/89–7/89
Walkersville, N.C. 1/1888—closed same year
Warner Robins, Ga. 5/64
Washington, #1 (Temple) 7/1885; made Harbor Light 4/51–6/78
Washington #2 (Central) 7/1888–6/89; 3/92–12/92; 1/97–1/01; 7/13 (Colored), changed to Sherman Avenue 11/68
Washington #3 (Southeast) 1/1897–1/01; 2/20–10/23; 8/25
Washington #4 (Georgetown) 10/24–11/64
Washington, DC (Ninth Street) 1/66
Washington #5, DC 11/27–4/51 (Northeast) moved to Colmar Manor, Md.
Washington, DC Industrial Home 10/03; now ARC
Washington Young Women's Residence (Evangeline) 1912–11/31; 9/39–4/51
Washington, N.C. 9/37
Waxahatchie, Tex. 1/00–12/04; 2/25–11/27
Waycross, Ga. 4/10
Waynesboro, Va. 7/20–1/21; 6/36
Waynesville, N.C. 10/36
Weatherford, Tex. 5/02–12/04
Weirton, W. Va. 10/30
Welch, W. Va. 1/24–6/83
Wellsburg, W. Va. (MSA 10/1884–5/1885) 1883–10/1884; Outpost 6/31–11/33; Corps 1944
Westernport, Md. 1888–7/90
Westminster, Md. MSA 8/1885–3/1886
West Palm Beach, Fla. 5/22
West Pasco, Fla. 10/80
West Tulsa, Okla. 8/14–7/89
Wewoka, Okla. 7/29–11/33
Wheeling, W. Va. (MSA 10/1884–12/1886) 1883 10/1884; 10/1889–1892; 1/91–1/92; 10/98
Wheeling Industrial Home 1/09–

11/33; turned over to corps 11/33
Wichita Falls, Tex. 2/10
Williamson, W. Va. (MSA 10/1884–12/1885) 1883–10/1884; 7/13
Wilmington, N.C. 1887–7/88; 2/05
Wilmington, N.C. Maternity Home 5/25–5/32
Wilson, N.C. 4/27
Winchester, Ky. MSA 1/1887–6/1887
Winchester, Va. 1/20
Winston-Salem, N.C. (Central) 1/07
Winston-Salem, N.C. (Southside) 4/41; Service Center 1/83
Winter Haven, Fla. 10/58
Woodbury, Md. 11/1892–1/97
York, Tex. 1/99–12/99
Yukon, Okla. 6/1894–3/96

BIBLIOGRAPHY

Allison, Evelyn. *The Baltimore Story*. Unpublished manuscript, 1980

Bailey, Kenneth K. *Southern White Protestantism in the Twentieth Century*. New York: Harper and Row, 1964

Blue Print for Progress in the Second Century. New York, The Salvation Army, 1971

Booth, Maud Charlesworth. *Beneath Two Flags*. Cincinnati, Cranston and Curts, 1894

Bouterse, Wesley. *Shepherdess of the Hills*. Unpublished manuscript, no date

Brantley, Harriotte. *The Little Harbor*. Washington, The Salvation Army, 1947

Carruth, Gordon. *The Encyclopedia of American Facts and Dates*. New York, Harper and Row, 1987

Cash, W. J. *The Mind of the South*. New York; Vintage Books, 1941

Century Advance Campaign for 1899. New York, The Salvation Army, 1899

Chesham, Sallie. *Born to Battle*. New York, Rand McNally, 1965

Daniel, Clifton. *Chronicle of the Twentieth Century*. Mount Kisco, NY, Chronicle Publications, 1987

Daniel, Clifton. *Chronicle of the Year 1987*. Mount Kisco, NY, Chronicle Publications, 1988

Dennis, Denise. *Black History for Beginners*. New York, Writer's and Reader's Publishing, 1984

Ellsworth, Scott. *Death in a Promised Land*. Baton Rouge, The Louisiana State University Press, 1982

Ezell, John Samuel. *The South Since 1865*. Norman, University of Oklahoma Press, 1975

Gearing, Winifred. *Salvation Patrol*. Atlanta, The Salvation Army, 1981

Gearing, Winifred. *The House That Juan Built*. Atlanta, The Salvation Army, 1979

Hall, Clarence. *Portrait of a Builder*. Atlanta, The Salvation Army, 1983

Hall, Lesslie. *Half Hours in Southern History*. Richmond, B. F. Johnson Publishing Co., 1907

Hansen, Lillian. *The Double Yoke*. New York, Citadel Press, 1968

History of Injunction Litigation—The Salvation Army v. The American Salvation Army. New York, The Salvation Army, 1910

Ingoe, Hal. *Soliloquies of a Bandsman*. Unpublished manuscript, 1939

Kennedy, Ralph C., Jr. and Thomas Rothrock. *John Brown of Arkansas*. Siloam Springs, Ark., John Brown University Press, 1966

Lavine, Sigmund A. *Evangeline Booth, Daughter of Salvation*. New York, Dodd, Mead and Co., 1970

Mayfield, Chris. *Growing Up Southern*. New York, Pantheon Books, 1981

McGill, Ralph. *The South and the Southerner*. Boston, Atlantic Monthly Press, 1959

McHenry, J. Patrick. *A Short History of Mexico*. Garden City, NY, Doubleday and Co., 1962

McKinley, Edward. *Marching to Glory*. San Francisco, Harper and Row, 1980

McKinley, Edward. *Somebody's Brother*. New York, The Salvation Army, 1986

Moore, Thomas. *All About The Salvation Army*. New York, The Salvation Army, 1884

Morrison, Samuel Eliot. *The Oxford History of the American People—Volume 3*. New York, New American Library, 1972

Origin and Development of The Salvation Army. London, The Salvation Army, 1973

Parker, Edward J. *My Fifty-Eight Years*. New York, The Salvation Army, 1943

Railton, George Scott. *The Authoritative Life of General William Booth, Founder of The Salvation Army*. New York, Reliance Trading Company, 1912

Report on Hurricane Camille, A. Atlanta, The Salvation Army, 1969

Report to International Headquarters. (Unpublished reports for private circulation) Atlanta: The Salvation Army, 1972–1987

Salvation Army and the USO, The. Atlanta, The Salvation Army, undated

Salvation Army Song Book, The. London, The Salvation Army, 1987

Salvation Army Year Book, The. London, The Salvation Army, various years

Satterlee, Allen, Editor. *Notable Quotables*. Atlanta, The Salvation Army, 1985

Troutt, Margaret. *The General Was a Lady*. Nashville, A. J. Holman Co., 1980

Waldron, John, Editor. *Pioneering Salvationists*. New York, The Salvation Army, 1986

Watson, Bernard. *Soldier Saint*. London, Hodder and Stoughton, 1970

Williams, Harry. *William Booth's First Gentleman.* London, The Salvation Army, 1980

Williams, Juan. *Eyes on the Prize.* New York, Viking Press, 1987

Wisbey, Herbert A., Jr. *Soldiers Without Swords.* New York, Macmillan Company, 1955

Wisbey, Herbert A., Jr. *The History of the Volunteers of America.* Unpublished manuscript, 1952

Woodard, C. Vann. *The Burden of Southern History.* Baton Rouge, The Louisiana State University Press, 1970

Zinn, Howard. *A People's History of the United States.* New York, Harper and Row, 1980

MAGAZINES AND PERIODICALS

All the World. London, The Salvation Army, 1886–

Conqueror, The. New York, The Salvation Army, 1892–

Historical News and Views. New York, The Salvation Army National Archives and Research Center, 1986–1988

Local Officer's Counselor. New York, The Salvation Army, 1930

Maytag News. New York, Maytag Corporation, 1932

Nashville Beat. Nashville, The Salvation Army, 1984–1987

Southern Spirit, The. Atlanta, The Salvation Army, 1983–1988

Texas Report, The. Dallas: The Salvation Army, 1970–1987

War Cry, The. Atlanta, The Salvation Army, 1927–1970

War Cry, The. Chicago, The Salvation Army, 1920–1926

War Cry, The. New York, The Salvation Army, 1881–1926; 1935; 1970–1988

War Cry, The. New York, The Salvation Army of America, 1884–1890

NEWSPAPERS

Atlanta Journal
Atlanta Constitution
Baltimore Sun
Birmingham Age Herald
Columbus Ledger-Enquirer
Edmund Sun-Democrat
Harrisonburg News-Record
Louisville Courier-Journal
Macon Telegraph
Memphis Commercial Appeal
Memphis Press Sentinel
Muskogee Times-Democrat
Nashville Banner
New Orleans Times-Picayune
New York Post
New York Times
Philadelphia Sunday Press
Roanoke Times and World-News
Texas City Sun
Washington Evening Star

INTERVIEWS, PERSONAL NOTES AND CORRESPONDENCE

Correspondence of Commissioner William C. Arnold, 1939–1946
Correspondence from W. L. Atwood, 1925–1928
Notes and interviews from Dr. F. A. Baker

Correspondence of Colonel Arthur Brewer to Major Barrett, 1925
Correspondence of Commissioner William Chamberlain, 1969–1976
Notes from Mr. Philip Collier
Correspondence of Lt. Colonel Beatrice Combs, 1971
Diaries of Commissioner Alexander Damon, 1930–1935
Interview and notes from Brigadier Verna Davis
Correspondence of Commissioner William Dray, 1953
Interview with Brigadier Mrs. Frances Eckstein
Interview with Lt. Colonel Leon Ferraez
Correspondence of Brigadier Bernard Flinn
Interview with Lt. Colonel Ruth Gibbs
Interviews with Commissioner W. R. H. Goodier
Interviews and notes from Commissioner Ernest W. Holz
"Provincial Officer's Brief—Ohio, Pittsburgh and Southern Province (1908)" Colonel Richard Holz
Interview with Lt. Colonel Mrs. Emma Howarth
Interview with Major James Hylton
Correspondence of Lt. Colonel C. William Jaynes
Correspondence of Mrs. Lt. Colonel C. William Jaynes
Notes and interview with Colonel James Klaas
Notes of Lt. Colonel W. Edward Laity, Sr.
Interview with CSM Jimmy Maiden
Notes of Mrs. Billie Jean McClure
Farewell brief of Adjutant Harry McDonald, 1932
Inaugural Address of Commissioner William McIntyre, 1927; various items of correspondence, 1926–1930
Interviews with Major Omer McKinney
Interviews with Mrs. Major Omer McKinney
Notes of Captain Meridian, 1910
Notes from Major John Merritt
Interview with Commissioner Andrew S. Miller
Interview with Ralph I. Miller
Correspondence between Thomas Moore, Jr. and The Salvation Army, 1910
Interview with Mrs. Commissioner John D. Needham
Interview with Mrs. Major Philip Needham
Interviews with Mrs. Colonel Lillian Hansen Noble
Interview with Commissioner James Osborne
Interview with Major Mary Peacock
Interview with Colonel Ernest Pickering
Interview with Commissioner Arthur Pitcher
Correspondence of Brigadier Hazel Pownell
Interview with Major Norma Roberts
Notes by Colonel Bertram Rodda, 1927

Interview with Lt. Colonel Orville Salmon
Interview with Major Maurice Smith
Notes and interviews with Colonel Gordon Swyers
Interviews with Lt. Colonel Walter Swyers
Interview with Colonel Bramwell H. Tillsley
Interview with Mrs. Lt. Colonel Harry Ward
Interview with Lt. Colonel Jack T. Waters
Interview with Major Michael Waters
Correspondence of Braxton Zuber, 1943

INDEX

N

CAPTAIN ALLEN SATTERLEE was born in Tampa, Fla. in 1953. After a move north he met The Salvation Army at the age of thirteen and was captivated by it. At fifteen he moved back to Florida with his family where he graduated from Lakeland Senior High School. Serving in the Lakeland Corps in various local positions he then entered The Salvation Army School for Officers Training in 1973 to be commissioned as an officer in 1975.

His Salvation Army service has included Key West and St. Petersburg, Fla.; command of corps in Florida, including Titusville, Melbourne, and Tallahassee. In 1980 he opened the corps in Port Richey (West Pasco), Fla. He has also commanded corps in Roanoke, Va., Selma and Birmingham, Ala. Satterlee served as well on the National Centennial Congress staff when the Army celebrated its one hundredth anniversary of its work in America. Counting it a high privilege, Satterlee has sent fourteen individuals into Salvation Army officership.

Captain Satterlee and his wife, Esther, who became a Salvation Army officer in 1979, have four children—Jay, Sharon, Jon and Anna. In addition to this book, Satterlee authored a collection of quotes from Salvation Army literature entitled *Notable Quotables;* also numerous articles for Salvation Army publications.